SECOND EDITION

Pronunciation Pairs

An Introduction to the Sounds of English

Teacher's Manual

ANN BAKER
SHARON GOLDSTEIN

CAMBRIDGE
UNIVERSITY PRESS

CAMBRIDGE UNIVERSITY PRESS
Cambridge, New York, Melbourne, Madrid, Cape Town, Singapore, São Paulo, Delhi

Cambridge University Press
32 Avenue of the Americas, New York, NY 10013–2473, USA

www.cambridge.org
Information on this title: www.cambridge.org/9780521678094

First published 1990
Second Edition 2008
2nd printing 2008

Printed in the United States of America

A catalog record for this publication is available from the British Library

Library of Congress Cataloging-in-Publication Data
Baker, Ann, 1939-
 Pronunciation pairs: an introduction to the sounds of English: teacher's manual / Ann Baker, Sharon Goldstein. – 2nd ed.
  p. cm.
 Summary: "This Teacher's Manual includes a diagnostic test, an answer key with helpful teaching tips, and detailed
information on student difficulties in producing each sound. Teachers who need help with teaching the sounds, rhythm,
stress, and intonation patterns of North American English will find the in-depth treatment of these features especially
useful." – Provided by publisher.
 ISBN 978-0-521-67809-4 (teacher's manual)
 1. English language–Pronunciation–Study and teaching. 2. English language–Pronunciation by foreign speakers.
 3. English language–Study and teaching–Foreign speakers. I. Goldstein, Sharon. II. Title.

PE1137.B226 2008
428.3'4–dc22

2007046696

ISBN 978-0-521-67808-7 student's book
ISBN 978-0-521-67809-4 teacher's manual
ISBN 978-0-521-67811-7 class audio CDs
ISBN 978-0-521-67810-0 class audio cassettes

Art direction and book design: Adventure House, NYC
Cover design: Adventure House, NYC
Layout: TSI Graphic Services
Audio production: Richard LePage and Associates

Contents

To the Teacher v

Overview vii

Section A • Vowels

Unit 1	/iy/ tea	Stressed Syllables in Words	**1**
Unit 2	/ɪ/ sit	Stress in Numbers; Moving Stress	**4**
Unit 3	/ɛ/ yes	Falling and Rising Intonation	**7**
Unit 4	/ey/ day	Stress in Sentences	**10**
Unit 5	/æ/ hat	The Most Important Word	**12**
Unit 6	**Review**	. . . .	**15**
Unit 7	/ʌ/ cup	Strong and Weak Pronunciations	**17**
Unit 8	/ə/ a banana	/ə/ in Unstressed Syllables and Words; *can* and *can't*	**20**
Unit 9	/ər/ letter	/ər/ in Unstressed Syllables and Words; Intonation in Choice Questions with *or*	**23**
Unit 10	/ɑ/ hot	Phrase Groups	**25**
Unit 11	/ɔ/ ball	Using Stress and Intonation to Show a Contrast	**28**
Unit 12	/ow/ go	Linking Vowel Sounds	**30**
Unit 13	/uw/ too	Stress and Pronouns	**33**
Unit 14	/ʊ/ book	Negative Contractions	**35**
Unit 15	**Review**	. . . .	**38**
Unit 16	/ay/ fine	Stress in Compound Nouns	**40**
Unit 17	/ɔy/ boy	Sentence Rhythm and Timing	**42**
Unit 18	/aw/ house	Stress and Linking in Phrasal Verbs	**44**
Unit 19	**Review**	. . . .	**47**
Unit 20	**Review**	. . . .	**48**
Unit 21	/ər/ word	Tag Questions with Falling Intonation	**50**

Section B • Consonants

Unit 22 /p/ pop   Intonation in Lists **53**

Unit 23 /b/ baby   Stress in Compound Nouns and Phrases.......... **55**

Unit 24 /t/ two   Linking a Final Consonant **58**

Unit 25 /d/ did   -*ed* Endings **61**

Unit 26 /k/ key   Stress in Noun Phrases with Compounds **63**

Unit 27 /g/ good   Gonna (*going to*) **66**

Unit 28 **Review** **68**

Unit 29 /s/ sun   Linking a Final Consonant Cluster **69**

Unit 30 /z/ zoo   -*s* Endings **72**

Unit 31 /ʃ/ shoe   Linking Words with /ʃ/ **75**

Unit 32 /ʒ/ television   Stress in Words with -*ion* **78**

Unit 33 /ʧ/ chips   Silent Syllables **80**

Unit 34 /ʤ/ joke   Didja (*did you*); Wouldja (*would you*); Didncha (*didn't you*); Doncha (*don't you*) **82**

Unit 35 **Review** **85**

Unit 36 /y/ yes   Useta (*used to*) **87**

Unit 37 /f/ fan   Intonation in Long Sentences **90**

Unit 38 /v/ very   Weak and Strong Pronunciations of *have* **92**

Unit 39 /w/ wet   *Wh-* Questions with Rising Intonation **95**

Unit 40 /h/ how   Dropped /h/; Intonation in Exclamations **99**

Unit 41 /θ/ think   Using Stress and Intonation to Show Surprise **102**

Unit 42 /ð/ the other   Weak Pronunciations for *the* and *than* **105**

Unit 43 **Review** **107**

Unit 44 /m/ me   Using Intonation to Change Meaning **108**

Unit 45 /n/ no   Syllabic /n/ **110**

Unit 46 /ŋ/ sing   Weak Pronunciation and Contraction of *be* **113**

Unit 47 /l/ light, fall   Weak Pronunciation and Contraction of *will* .. **116**

Unit 48 /r/ right   Stress in Long Words **119**

Unit 49 /r/ after vowels   Intonation in Polite Questions **122**

Unit 50 **Review** **125**

Diagnostic Test **126**

To the Teacher

*P*ronunciation Pairs, Second Edition, is a comprehensive pronunciation course that covers all the individual consonant and vowel sounds of North American English, as well as stress, rhythm, intonation, linking, and other features of connected speech. It is designed for learners at the high beginning through intermediate levels. Often pronunciation practice is not adequately incorporated into the beginning and intermediate levels of language teaching. As a result, mistakes made in those early stages become fossilized – repeated so many times that they become difficult, if not impossible, to eradicate. *Pronunciation Pairs* is designed to help teachers incorporate pronunciation practice at these earlier levels, when pronunciation practice is likely to do the most good.

Organization of the Student's Book

The Teacher's Manual for *Pronunciation Pairs*, Second Edition, follows the same general organization as the Student's Book. The Student's Book is divided into two sections – one on vowels and one on consonants. After an introductory unit, which introduces the basic mouth positions and movements needed to produce the sounds in that section, each unit presents a specific sound, often in contrast with a sound that has been practiced in an earlier unit.

- **Overview.** The Teacher's Manual begins with an Overview that describes the organization of each unit, with suggested classroom procedures for presenting tasks, such as word pairs and dialogs, that occur in almost all the units of the Student's Book.

- **Student Difficulties.** Each unit of the Teacher's Manual begins with a description of the problems that speakers of different languages are likely to have with the target sound in the unit. This provides teachers with an indication of how relevant each unit is to their students.

- **Description of the tasks.** The main section in each unit of the Teacher's Manual describes each of the tasks in the Student's Book, with suggested procedures for using the material and background information on specific language items. This section also often includes ideas for additional practice.

- **Answer keys and audio scripts.** Each unit of the Teacher's Manual includes answer keys for all the tasks in the Student's Book. The answer keys incorporate audio scripts for all the material on the audio program that is not shown in the Student's Book.

- **Connecting pronunciation to the classwork.** The detailed notes for each unit provide suggestions for linking the teaching of pronunciation with other classwork. These suggestions are found under the headings *Further Practice* and *Linking Pronunciation with Other Classwork*.

- **Diagnostic Test.** Following the individual units, there is a Diagnostic Test on pages 127–131 of the Teacher's Manual that can be used to help determine the pronunciation needs of the students.

Selecting Material

The units in the Student's Book may be taught in whatever order seems most useful. Particularly at beginning levels, some students may be happy to spend time on sounds that are easy for them. But many classes will not have enough time to work through all the material in the book. If class time is limited, focus on the sounds and features of connected speech that are important for your students. Students with different native languages will have different pronunciation problems. The Diagnostic Test on pages 127–131 of the Teacher's Manual can be used to help determine the pronunciation problems of individual students. A List of Likely Errors on the Web site (www.cambridge.org/pp/student) summarizes information on the difficulties speakers of different languages are likely to have, to help you decide which units are the most important for your students.

It is also important to consider the needs and goals of your particular students. For example, will most of their communication be with native speakers of English? Or will most of their contact be with other nonnative speakers? Some features will affect intelligibility regardless of the context – for example, substituting the sound /p/ for /f/ in a word like *fork* or /r/ for /l/ in a word like *glass*. But other substitutions, such as using /z/ in place of /ð/ in a word like *other*, are less likely to cause breakdowns in communication, especially among nonnative speakers. For students who aim at a native or near-native accent (and some language learners do, regardless of the context in which they will use the language), of course, mastery of all the sounds is important. Remember, too, that each unit in the Student's Book practices a feature of connected speech, so that even if the particular sound in a unit is not problematic for your students, the material from the Dialog onward may be useful for them.

The Audio Program

The classroom audio program, available in CD or cassette format, contains all the examples and practice material marked with the 🎧 symbol in the Student's Book. For each unit, this material includes the instructions for producing the sound, the illustrated word pairs, the words and sentences in the Test Yourself task, the vocabulary list, the dialog or other listening selection, examples of the feature of connected speech that is practiced, and the list of common expressions.

The Student's Book for *Pronunciation Pairs*, Second Edition, includes a separate student audio CD. This contains all the dialogs (or similar listening selections) in the Student's Book. Since repeated listening practice and self-monitoring are often crucial for improving pronunciation, it is recommended that your students have a CD player or computer for listening to the audio CD that accompanies the Student's Book, as well as equipment for recording their own pronunciation and a mirror for checking the position of the mouth for producing the sound in each unit.

Overview

Each unit of the Teacher's Manual follows the general format described below.

Student Difficulties

Often students learning a language have difficulty with the sounds of the new language, hearing a new sound as being more like a sound in their own language than it is or hearing two different sounds in the new language as the same. The opening section of the teaching notes in each unit gives information on the problems students with different native languages are likely to have with the target sound.

A summary of common problems that speakers of different languages have appears in a List of Likely Errors on the Web site at www.cambridge.org/pp/student. For more details on the pronunciation problems of speakers of various languages, consult *Learner English* (Cambridge University Press, 2001).

Making the Sound

When learning a language, students often have difficulty hearing unfamiliar sounds or hearing the differences between some sounds. It helps to show students how sounds are produced. Each unit of the Student's Book for *Pronunciation Pairs* begins with an illustration that shows the positions of the mouth and tongue for producing the sound introduced in that unit, accompanied by directions that explain how to make the sound. In many units, there is also an illustration comparing the mouth and tongue positions for making a sound that students often confuse with the target sound.

Make sure that students understand how the sound in each unit is made. Demonstrate where possible and model the sound, in addition to using the recording. Students should watch your mouth as you make the sound. For many sounds, it is also helpful for students to use small hand mirrors to watch their own mouths as they say the sound. The detailed teaching notes for each unit often include amplified instructions or additional notes on the sound and suggestions for dealing with particular problems described under *Student Difficulties*. These notes can be read or paraphrased to the class according to the teacher's discretion.

Students briefly practice the sound in isolation. Even with a large class, it should be possible to check every student's performance at this stage. The teacher can give further individual help to those who need it during the group practice later on.

Do not dwell too long on the production of individual sounds. Students may become discouraged if they are expected to pronounce isolated sounds perfectly. Note, too, that sounds become modified in the stream of speech, in other words, as they occur surrounded by other sounds. Sounds pronounced in isolation often have an artificial quality.

Variation in the sound The teaching notes often include a section on variation to point out different ways the sound may be said by different speakers of English or in different contexts. These sections are included for reference. They can be discussed with students at the discretion of the teacher, according to the level of the class and the relevance of the note to the students.

Word Pairs

Illustrated word pairs appear in almost every unit of the Student's Book. Word pairs (also known as *minimal pairs*) are pairs of words, like *sheep* and *ship* or *time* and *dime*, that differ by only one sound. The illustrations of the word pairs in the Student's Book help students understand that altering a single sound in a word can change its meaning completely, demonstrating the importance of accurate pronunciation.

Each set of word pairs contrasts two sounds that students often confuse or hear as being the same. Practice with the word pairs can help students learn to recognize and produce the target sound in each unit and to distinguish it from other sounds in English with which it might be confused. You can use the *Student Difficulties* section in the Teacher's Manual to help determine which sounds students of particular language backgrounds are likely to confuse.

Check that students understand the vocabulary in the illustrated word pairs. If necessary, demonstrate the meaning of the word, or use the word in a sentence suitable to the class level. Students should listen to the recording or to the teacher and repeat the words, reading from the list first vertically and then horizontally. If possible, initially have students cover the words and focus only on the pictures.

Additional examples of word pairs are given in the teacher's notes for each unit. Sometimes these examples include more advanced vocabulary items than the words generally used in the Student's Book. Teachers can decide whether to use these additional examples based on the students' level and need for further practice and on their own ability to illustrate or explain the words.

To give students extra practice in recognizing the sounds, you can follow one of the procedures below, giving immediate feedback on students' responses:

1. Read two words from the list of word pairs. Students say whether the words were the same or different.

2. Read words at random from the list of word pairs in the Student's Book or the additional pairs given in the Teacher's Manual. Students indicate if they heard sound 1 or sound 2, for example by saying the numbers or holding up one or two fingers.

3. Point to a picture and say one of the words in the word pair. Students say whether the word was the correct one or not.

4. Say three words, two of which are the same. Students identify the word that was different.

5. Say one of the words in a pair. Students choose an appropriate paraphrase (e.g., written on the board or a paper handout). For example, Teacher: "Ship." Students: "A boat." Teacher: "Sheep." Students: "An animal."

For vowel or consonant contrasts where there is a clearly visible difference in the mouth position (e.g., the vowel sounds /ɑ/ as in *hot* and /ʌ/ as in *cup*), you may want to try saying one of the contrasted sounds or one of the words in a word pair silently and have students identify which sound or word was said. Then, facing away from the class, try saying one of the sounds or words to see if students can hear the difference without seeing the shape of your mouth. Students can try these procedures, too, either working in pairs or with the whole class.

Test Yourself

Every unit with word pairs in the Student's Book also includes practice recognizing the two sounds contrasted in the word pairs. Practice moves from word level to sentence level and from recognition to production.

In step 1, students either listen to two words and say whether the words were the same or different or listen and identify which of the words in their books they heard. In step 2, students look at the sentences in their books and identify which of the words in parentheses was said on the recording. This gives students practice in hearing the target sound in connected speech.

In step 3, students practice the sentences from step 2 with a partner. Working in pairs allows everyone to practice speaking and listening, even in a large class. One person says each sentence, choosing a word from the word pair in parentheses. The other person points to the word that was said. After the first person has read all the sentences, students should switch roles. You may want to remind students not to consistently choose the same word heard on the recording. Walk around the room and listen while students practice. Rather than correcting every error, you may want to take notes as you move around the room and deal with common errors with the whole class at the end. This helps keep students focused on talking and listening to their partner and helps avoid making students self-conscious by calling attention to their errors.

Vocabulary

Each unit of the Student's Book includes a list of words or phrases, usually taken from the dialog, that contain the target sound. For the most part, the vocabulary lists use simple, everyday words. Practicing the vocabulary helps prepare students for the activities, especially the dialog, that follow. Students practice the vocabulary words in various ways, both in the vocabulary section and the activities that follow.

In many of the units, students use the vocabulary words in a task – for example, matching words with pictures, identifying words that do not have the target sound, or completing rules. In all of the units, students have the opportunity to hear and repeat the vocabulary words. Play the recording and have students repeat each word chorally. A few individual students could be asked to repeat some of the more difficult words. If additional practice is needed, read words at random from the list and have students repeat them. For consonant sounds, you may want to note whether students have more difficulty with the sound in a particular position (beginning, middle, or end) in words.

Discuss any unfamiliar vocabulary that is essential for understanding the dialog that follows. You may prefer, however, to let students listen to the dialog before discussing vocabulary so that they can hear the words in context.

Dialog

Each unit of the Student's Book contains a dialog or other listening selection with a high concentration of the sound (or sounds) being practiced in the unit. The dialog also incorporates the feature of connected speech that is practiced later in the unit. Each dialog includes a guided listening task that involves use of the target sound. Additional suggestions for practice are often given in the Teacher's Manual. Work on pronunciation calls for extended practice, and students are likely to be more motivated to listen to, repeat, and learn dialogs or other contextualized practice material than to practice isolated sentences. The dialogs are written to sound as natural as possible, and students do not need to understand every word. Students are given several opportunities to work with the material in the dialog.

Each dialog is introduced by a descriptive line, shown in italics, that briefly describes the setting and characters. An accompanying illustration also helps set the context. Introduce the dialog by reading or paraphrasing the descriptive line or directing attention to the illustration. Alternatively, ask students to look at the illustration and predict what the dialog will be about.

Explain the task in step 1. In many units the task involves a listening goal – for example, answering questions, listening for particular items, or making corrections in the written text. In other units, students work with a partner to fill in blanks or circle the correct items in their books. In either case, students use words from the preceding *Vocabulary* section to complete the task. In step 2, students listen to the dialog and check their answers. You may want to have students compare their answers with a partner before listening to the recording to check their answers.

Although most of the dialogs are intended primarily for practice in listening to the target sound in context, they can also be used for oral practice. Longer dialogs or lines from dialogs can be shortened for student practice, according to the class level. After students listen to the dialog in step 2, play the dialog again, pausing after each sentence for students to repeat chorally. If students have difficulty in saying a line smoothly or with the appropriate rhythm, try using "backward buildup." With this technique, sentences are broken down into words and increasingly larger phrases, working from the end of the sentence backward. Students repeat each segment after the teacher, for example:

> My eyes are closed, and I'm going back to sleep.
> to sleep
> back to sleep
> going back to sleep
> and I'm going back to sleep
> etc.

When students practice the dialog, encourage them to look up as they say each line, rather than looking down at their books. Students should read each line (or phrase, if the line is long) silently and then look up as they say the line. Demonstrate this to the class. The "read and look up" technique helps students to group words into phrases said with natural rhythm and intonation rather than reading word by word.

Depending on student interest, dialogs could also be practiced in groups, with the teacher moving around the room checking pronunciation and students taking turns performing. However, before spending a great deal of time practicing the dialog at this point, keep in mind that the guided pronunciation practice later in the unit is usually based on the dialog and incorporates both the target sound and the feature of connected speech presented in the unit.

Stress, Rhythm, and Intonation

Even if students can pronounce and recognize every English sound, they may still have difficulty understanding spoken language and being understood if they have not mastered the suprasegmental features of English – features such as stress, rhythm, and intonation that occur along with individual consonant and vowel sounds. In addition to practicing a sound, each unit also practices a suprasegmental feature.

After the dialog, a section with boxed information presents a feature of connected speech that students have been exposed to receptively in the dialog. Read or summarize the information in the box with the class. Then have students listen and repeat the examples, which are usually taken from the dialog. It is a good idea for students to listen to the examples several times before they repeat, to help them memorize the pattern. It is also helpful for students to repeat the examples chorally at the same time as they are said on the recording, or at the same time that you say them.

In units practicing stress or intonation, stressed syllables are shown in darker, boldfaced type. Arrows indicating the direction of the intonation are shown over the part of a sentence where there is a change in intonation. In units that practice linking words together, curved linking lines are shown under the relevant parts of the words.

Detailed background notes on the feature of connected speech that is practiced, including a description of likely student difficulties and suggested teaching procedures, appear in the teaching notes for each unit.

Practice Activities

After the suprasegmental feature has been presented, each unit has one or more interactive activities that practice both that feature and the target sound introduced in the unit. In some units, the practice is more structured, for example, using guided conversations or scrambled sentences. In others the practice is less structured, using activities such as surveys, games, discussions, or role plays, giving students opportunities to exchange information, express opinions, and use language more freely. Some units include both types of practice.

Make sure that students understand the task. Go over a few examples with the whole class listening. While students are involved in group work, the teacher should be free to give further individual help to those who need it. Students who finish the group activity early can practice acting out the dialog.

Spelling

Students are very often puzzled by English spelling. It may seem not only arbitrary to them but also unrelated to any other part of their class. Linking spelling and pronunciation provides a systematic approach to the teaching of spelling, as well as an opportunity for further practice and review of pronunciation material. Each unit of the Student's Book includes a spelling section that lists basic spelling patterns for the sound being practiced. These spelling lists use words taught in the unit as examples, as well as other words that illustrate the patterns.

It is suggested that the spelling material in the Student's Book be left until the rest of the unit has been completed and introduced in a later lesson. In the initial practice of a new sound, the spelling of words very often distracts students from the correct pronunciation rather than helping them. The spelling sections provide an opportunity for further practice and review of the words presented in the unit. The additional words, not taken from the unit, can be used for practice according to the level of the class. Teachers may want to add or substitute other words familiar to students.

The simplest way of introducing the spelling material is to ask students, for example, "How do you write/spell the sound /iy/?" and to make a list of words on the board for each spelling of the sound, using students' suggestions whenever possible. Note that spaces are provided in the Student's Book for students to write example words that illustrate the most common spellings for each sound. Add spellings that students miss, underlining the spelling that represents the sound in an example word. Ask a student to try pronouncing the word, or say the word and have students repeat it. Call attention to generalizations that can be made about a particular spelling pattern (e.g., that it occurs only at the end of a word).

The Teacher's Manual often gives suggestions for further practice of the spelling patterns, such as practice distinguishing between similar spellings for different sounds.

One way to review spelling patterns, especially for vowel sounds, is to use a list of rhyming words as the basis for a game of Concentration (matching pairs), in which the object is to find pairs of words that rhyme. The game can give students practice with the use of different spellings to represent a single sound (as in *sun*, *touch*, *blood*) and with the use of the same spelling to represent different sounds (as in *love*, *stove*, *move*). Both ideas are often difficult for students who speak languages in which spelling is more or less phonetic and a single sound usually has a single spelling. To prepare the game, write each word on a small card, using about twenty to thirty words (ten to fifteen pairs). To play, the cards are shuffled and turned facedown. A student turns two cards faceup and says the words on them. Other players should be able to see the cards, to check the student's pronunciation and judgment as to whether the words rhyme. If the words rhyme, the student keeps the cards and turns over another pair. If the words do not rhyme, the student puts the cards facedown in their original places and the next student follows the same procedure. The player who accumulates the most pairs is the winner. The game can be played using one large set of cards for the whole class or with separate sets of cards for groups of students. Here is a sample list of matching pairs:

/ow/	/ʊ/	/ʌ/	/uw/	/aw/
phone/groan	good/could	sun/done	move/prove	how/now
know/sew	wool/full	much/touch	food/rude	loud/crowd
stove/drove		love/glove		
home/comb		gum/some		
		mud/blood		

Common Expressions

Each unit of the Student's Book ends with a boxed list of about six common expressions that illustrate use of the target sound in everyday phrases and sentences. If possible, have students listen and repeat the sentences several times to help them absorb the rhythm of the sentences and to improve fluency. In many cases other words could be substituted for one of the words in the sentence to extend practice and encourage students to use the target sound outside the classroom. For example, in Unit 2 other words could be substituted for the underlined words in these common expressions:

I think it's interesting.
Where do you live? I live in the city.

Further Practice

The teaching notes for some units provide teaching material for further practice, if needed. Practice may involve the target sound, the stress or intonation pattern taught in the unit, or a related feature of pronunciation.

Linking Pronunciation with Other Classwork

Teachers sometimes find that students can master a pronunciation point in pronunciation lessons but lapse in general classwork or in ordinary speech. The answer to this problem is to tie pronunciation in with general language teaching as much as possible. For example, if students have difficulty with the sound /ʃ/, it can be practiced in lessons on:

1. describing actions using *she* ("She's sleeping.")
2. talking about nationality ("What nationality is she? Is she Russian?")
3. asking for advice ("What should I wear?")

Few pronunciation difficulties will be overcome with one isolated pronunciation lesson. The teacher should be prepared for a slow process in which the problem is approached in as many different contexts, on as many different occasions, using as many different materials as possible.

The teaching notes for each unit provide suggestions for linking the teaching of pronunciation with other classwork. Sometimes the link is made with teaching a grammatical structure (for example, continuous tenses with *-ing* verb endings in Unit 46); in other cases the link is more functional (for example, complaining about problems in an apartment or a house, also in Unit 46).

In some cases, specific ideas are given for practicing the sound in the suggested context. In most cases, only the context is mentioned; teachers should teach the grammatical structure or other item in whatever way they would normally teach it, but with attention given to the sound or other feature of pronunciation in question. Only a few suggestions for practice are given in each unit. These are merely sample ideas, and teachers should look for other opportunities to tie in their own general coursework with teaching pronunciation.

Word Stress Practice

Since stress is such an important part of the pronunciation of English words, the teaching notes for almost every unit end with a suggested exercise for practicing stress in words from the unit. The format varies, though often the material takes the form of a recognition test. Stress patterns are usually illustrated with dots of varying sizes (e.g., the dots • ● representing the stress pattern of *today*).

You may want to have students practice the stress patterns before doing the recognition test. To do this, draw one of the stress patterns shown in the teaching notes on the board, making larger and darker dots to represent stressed syllables and smaller and lighter dots to represent unstressed syllables. Tap out the stress pattern with a ruler or pencil and / or show the pattern by clapping. Students should join in. Then read aloud the words that have this stress pattern. Students listen and repeat the words, accompanied by tapping or clapping. If possible, include other words with the stress pattern that your students know. Repeat these steps for the other stress pattern(s) shown before proceeding with the exercise.

Section A Vowels

The introduction to Section A in the Student's Book presents the vocabulary that students will need in order to follow the directions for making the vowel sound that begin each unit. It also introduces the basic mouth positions and movements that students will need to use for producing English vowel sounds.

Work through this unit with the class. It would be helpful for students to use mirrors to watch their own mouths as they follow the directions in the Student's Book.

Practice moving your mouth

Students begin by practicing the basic movements of the mouth and lips for making different vowel sounds.

Practice moving your tongue

Steps 1–5 (page 2) Students practice the basic ways that the tongue moves in making English vowel sounds. The tongue is pushed forward in the mouth for the vowels /iy/, /ɪ/, /ɛ/, /ey/, and /æ/. The tongue is pulled back for the vowels /uw/, /ʊ/, /ow/, and /ɔ/. Vowels such as /iy/ and /uw/ are made with either the front or back of the tongue high in the mouth. Vowels such as /ɑ/ are made with the tongue low in the mouth. The tongue is curled up and back to make /ər/.

Steps 1–3 (page 3) Students practice the positions for making the sounds /iy/, /ɑ/, and /uw/. These three basic vowels (or close equivalents) occur in nearly all languages.

Have students practice saying /iy/ – /ɑ/ – /uw/ slowly, making the sounds long. Model this, asking students to watch your mouth as you say the sounds. Have students practice saying the sounds several times. Ask them to feel the way their mouths and tongues move as they say these sounds. Becoming aware of how the mouth and tongue move in making these sounds should make it easier for students to focus on the subtler movements needed to make other vowel sounds.

Practice making tense and relaxed vowel sounds

Students practice tensing their mouth muscles and then relaxing them as they say the tense vowels /iy/ and /uw/ and the lax vowel /ʌ/.

The distinction between tense and lax (or relaxed) vowels is crucial for distinguishing pairs of vowels like /iy/ – /ɪ/, /ey/ – /ɛ/, and /uw/ – /ʊ/, which students often confuse. If students have difficulty feeling the change in their mouth muscles, have them tighten and relax other muscles, for example clenching and unclenching their fists, as they practice the tense and lax vowels. Point out the difference in the lips. The lips are often spread or rounded for tense vowels, but in a more relaxed, neutral position for lax vowels.

UNIT 1 /iy/ • tea   Stressed Syllables in Words

Student Difficulties

Most students do not have trouble producing a sound close to /iy/. Many students, however, make the sound too short and omit the /y/ glide sound at the end. In many languages, including French, Greek, Hebrew, Japanese, Russian, and Spanish, the sound that resembles English /iy/ is a shorter, pure vowel without the /y/ ending. Speakers of these languages may substitute this shorter sound for /iy/ in English or confuse /iy/ with /ɪ/ (practiced in Unit 2).

Speakers of some languages, including Arabic and Thai, have a strong tendency to put a glottal stop before all vowels at the beginning of words.

Making the Sound

The first vowel practiced in this book is the vowel made with the tongue in its highest and farthest forward position. It is a good sound to start with because most languages have a similar vowel, and students will probably not have a great deal of difficulty producing a sound close to English /iy/. Being able to say the sound /iy/ correctly is helpful for contrastive work in the next unit with /ɪ/, which most students do find difficult.

Have students read the directions for making the sound /iy/ as they listen to the audio and look at the illustrations. When modeling the sound, you may want to exaggerate the /y/ glide to make it easier for students to hear. Students should feel the tongue move up slightly for the second, glide part of the vowel. When the sound /iy/ comes before another vowel sound, the /y/ sound is used to link the vowels smoothly together: coffee /y/ or tea.

Variation in the sound

1. The sound /iy/ is longest when it is stressed and at the end of a word, as in *tea*, or followed by a voiced consonant, as in *cheese*. It is shorter, and the /y/ glide sound is less noticeable, before a voiceless consonant, as in *sheep*. Compare *need/neat, feed/feet, bead/beat, seed/seat, league/leak, peas/piece, leave/leaf.*

2. The sound /iy/ is shortest when it is in an unstressed syllable, as at the end of *city, coffee,* or *movie*. In an unstressed syllable, there may be no glide at all.

A Vocabulary See Overview, p. ix.

Step 1 Students first practice the sound /iy/ in words where it is long and the /y/ glide is most noticeable – at the end of a word or before a voiced consonant sound. If students do not make the vowel long enough, it may be helpful to tell them to say /iy/ twice.

Step 2 Students practice the sound /iy/ in words where the vowel sound is shorter and the glide sound is much less noticeable.

Step 3

ANSWER
/iy/ is longer in the words on the left.

B Dialog See Overview, pp. ix–x.

Step 1 Introduce the dialog, directing students' attention to the menu. Three friends are talking about what they are going to order at a pizza restaurant.

Have students cover the dialog (e.g., with a piece of paper). They should not cover the questions in step 1.

Step 2 Play the recording of the dialog again and go over the answers to step 1.

ANSWERS
1. meat
2. two meat pizzas and one cheese pizza
3. Greek salad

You may want to add other questions with answers that use the sound /iy/, for example: "How much is the lunch special?" "What is Deena having to eat?" "Who wants coffee?"

Ask students what they like on pizza. If they name any foods that have the sound /iy/, write them on the board.

C Stressed Syllables in Words

Background notes This section introduces syllables and stress within words, including some tips for predicting which syllable will be stressed in two-syllable words. Each English syllable normally has a vowel sound, except for words that have a syllabic /n/ or /l/, as in the second syllables of *written* and *little*.

In English, the stressed syllable in a word is longer, sounds louder, and is often said at a higher pitch than an unstressed syllable. The vowel in the stressed syllable has a clear sound. Though some words have both a strongly stressed syllable and a syllable with lighter stress, only the distinction between stressed and unstressed syllables is presented here.

The stress pattern of a word is a basic part of its pronunciation. Putting the stress on the wrong syllable can make a word very hard to understand. Some languages do not make a clear difference between stressed and unstressed syllables. And in many languages, stress is predictable, always falling on the same syllable (for example, the first) in a word. English stress is much less predictable, but there are some rules that can help.

The vast majority of two-syllable nouns in English are stressed on the first syllable. Many two-syllable verbs are stressed on the second syllable, though the percentage of verbs that follow the rule is not as high as the percentage of nouns. Some words can be used as either a noun or a verb, depending on the stress. For example, **record, ob**ject, **con**duct, **des**ert, and **pres**ent are nouns, but re**cord**, ob**ject**, con**duct**, de**sert**, and pre**sent** are verbs. For more on word stress, see the notes for Unit 20, task B.

Read or summarize the information in the box with the class. Make sure students understand that *syllable* here refers to the way a word is said, not to its written form.

Step 1 Have students tap out or clap the stress pattern of each word as they say it. You may also want to use a visual device, such as large and small circles, to show the stress pattern: ● • for *pizza,* • ● for *repeat.*

Step 2 Encourage students to tap out the syllables, using their fingers, feet, or a pencil, as they listen to the words.

Instead of having students underline the stressed syllable, you could ask them to hold up one finger if the first syllable is stressed and two fingers if the second syllable is stressed. That way, you can check their answers as they do the task.

Step 3 Encourage students to make the stressed vowels long when they repeat the words.

Note that *evening* has two spoken syllables, even though it may look like it has three. The second *e* is silent: ev∅ning.

Step 4 If students have not studied grammar recently, check that they can identify the nouns (*pizza, coffee, cheesecake, people, season, ice cream, evening*) and verbs (*repeat, believe*). Note that some two-syllable adjectives have stress on the first syllable (e.g., *ready*) and some have stress on the second syllable (e.g., *complete*), though first-syllable stress is more common.

Extra practice At a later time, show students how changing the stress can change a word from a noun to a verb in words like *record, present, object, conduct, suspect, desert,* and *rebel.* For example, give students a list of these words. Review the rule about stress in two-syllable nouns and verbs. Read the words, choosing whether to stress each one as a noun or a verb. For each one, students say whether they heard a noun or a verb. Then have students practice the words in sentences.

D Role-Play

In groups of three or four, students role-play ordering food in a restaurant. If possible, rearrange tables and chairs to create a more realistic setting. You may want to suggest or elicit other phrases students might need for their role plays, such as "Are you ready to order?" "Yes, I'll have . . . / I'd like . . . / No, not yet. / No, we need another minute." "Anything else?"

Alternatively, you can wait until students have practiced the sound /ɪ/ in Unit 2 to do this activity. Write Sound 1 (/iy/) and Sound 2 (/ɪ/) on the board, and say the sounds. Say the names of foods and ask students to tell you which sound to write them under. Or give two names (e.g., *Steve* with the sound /iy/ and *Nick* with the sound /ɪ/) and ask students which foods each one likes. Foods with the sound /ɪ/ include: fish, chicken, shrimp, spinach, vanilla, milk. Then proceed as above.

Note the intonation of the question "Would you like bean soup or Greek salad?" The voice rises in pitch on the first choice and falls in pitch on the second choice (see Unit 9, task C).

E The Alphabet

Spelling aloud is a very important skill for learners. Even fairly advanced learners may have trouble spelling words aloud or understanding oral spellings. They may, for example, confuse the letters *e* and *a* or *e* and *i* or mispronounce letters, such as *c* and *k*, that use these vowel sounds.

Step 1 If their native language uses an alphabet, you can ask students to point out the names of letters that are either the same as or different from the letters in their own alphabet.

Step 2 Note that z = /ziy/ in American English, but /zɛd/ in British English.

Step 3

Step 4 Working in pairs, students take turns spelling their first and last names (and middle names, if they have them) as their partner writes down the letters. If they need more practice, you can have them switch partners with other pairs.

Extra practice For review at a later time:

1. Prepare a short list of words, including words with letters such as *a, e, i, g,* and *j* that might cause confusion, for example: *repeat, eighteen, believe, chicken, orange juice.* Either dictate the words or divide the class into pairs, with one student spelling the words aloud and the other writing them down. Students compare their lists at the end.

2. Respell words as letters of the alphabet, as often done in text messaging. Have students "translate" these. They will need to know how to pronounce the names of the letters to do this, for example: CU (= See you), EZ (= easy), NE (= any), MT (= empty), IC (= I see).

F Spelling

The variety of spellings for the sound /iy/ may be confusing to students, especially those who speak languages in which spelling is regular and more or less phonetic, with a single spelling representing a single sound. Point out that even though there are many spellings for the sound /iy/, almost all contain the letter *e*. In English, unlike many other languages, the letter *i* does not usually represent the sound /iy/, except in a few words, such as *visa, machine,* and *ski.*

Note that at the end of a word, the sound /iy/ is usually spelled with the letter *y.*

G Common Expressions See Overview, p. xii.

Linking Pronunciation with Other Classwork

Tie pronunciation in with practice of:

1. Introductions: "Pleased to meet you." / "Nice to meet you." / "Nice to meet you, too."

2. Requests with *please*: "Could you repeat that, please?" / "Can I please speak to _____?" Note that some students tend to put too much stress on the word *please.*

3. Nationalities and language names, for example: "Do you speak Chinese / Japanese / Portuguese / Vietnamese / Swedish / Norwegian?"

UNIT 2 /ɪ/ • sit   Stress in Numbers; Moving Stress

Student Difficulties

Nearly all learners have difficulty with the sound /ɪ/. Usually they confuse it with /iy/, since many languages have only one vowel in the area of /iy/ and /ɪ/. Arabic speakers may also confuse the sound /ɪ/ with /ɛ/. Unfortunately, there are many pairs of words in English that are distinguished only by whether they contain the sound /iy/ or /ɪ/, so failure to hear and produce the difference between these two sounds can easily result in misunderstandings.

Making the Sound

Have students read the directions for making the sound /ɪ/ as they listen to the audio and look at the illustrations. Demonstrate and model the two vowels /iy/ and /ɪ/. The tongue is a little lower in the mouth for the sound /ɪ/ than for /iy/. Students should not move their tongues up toward /y/ when saying /ɪ/.

To help students who have difficulty distinguishing between /iy/ and /ɪ/, focus on the difference in the shape of the lips and the fact that /ɪ/ is a much more relaxed sound than /iy/. By placing their fingers under their chins, students should be able to feel the tension in their muscles when saying /iy/ and the lack of tension in their muscles when saying /ɪ/. They can use a mirror to check the position of their lips.

Variation in the sound

1. The sound /ɪ/ is longer before a voiced consonant and shorter before a voiceless consonant. Compare *hid / hit, rib / rip, ridge / rich, his / hiss, Ms. / Miss.*

2. The sound /ɪ/ is common in unstressed syllables as well as in stressed syllables. In many unstressed syllables, the pronunciation of the vowel may vary between /ɪ/ and /ə/, as in *American* or *college,* or between /ɪ/ and /iy/, as in *because.*

A Word Pairs See Overview, p. viii.

Word pairs for additional practice:

/iy/–/ɪ/: leave/live, eat/it, feet/fit, beat/bit, heat/hit, cheap/chip, green/grin, bean/bin (*or* been), reach/rich, least/list, meal/mill, peel/pill, bead/bid, ease/is, cheeks/chicks

B Test Yourself See Overview, p. ix.

Step 1

ANSWERS	
1. S (leave, leave)	4. S (sit, sit)
2. D (sheep, ship)	5. D (sleep, slip)
3. D (feel, fill)	6. S (heel, heel)

Step 2

ANSWERS	
1. He isn't going to leave.	4. Those hills are very high.
2. Try not to slip.	5. Did you fill the glass?
3. They want to buy a sheep.	6. Do you want a seat?

C Vocabulary See Overview, p. ix.

Remind students that in words with more than one syllable, one syllable is stressed, or stronger than the others (see Unit 1, task C). This syllable is shown in bold type. Note that some learners pronounce *interesting* as four syllables and put stress on the third syllable: *interesting*. Native speakers usually say "**in**teresting" /'ɪn•trəs•tɪŋ/ – three syllables, with stress on the first syllable.

Some students have difficulty pronouncing the /ts/ in *it's,* which can sound like a mistake in grammar (*Is a book). Forward and backward buildup of the word may be helpful. Write on the board and have students practice: it, it's, s, ts, it's.

The titles *Mrs., Mr., Ms.,* and *Miss* are all pronounced with the sound /ɪ/.

D Dialog See Overview, pp. ix–x.

Step 1 Have students work with a partner to fill in the blanks. Encourage them to say the words aloud as they fill them in.

The original *King Kong,* a movie about a fictional giant gorilla, was made in 1933. There have been several remakes of the film, including one released in 2005. Ask students if they have seen any of the King Kong movies.

Step 2 The linking together of words that naturally occurs in connected speech can sometimes make it hard for learners to tell where one word ends and another begins. You may want to point out, for example, that *Is he,* as in the second line of the dialog, often sounds like "izzy" in conversation.

Ask students what they would do if they stayed home sick from school or work. Would they go to a film in the evening?

ANSWERS	
Mrs. Kim	Hello, Cindy.
Cindy	Hi, Mrs. Kim. Is William in? Is he coming with me to the film? I picked up a ticket for him.
Mrs. Kim	Oh, William's sick.
Cindy	Here he is! Hi, William! Are you sick?
William	What film is it? Anything interesting?
Cindy	It's *King Kong.* And it begins in fifteen minutes.
William	Fifty minutes? Come in and sit down.
Cindy	Not fifty minutes, fifteen!
Mrs. Kim	Listen, William, if you're sick, I don't think . . .
William	Quick! Or we'll miss the beginning of the film!

E Stress in Numbers

Background notes Students often confuse numbers like *fourteen* /fɔr•'tiyn/ and *forty* /'fɔr•tiy/. When counting (13, 14, 15, etc.), native English speakers tend to stress the first syllable of each number more than they otherwise would. Since students usually learn numbers by counting, they often continue to stress the first syllable of *-teen* numbers in other contexts, making it hard to distinguish -teen from -ty numbers. If students don't pronounce final /n/ clearly, it can add to the confusion. Alternatively, especially when there is a question about which number was said, students may stress the last syllable of -ty numbers, making the problem worse.

Have students repeat the numbers, reading the columns horizontally. Emphasize the stress by tapping, for example with a ruler. Notice that in North American English, the pronunciation of the /t/ in -teen and -ty differs. At the beginning of -teen, /t/ is voiceless and aspirated (pronounced with a puff of air). In unstressed -ty, except in *fifty* and *sixty*, /t/ is pronounced more like a quick English /d/ sound (see Unit 24, task A).

Write the numbers on the board. Ask a student to stand at the board and point to the numbers as you say them. Then have students take turns saying the numbers clearly enough for another student to point to the correct numbers.

F Moving Stress

Background notes Usually, the stressed syllable in a word does not change. It is part of the pronunciation of the word. But in some words the stress can move to a different syllable when another word follows. This happens especially in numbers and adjectives that have strong stress at the end. English rhythm tends to avoid having two strong stresses next to each other, so when these words are followed by a stressed word or syllable, the stress often moves to a syllable earlier in the word, for example: *Chinese* – but **Chi**nese re**s**taurant, *Japanese* – but a **Jap**anese **paint**ing.

Read or summarize the information in the box with the class. Explain that in most words in English, the stress doesn't change. But in some words, there can be a difference in the stress when the word is said alone and when another word comes after it. The stress moves to an earlier syllable in the word.

Extra practice For practice in hearing the difference between -teen and -ty numbers, read sentences such as the ones below and ask students to say the number they hear.

The meal cost 15 / 50 dollars.
We live at 19 / 90 King Street.
I invited 18 / 80 people to the party.

G Conversation Practice

Students practice the conversation in pairs, substituting different -teen numbers and the corresponding -ty number in the blanks. Check that they use the correct stress when they practice, following the model in task F.

H Bingo Game

Students play bingo in a group of three, four, or five people. The student who calls out the numbers should check them off as they are called, without letting the other students see. Alternatively, you can write the numbers on small pieces of paper that the student can pick up at random. Check that the caller uses the stress shown in task E.

The other students cross out each number as it is called. Alternatively, the grids can be copied and enlarged, and the players can cover the numbers with small pieces of paper.

I Spelling

The tendency of many learners to confuse the sounds /iy/ and /ɪ/ may also involve confusion over spelling. In many other languages, the letter *i* represents a tense vowel sound that resembles English /iy/. In English, however, the letter *i* usually represents the sound /ɪ/ or /ay/, not /iy/. Although *i* does represent the sound /iy/ in a few words (e.g., *ski* and *police*), it is not a regular spelling for this sound.

Background notes

1. The consonant is doubled in words like *sitting* and *winner* to maintain the sound /ɪ/. The letter *i* followed by a single consonant and then a vowel normally has the sound /ay/: compare *diner / dinner*.

2. English words do not end with the letter *v*. An *e* is added in the spelling. Words like *give* and the verb *live* end in *e*, even though *i . . . e* usually spells the sound /ay/, not /ɪ/.

3. Some speakers of American English pronounce the word *been* with the vowel /ɛ/ rather than /ɪ/.

4. The spelling list in the Student's Book does not include spellings for unstressed /ɪ/, as in *example* or *because*.

J Common Expressions See Overview, p. xii.

Further Practice

Have students practice short sentences that contrast the sounds /iy/ and /ɪ/, for example:

It isn't easy.
Read this.
I'm really busy.

Do you need this?
Did you see it?
Sit on this seat.
Did you speak to him?
When did you meet him?
I feel sick.
Please speak English.

Linking Pronunciation with Other Classwork

Tie pronunciation in with practice of:

1. It / is / it's / isn't: For example, play the game 20 Questions. In this game, one student thinks of an object. You can limit the object in some way, for example to items in the classroom. The other students then ask *Yes / No* questions to try to identify the object, for example: "Is it bigger than this book?" "Yes, it is. / No, it isn't."

2. Introductions: "This is Mr. / Ms. / Mrs. X. He's / She's . . ."

3. Conditional sentences with *if* (e. g., "If you're sick, stay home.").

4. *This* vs. *these.*

5. Prices, especially with *-teen* and *-ty* numbers.

UNIT 3 /ɛ/ • yes Falling and Rising Intonation

Student Difficulties

Students may have the following difficulties with the sound /ɛ/:

- Some students, including speakers of Arabic, may confuse /ɛ/ with /ɪ/.

- Chinese speakers may confuse /ɛ/ with /ʌ/.

- Other students may pronounce /ɛ/ with the mouth too open, causing confusion with /æ/ (for example, pronouncing *pen* more like *pan*).

- Some students, including speakers of Spanish and Italian, may pronounce /ɛ/ as a tense rather than a relaxed sound, creating confusion with /ey/. These students often substitute the same pure (without a glide) tense vowel /e/ for both /ɛ/ and /ey/. This problem may be reinforced by spelling, since in many languages the letter *e* represents the tense vowel sound /e/.

Making the Sound

Have students read the directions for making the sound /ɛ/ as they listen to the audio and look at the illustrations.

Students who pronounce the sound /ɛ/ as /ɪ/ need to open their mouths a little more for /ɛ/. Students who pronounce the sound /ɛ/ as /æ/ need to close their mouths a little. In either case, model the two sounds or direct attention to the mouth diagrams in the book. Students can use a finger or pencil to help judge how wide their mouths should be open. A finger or pencil would just barely fit between the teeth for /ɛ/, but would fit easily for /æ/ and would not fit at all for /ɪ/.

Variation in the sound

1. In some (e.g., Southern) dialects of American English, the sound /ɛ/ may be pronounced like /ɪ/ before a nasal consonant such as /n/. In these dialects, *pen* and *pin* often both sound like /pɪn/.

2. As with other vowel sounds, /ɛ/ is longer when it comes before a voiced consonant and shorter before a voiceless consonant. Compare: *bed / bet, said / set, led / let, peg / peck, edge / etch.*

A Word Pairs See Overview, p. viii.

Word pairs for additional practice:

/ɪ/–/ɛ/: lift/left, fill/fell, bitter/better, if/F, bit/bet, pit/pet, miss/mess, big/beg, did/dead, wrist/rest, disk/desk, pick/peck, six/sex, Ginny/Jenny

B Test Yourself See Overview, p. ix.

Step 1

ANSWERS		
1. bell	3. rest	5. spell
2. pen	4. chicks	6. bitter

Step 2

C Vocabulary See Overview, p. ix.

Step 1 Students can work individually or in pairs to underline the stressed syllables.

Step 2 Check the pronunciation of *everything* and *everybody* when students repeat the words. Note that the second *e* in *every* and compounds with *every* (such as *everything* and *everybody*) is silent: /ɛvriy/. If students pronounce the second *e*, respell the words on the board: "evrything," "evrybody." Stress in words like *everybody, everything, someone, somewhere, anything,* and so on, is on the first syllable.

D Dialog See Overview, pp. ix–x.

Step 1 Have students read the *True / False* questions before they listen to the dialog. Explain that they will listen for the answers to these questions as they listen to the dialog. Students should not look at the dialog in their books when they listen.

Step 2 Play the recording of the dialog again and go over the answers to step 1. You may want to ask students to write one more *True / False* question about the dialog.

E Falling and Rising Intonation

Background notes This section introduces two basic intonation patterns of North American English: falling intonation and rising intonation. In falling intonation, the voice usually jumps up to a high note on the stressed syllable of the most important word and then falls abruptly just after the stressed syllable. The voice continues to fall to a low note at the end of the sentence. If the stressed syllable is at the end of the sentence (e.g., "I went with a **friend**"), the voice jumps and then falls on the same syllable.

In actual speech, the intonation may not follow the rules given in the Student's Book. For example, *Wh-* questions end with rising intonation when they ask for old (repeated) information (see Unit 39, task E). And it is not unusual for *Yes / No* questions to end with falling, instead of rising, intonation. The intonation patterns presented in the Student's Book are common patterns that can be used with a neutral, matter-of-fact meaning for each type of sentence.

Go over the information in the box with the class. You may want to have students repeat the examples several times. To help students learn the intonation, it can be helpful to have them say the sentences at the same time as they are said on the recording, or at the same time that you say them. Use hand gestures to show the direction of the rising and falling intonations.

If students have difficulty with falling intonation for *Wh-* questions, practice with shorter questions, such as "What's this / that?" "Who's this / that?" or "What's her name?" before continuing with the lesson.

F Conversation Practice

Step 1 Students listen to and repeat place names with the sound /ɛ/. Some of the place names here have variant pronunciations. Note that *Kenya* can be pronounced with either the sound /ɛ/ or /iy/. Ask students which places they have been to or which places they would like to go to for a vacation.

Extra practice Ask students: "Which place do you think has the wettest weather / has the best weather / has the friendliest people / has the best restaurants / is the most expensive?"

Step 2 Students can practice the conversation either in pairs or as a whole class. Model the conversation by asking a student the questions.

That student then chooses another student to question, and so on. If possible, add other place names with the sound /ɛ/ that are familiar to students.

Notice the change in stress after the first person asks "Where did you spend your va**ca**tion?" The second person who asks the question should move the main stress to *your* for contrast: "Where did you spend **your** vacation?"

G Discussion

Students practice asking and answering questions about their best vacation. They can use the example conversation and the dialog in task D as models or their own ideas. Encourage them to use words with the sound /ɛ/. Students can be asked to keep track of the words with /ɛ/ that their partners used. As they practice, move around the room checking their intonation and pronunciation of words with the sound /ɛ/.

After students practice in pairs or small groups, have individual students tell the class about their partners' vacations.

H Spelling

Compare common spelling patterns for the sound /ɛ/ and /iy/ using the letter *e*. Note the doubling of the consonant to maintain the sound /ɛ/, rather than the sound /iy/, in words like *getting* and *redder*.

Extra practice For review, give students a list of words such as the one below. Students indicate whether the *e* spelling in each word has the sound /ɛ/ (Sound 1) or /iy/ (Sound 2).

1. friend   6. equal
2. complete   7. jealous
3. piece   8. meat
4. everywhere   9. cream
5. met   10. breakfast

I Common Expressions See Overview, p. xii.

Encourage students to practice asking and answering the question "How do you spell _____?", substituting their own words for *weather*. Check to make sure they use falling intonation on both the question and the answer. You can use hand gestures to show the way the intonation jumps up and then falls.

Further Practice

1. For additional practice of some of the vocabulary in this unit, ask students to find a word in the unit that is the opposite of:

   1. dry (wet)
   2. cheap (expensive)
   3. crowded *or* full (empty)
   4. terrible (excellent)
   5. unfriendly (friendly)
   6. worst (best)
   7. expensive (inexpensive)
   8. nothing (everything)

2. The following letters are pronounced with the sound /ɛ/: *f, l, m, n, s,* and *x*. If students have trouble with oral spelling, have them say these letters aloud. Then write a few words using these letters on the board, and ask them to spell the words aloud, for example:

   1. left   3. listen   5. excellent   7. spelling
   2. many   4. lemon   6. lesson   8. Mexican

Linking Pronunciation with Other Classwork

Tie pronunciation in with practice of:

1. *Wh-* questions.

2. Comparatives and superlatives with *better* and *best*.

3. Comparing the cost of living in different cities, using a chart that shows relative costs, for example:

   Venice   Hotels $$$ Restaurants $$ Rent $$$$

Word Stress Practice

Write some of the following words on the board or on flash cards. Say a few of the words and have students repeat them. Tap out the stress or show a large dot over the stressed syllable and smaller dots over the other syllables. Then point to other words or add them to the list and have students try pronouncing them. Point out or elicit that all these compounds have the strong stress on the first syllable.

anything	anyone	anybody	anywhere
everything	everyone	everybody	everywhere
nothing	no one	nobody	nowhere
something	someone	somebody	somewhere

UNIT 4 /ey/ • day   Stress in Sentences

Student Difficulties

Many students do not have trouble producing a sound close to English /ey/. In many languages, however, there is only one vowel sound in the area of /ey/ and /ɛ/ – a pure tense vowel /e/. Speakers of these languages are likely to substitute this /e/ sound for /ey/ in English and to make the sound too short. They may also confuse the sounds /ey/ and /ɛ/.

- Students who tend to have difficulty with /ey/ include speakers of Arabic, French, Italian, Greek, Hebrew, Japanese, Thai, German, Russian, and Scandinavian languages.
- Some students, including some Spanish and Scandinavian speakers, make the second part of the /ey/ too long.
- Some students, including some Chinese speakers, have difficulty with the sound when it comes before a final consonant and may drop the consonant sound.

Although the most common error is to confuse /ey/ with /ɛ/, some students may confuse /ey/ with /ay/.

Making the Sound

Have students read the directions for making the sound /ey/ as they listen to the audio and look at the illustrations. Explain that in the side view picture, the solid line shows where the tongue is at the beginning of the sound, and the dotted line shows where the tongue moves for the /y/ glide at the end.

Demonstrate and model the two vowels /ɛ/ and /ey/. Students should make their mouth muscles tense for the sound /ey/. Emphasize that /ey/ has two parts: /e/ and /y/. It is not the pure vowel sound /e/ found in many other languages.

You may want to have students practice making the sound /ey/ silently or while whispering the sound, so they can feel the way their mouths move, with the tongue moving up a little and the jaw closing as they make the sound. Emphasize the gradual change in lip position in saying /ey/.

Variation in the sound The sound /ey/ is longest and the /y/ glide is clearest when /ey/ is stressed

and at the end of a word (as in *day*) or followed by a voiced consonant (as in *train*). It is shorter before a voiceless consonant (as in *late*). In an unstressed syllable, there may be no glide at all. Compare *plays/place, stayed/state, played/plate, age/H*.

A Word Pairs See Overview, p. viii.

Word pairs for additional practice:

/ɛ/–/ey/: tell/tail, fell/fail, sell/sail, letter/later, edge/age, chess/chase, get/gate, let/late, west/waist, men/main, Ed/aid

/ay/–/ey/: I/A, my/may, die/day, why/way, light/late, right/rate, white/wait, like/lake, bike/bake

B Test Yourself See Overview, p. ix.

Step 1

ANSWERS	
1. pen	4. pepper
2. shade	5. taste
3. wet	6. sell

Step 2

ANSWERS
1. Can I have some more <u>pepper</u>?
2. Put it in the <u>shed</u>.
3. This <u>pain</u> is terrible.
4. Did you see her <u>later</u>?
5. I want to <u>sail</u> the boat.
6. <u>Test</u> the cake and see if it's done.

C Vocabulary See Overview, p. ix.

Students practice /ey/ first in words where it is most easily distinguished from /ɛ/ – in words where /ey/ is longest and has a clear /y/ glide sound (see *Variation in the sound*).

D Dialog See Overview, pp. ix–x.

Step 1 Have students work with a partner to fill in the blanks. Encourage them to say the words aloud as they fill them in.

Step 2

E Stress in Sentences

Background notes The pattern of stressed and unstressed syllables in a sentence helps give English its rhythm. Just as some syllables in words are stressed and other syllables are weaker, some words in a sentence are stressed and others sound weaker. Stressed words stand out from the words around them. They sound louder and take longer to say. They are also often said at a higher pitch. Stress helps the listener notice the important words in a sentence.

The words that are stressed are usually *content words* – the nouns, main verbs (other than *be*), adjectives, adverbs, and *Wh-* words that carry most of the meaning in a sentence. Structure words, often called *function words*, are words that are needed for the grammar of a sentence but do not have much meaning of their own. Structure words include articles, prepositions, pronouns, conjunctions, and auxiliary verbs. They can be stressed if there is a choice or contrast involved – "Can *you* take her to the airport? I can't." – but otherwise they are usually unstressed.

Read or summarize the information in the box with the class. To check their understanding, you may want to ask students for examples of words that would typically be stressed and words that would usually be unstressed.

Step 1 Sometimes all the syllables in a sentence are stressed: **This train's late.** But in most sentences, some words and syllables are stressed and some are unstressed. Notice that the first example in step 1 has two stressed syllables, the second has three, and the third has four. You can tap with a ruler or clap to show the rhythm. You can also demonstrate the rhythm by saying the sentences using nonsense syllables. For example, the first two sentences would be: "də də DAH də də DAH də"; "də də DAH də DAH də də DAH."

Step 2

F Conversation Practice

Step 1 Explain the task: Working with a partner, students underline the stressed syllables in each of B's lines. Students should try not to look at the stressed syllables they underlined in task E. The sentences in task E show the stress in A's lines.

Step 2

Step 3 Check that students use the appropriate stress and intonation as they practice the conversation in step 1 with a partner. If necessary, they can look at task E to check the stress in A's lines. Student B should use rising intonation on the questions.

Encourage students to link the shorter, quieter structure words to the longer, stressed words. This will help the rhythm sound more natural.

When the sound /iy/ or /ey/ at the end of a word comes before another vowel sound, use the /y/ sound to link the vowels smoothly together.

the **eighth** of **May**   a**way** on va**ca**tion

G Spelling

See Unit 5, task G, to compare common spelling patterns for the sounds /ey/ and /æ/ using the letter *a*.

Background notes

1. The letter *a* is almost always pronounced as the sound of its name – /ey/ – in the spellings with *a* + another vowel letter, such as *a* + final *e*, *ay*, and *ai*. The second letter in all these spellings is silent. You may want to teach this traditional English spelling rule: "When two vowels go walking, the first one does the talking."

2. The spelling *ea* has the sound /ey/ in only a few words. This spelling usually has the sound /iy/.

3. The word *gray* is also spelled *grey*, especially in British English.

H Common Expressions See Overview, p. xii.

Further Practice

Review letters of the alphabet that have the sound /ey/: *a, h, j,* and *k*.

Linking Pronunciation with Other Classwork

Tie pronunciation in with practice of:

1. Asking about and saying the date, for example:

   What's today's date?
   May eighth / April eighteenth / May twenty-eighth (or just: the eighth / the eighteenth / the twenty-eighth).

2. Polite apologies beginning with "I'm afraid . . .", for example:

   I'm afraid you've made a mistake / you'll have to wait / you're too late.

   I'm afraid I'm late / I've forgotten your name / I lost the paper / I broke the plate / I don't have change/ I can't stay.

Give brief descriptions of situations that would call for apologies like these and ask students to supply appropriate apologies.

Word Stress Practice

Use the Vocabulary words and other words from the unit to practice word stress. Write large and small circles on the board showing these two stress patterns:

   A ● •   B • ●

Read the following words. Students say whether they heard stress pattern A or B.

1. today (B)   5. station (A)
2. mistake (B)   6. birthday (A)
3. April (A)   7. away (B)
4. afraid (B)   8. neighbor (A)

UNIT 5 /æ/ • hat   The Most Important Word

Student Difficulties

Almost all learners have difficulty with the sound /æ/.

- Speakers of Russian, Korean, Turkish, Farsi, Dutch, German, and Scandinavian and Indian languages usually confuse /æ/ with /ɛ/. This results in confusion between words like *pan* and *pen*.

- Spanish, French, Italian, Portuguese, Greek, Japanese, Swahili, and West African speakers confuse /æ/ with /ɑ/ (as in *hot*) and/or /ʌ/ (as in *hut*).

- French, Italian, Greek, and Swahili speakers may also confuse /æ/ with /ɛ/.

- Many Chinese speakers nasalize /æ/. They may also confuse it with the sounds /ɛ/, /ʌ/, or /ɑ/.

■ Thai speakers often make the sound /æ/ too long.

Many languages do not have a sound exactly like either English /æ/ or /ɑ/, but have a sound that is somewhere between the two English sounds. Students often substitute this sound for /æ/ in English. This non-English vowel sound is usually spelled with the letter *a* in these languages, increasing students' confusion.

Making the Sound

Have students read the directions for making the sound /æ/ as they listen to the audio and look at the illustrations. Demonstrate and model the two vowels /ɛ/ and /æ/. The tongue is a little lower in the mouth for /æ/ than for /ɛ/, and the mouth is open wider.

The difference in the mouth positions for /ɛ/ and /æ/ is easy to see. The mouth is open wide and the tongue is pushed forward for /æ/. The tongue should rest at the bottom of the mouth with the tip against the bottom front teeth for /æ/. Have students watch the change in mouth position as you say /ɛ/ and /æ/. Encourage them to practice the two sounds in front of a mirror.

A Word Pairs See Overview, p. viii.

Word pairs for additional practice:

/ɛ/–/æ/: dead/Dad, send/sand, met/mat, set/sat, bet/bat, pet/pat, bed/bad, head/had, Ed/add, end/and, guess/gas, ten/tan, bend/band, lend/land, dense/dance, Beth/bath, peck/pack, shell/shall, M/am, gem/jam, better/batter, letter/latter

B Test Yourself See Overview, p. ix.

Step 1

ANSWERS
1. S (pen, pen)   4. S (said, said)
2. D (X, axe)   5. D (left, laughed)
3. D (men, man)   6. S (Dad, Dad)

Step 2

ANSWERS
1. Where did you put the <u>pan</u>?
2. Is that man in the picture <u>dead</u>?
3. He drew an <u>X</u> on the board.
4. I talked to the <u>men</u> in the store.
5. They are <u>sad</u> to be leaving.
6. She <u>laughed</u> when I said that.

C Vocabulary See Overview, p. ix.

Step 1 Note that most of the two-syllable words here are stressed on the first syllable: **glass**es, **back**pack, **jack**et, **plas**tic. The word *mustache* can be stressed on either the first or second syllable: **mus**tache or mu**stache**.

Step 2 Students work in pairs to match the words in step 1 with the illustrations in step 2. You may want to go over the first item with the class.

ANSWERS
1. glasses   5. a hat
2. a backpack   6. a mustache
3. a plastic bag   7. a plaid jacket
4. a black jacket   8. black pants

D Dialog See Overview, pp. ix–x.

Step 1 Students listen to the dialog and check the words in task C that Alice and the detective use to describe the bank robber. Students should look at the vocabulary words in task C, and not at the dialog, as they listen.

Step 2 Play the recording of the dialog again and go over the answers to step 1.

ANSWERS
black pants, a mustache, a plaid jacket, a plastic bag

To practice some of the other vocabulary in the dialog, you could ask students to tell what happened at the bank on Saturday. Make sure they do not add an extra syllable for the *-ed* in *happened, grabbed, robbed,* or *stuffed* (see Unit 25, task E). If necessary, write these words on the board, drawing a line through the *e,* or respell them without the *e* (e.g., "happend").

E The Most Important Word

Background notes Several words in a sentence may be stressed, but in a short sentence one stressed word stands out more than the others. This word usually has the major pitch change in the sentence. The intonation jumps up or sometimes down on this word. In a longer sentence, more than one word may stand out in this way.

Any word can be the most important in a sentence, but at the beginning of a conversation, the most important word is typically the last content word. As a conversation continues, the information or idea that is new, added, or different is highlighted by having the major pitch change in the sentence. Other languages may highlight new information in different ways – for example, by changing the word order. If students are not aware of the way English uses intonation to highlight new information, they are likely to miss important signals when listening. And failing to use intonation to highlight important information in their own speech makes it harder for the listener to process what they are saying. This use of intonation is pervasive in English, and it is important for students to be aware of it.

Step 1 After students listen to the two short conversations, point out how the most important word changes.

A He stuffed the cash in a **bag**. (The most important word is the last content word.)

B What **kind** of bag? (The new idea is *kind*.)

A A **plas**tic bag. (*Plastic* gives new, added information.)

A He was wearing a **jack**et. (The most important word is the last content word.)

B A **black** jacket? (*Black* gives new, added information.)

A **No**, a **plaid** jacket. **Red** plaid. (*Plaid* gives different, contrasting information. *Red* adds new information.)

Note that repeated words in the second and third lines of each conversation – *bag* in the first conversation, *jacket* in the second – are not stressed, since they give old information.

Step 2 Play the audio again. Have students repeat the conversations. To illustrate the melody, you can hum each sentence, or say the sentence through a kazoo.

Extra practice Give students the following short conversation, and ask them to identify (e.g., underline) the most important word in each line.

> **Detective** And this happened around <u>one</u>?
> **Alice** A little <u>after</u> one.

F Conversation Practice

Step 1 Students listen to the model conversation. Check to make sure they understand that the speakers are talking about the person in the first illustration.

Step 2 Students practice in pairs, following the model in step 1. They should talk about the pictures in random order. Move around the room while students practice, checking to see that they stress the correct word in each sentence.

G Spelling

Note the doubling of the consonant to maintain the /æ/ sound in words like *grabbed, grabbing, sadder,* and *saddest.*

Compare common spelling patterns for the sounds /æ/ and /ey/ using the letter *a*. Note that the word *have* is an exception to the rule that *a . . . e* spells the sound /ey/ and not /æ/. English words do not end with the letter *v*. An *e* is added in the spelling.

Extra practice Give students a written list of words such as the one below. Students say whether the *a* spelling in each word has the sound /æ/ (sound 1) or /ey/ (sound 2).

1. ages	6. grab
2. mistake	7. famous
3. family	8. happen
4. change	9. waiting
5. jacket	10. April

H Common Expressions See Overview, p. xii.

Linking Pronunciation with Other Classwork

Tie pronunciation in with practice of:

1. Short answers with *am, can/can't, have/haven't, has/hasn't*. For example, have students give short answers to rapid oral questions such as these: "Are you listening / hungry / studying English?" "Can you understand Spanish / drive a car / dance / swim?" "Have you ever been to Japan / France?"

2. Describing people to show which person is meant, for example: "Look at that man." "Which one? The one with the black jacket?" "No, the one with the tan jacket."

Word Stress Practice

Matching exercise: Read the words in column A, on the next page, aloud. For each word, students find a word in column B that has the same stress pattern. Students can draw a line connecting the two words or say the answers aloud.

	A	B
1.	plastic	absolutely
2.	understand	again
3.	detective	afternoon
4.	suddenly	exactly
5.	police	jacket
6.	conversation	manager

UNIT 6 Review /iy/, /ɪ/, /ɛ/, /ey/, and /æ/

This unit provides additional practice and review of the vowels /iy/, /ɪ/, /ɛ/, /ey/, and /æ/, presented in Units 1 through 5.

A Test Yourself

The set of words with contrasting vowels is not on the audio program. Before proceeding, you may want to have students listen to and repeat some or all of these words, reading across or reading first down and then across. They can use dictionaries to check the meaning of unfamiliar words, but they do not have to understand every word to do the task.

Play the audio. Students write or say aloud the number of the vowel they hear in each word, using the numbers at the top of each column in the table. Explain that they do not need to write the word – just the number.

B Vocabulary

Step 1 Students sort the words by sound, grouping words with the same vowel sound together. In words that have more than one vowel sound, students should pay attention only to the vowel in the stressed syllable, which is underlined.

Step 2

C Dialog See Overview, pp. ix–x.

Step 1 Students cover the dialog in their books and listen to the audio. You may want to give them questions to direct their listening. For example, tell them to listen to the dialog and then answer these questions:

1. What are Ben and Anna having for dinner?

2. Do they have dinner in the backyard? Why?

Step 2 Students, working alone or with a partner, add more words from the dialog to each column of the table in task B. Alternatively, arrange students in groups of 5. Each student in a group chooses one sound and tries to find as many words as possible that have that sound in the dialog.

You may want to tell students to pay attention only to the stressed vowel in each word, ignoring the vowels in unstressed syllables.

Note Words like *and,* which would normally be unstressed and pronounced with /ə/ (see Unit 8), are shown in parentheses.

1 /iy/: everything, ready, we, any, bakery, cheesecake, eat, idea, really, pretty, evening, carrying, be, me

2 /ɪ/: with, dinner, everything, having, did, pick, interesting, it, it's, delicious, in, pretty, this, evening, carrying, napkins, minute, sit, sitting, beginning, standing, figures, bring

3 /ɛ/: help, everything, any, vegetables, yes, bread, let's, get, smells, Ben

4 /ey/: made, tomato, bakery, cheesecake, tasted, OK, plates, wait

5 /æ/: having, (and), (at), that, backyard, carrying, (can), napkins, grass, can't, standing, back, Anna

D Syllables and Stress

Students first practice counting syllables in words and then identify the stressed syllable. Explain that in English, some words have vowel letters, and therefore syllables, that are not pronounced. For example, *everything* looks like it would have four syllables, but it has three syllables because the second *e* is silent. Write the word *everything* on the board and draw a slash through the second *e* to show that it is not pronounced, or respell the word to show the pronunciation: EV-ry-thing. (For more on silent syllables, see Unit 33, task E.)

Encourage students to tap out the syllables, using their fingers, feet, or a pencil, to help them count. Remind them to think about the pronunciation, not the spelling, of the word.

Check the answers at the end, making sure that students do not add extra syllables in words like *ev∉ning* and *veg∉tables.* If necessary, remind students that in nouns with two syllables *(evening, salad, minute, cheesecake)* the first syllable is usually stressed.

1.	everything	3	6.	vegetables	3
2.	evening	2	7.	tomato	3
3.	salad	2	8.	cheesecake	2
4.	minute	2	9.	delicious	3
5.	beginning	3			

E Puzzle

Students circle or say the word in each group that does not have the same vowel sound as the other words. Go over the example. If necessary, remind students to focus on sounds, not spellings. Students can work alone or with a partner.

Check the answers at the end. You can use the numbers for the sounds from the *Test Yourself* task at the beginning of the unit, for example: "Which vowel sound does *steak* have?" (4) "Which vowel sound do the other words have?" (1)

If students need the practice, have them listen to and repeat the words to check their answers.

1.	steak	3.	bakery	5.	jealous
2.	evening	4.	taste	6.	bread

Spelling Review

Give students a list of words, on paper or on the board, with the sounds practiced in Units 1–5. Students sort the words by sound, grouping words with the same vowel sound together. Alternatively, write each word on a card, preparing more than one set of cards for larger classes, and have students work in groups to sort them.

Sample list of words to be given in scrambled order:

/iy/	please, people, thirteen, these, leave
/ɪ/	minute, women, quick, English, miss
/ɛ/	says, friend, left, jealous, any
/ey/	they, wait, late, great, change, eight
/æ/	black, laugh, happen, glasses, cash

Word Stress Practice

Write large and small circles on the board showing these two stress patterns:

A ● •   B • ●

Read the following words. Students say whether they heard stress pattern A or B.

1. review (B)		6. complete (B)
2. salad (A)		7. lemon (A)
3. minutes (A)		8. begin (B)
4. jacket (A)		9. happen (A)
5. yourself (B)		10. mistake (B)

Student Difficulties

Most students have difficulty with the sound /ʌ/. Many learners substitute /ɑ/ or a sound from their own language that is between English /ɑ/ and /æ/, often creating confusion in English between both /ʌ/ and /æ/ (as in *cut/cat*) and /ʌ/ and /ɑ/ (as in *cut/cot*).

■ Students likely to replace /ʌ/ with /æ/, /ɑ/, or a similar sound include speakers of Arabic, Chinese, Farsi, Greek, Italian, Japanese, Portuguese, Spanish, and African languages.

■ French speakers may substitute a sound similar to the vowel in English *bird,* but without the /r/ sound.

■ Some students may pronounce /ʌ/ too far back in the mouth, creating confusion with /ɔ/ or /ʊ/.

Many students, even those who can pronounce /ʌ/, have problems with the sound caused by confusion over the spelling. They may pronounce the letter *o* as /ow/ or /ɑ/ in words where it represents /ʌ/, saying, for example, /lowv/ for *love* or /ˈnɑ•θɪŋ/ for *nothing.* Or they may use the sound /uw/ in words like *study* or *bus,* where /ʌ/ is spelled with the letter *u.*

Making the Sound

Have students read the directions for making the sound /ʌ/ as they listen to the audio and look at the illustrations. The sound /ʌ/ is a very relaxed sound. It is the sound English speakers use to express hesitation: *uh . . .*

Call attention to the front view of the lips, which shows that the mouth is open only a little. The lips and jaw are relaxed, and the tongue rests in the middle of the mouth. If students substitute /ɑ/ for /ʌ/, tell them to close their mouths a little. Focus on the difference in mouth position, which is easy to see. The mouth is wide open for /ɑ/, while the lips are open just a little for /ʌ/. The tongue should also be just a little farther forward in the mouth for /ʌ/.

If students substitute a sound closer to /æ/, have them relax their lips and close them a little. The tongue should be pulled back a little, not pushed against the lower front teeth, as for /æ/.

Variation in the sound The sound /ʌ/ is longer before a voiced consonant and shorter before a voiceless consonant. Compare *buzz/bus, cub/cup, dug/duck, bud/but.*

A Word Pairs See Overview, p. viii.

Word pairs for additional practice:

/æ/ – /ʌ/: ran/run, bat/but, bad/bud, fan/fun, match/much, cab/cub, track/truck, rag/rug, mad/mud, calf/cuff, tan/ton, dam/dumb, lack/luck, lamp/lump, sadden/sudden, rang/rung, sang/sung, drank/drunk, sank/sunk, swam/swum

B Test Yourself See Overview, p. ix.

Step 1

ANSWERS	
1. D (bag, bug)	4. D (rag, rug)
2. S (cat, cat)	5. D (ankle, uncle)
3. S (cup, cup)	6. S (run, run)

Step 2

ANSWERS
1. Don't sit on the bug!
2. This cup is too small.
3. I threw away the old rag.
4. What happened to your uncle?
5. They ran quickly.
6. How did he get that cut?

C Vocabulary See Overview, p. ix.

This task focuses on some common spellings for /ʌ/. Some students expect /ʌ/ to be spelled only with the letter *u.* The words in this task show that *o* and *ou* are other common spellings for /ʌ/, though these letters also spell other sounds. The letter *a* is not a common spelling for this sound.

Step 1 Explain the task and go over the example. Make sure that students understand that they should focus on the sound, not the spelling.

Step 2

D **Dialog** See Overview, pp. ix–x.

Step 1 Have students work with a partner to fill in the blanks. Encourage them to say the words aloud as they fill them in. All the missing words have the sound /ʌ/ spelled with the letter *o*.

Step 2

E **Strong and Weak Pronunciations**

Background notes This task introduces the concept of weak pronunciations in preparation for the next unit, on the unstressed vowel /ə/. Many short structure words, or function words, have two pronunciations – a strong pronunciation and a weak pronunciation. The weak pronunciation is much more commonly used. The strong pronunciation is used when the word is said on its own or at the end of a sentence or clause or when the word is given special emphasis. Otherwise, these words are usually unstressed and pronounced with their weak form. Weak pronunciations often have the short, unstressed sound /ə/. (For more about stress in sentences, see Unit 4, task E.)

Students listen and repeat the weak and strong pronunciations of some auxiliaries. The weak pronunciations of *was, does,* and *do* all have the short, unstressed vowel /ə/. It is easiest to hear the difference between strong and weak pronunciations with *do,* since the strong pronunciation has the vowel /uw/, which sounds clearly different from /ə/. The difference is harder to hear with *was* and *does*; since the strong pronunciations have the sound /ʌ/, the difference mainly involves stress.

Note that negative contractions always have a strong pronunciation, with a full, clear vowel sound.

F **Scrambled Conversations**

Step 1 Students listen and fill in the missing auxiliary and pronoun at the beginning of each question. In conversational speech, both the auxiliary and the pronoun normally have weak pronunciations in questions like these and can be hard for students to hear.

Step 2 Working in pairs, students find the sentence on the right that answers each question on the left. Go over the example. You may want to have Student A cover B's answers, and Student B cover A's questions while they practice.

Step 3 If some pairs finish early, you can ask them to write two or three more questions with *do, does,* and *was* to ask their partner.

ANSWERS

Does he have any brothers?
Yes, he does – a younger brother.

Do you come here often?
No, I don't. Just once a month.

Do you have enough money?
I think I do. How much is it?

Was he late for lunch?
No, he wasn't.

Does she understand Russian?
No, she doesn't, but her husband does.

Was she in love with his cousin?
No, she wasn't.

Do they have any children?
Yes, they do. They have two sons.

G Spelling

Problems with the sound /ʌ/ are often complicated by confusion caused by spelling. All of the spellings for this sound are also common spellings for other sounds – often sounds that students may confuse with the sound /ʌ/:

1. The letter *u* is a common spelling for the sounds /uw/ and /ʊ/, as well as for /ʌ/. Note the doubling of the consonant to keep the /ʌ/ sound in words such as *sunny* and *running*. Before a single consonant followed by another vowel, *u* would normally be pronounced as /uw/: compare *student* and *sudden*.

2. The letter *o* usually has the sound /ow/ or /ɑ/. Before the consonants *n, m, v,* and *th* (especially the voiced *th* sound), however, it often has the sound /ʌ/ (as in *sun, some, love, mother*).

3. *ou*, which represents /ʌ/ in *country, touch, enough,* etc., usually has the sound /aw/.

4. *oo (blood, flood)* usually has the sound /uw/ or /ʊ/.

5. *oe (does, doesn't)* usually has the sound /ow/.

Extra practice Remind students that many words spelled with *o* have the sound /ʌ/. As a review activity at another time, ask students for words spelled with the letter *o* and pronounced with the sound /ʌ/. Write the words on the board.

H Common Expressions See Overview, p. xii.

Linking Pronunciation with Other Classwork

Tie pronunciation in with practice of:

1. Family relationships: For example, draw a family tree on the blackboard. As you point to names on the family tree, have students make sentences that describe the relationship (e.g., "Sam Douglas is Janet Young's husband"). If necessary, practice the pronunciation of words with the sound /ʌ/ before you begin: *mother, son, husband, brother, uncle, cousin, grandmother, grandson, mother-in-law,* and *brother-in-law*.

2. Short answers using *does / doesn't* and *was / wasn't*.

3. Questions with *How much*.

4. *Must*.

5. Past participles, for example contrasted with other forms of the verb: ring / rang / rung – sing / sang / sung – drink / drank / drunk – sink / sank / sunk – shrink / shrank / shrunk – swim / swam / swum – begin / began / begun – run / ran / run – come / came / come – become / became / become – cut / cut / cut – shut / shut / shut – stick / stuck / stuck – hang / hung / hung – sting / stung / stung – win / won / won – do / did / done.

   For practice discriminating between the sounds /æ/ and /ʌ/, you could ask students to circle the words they hear in sentences like these:

   (I drank / I've drunk) all the juice.

   (He ran / He's run) in every race.

6. Using expressions like *Uh-huh* (meaning "Yes"), *Unh-unh* (meaning "No"), and *Uh . . .* (to express hesitation) in conversation.

Word Stress Practice

Read the following pairs of words. Students indicate whether the stress pattern for the two words is the same or different.

1. nothing, funny (S)
2. company, unhappy (D)
3. understand, government (D)
4. unhappy, remember (S)
5. comfortable, wonderful (S)
6. butterfly, umbrella (D)
7. sunglasses, grandmother (S)
8. unusual, uninteresting (S)

UNIT 8 /ə/ • a banana

/ə/ in Unstressed Syllables and Words; *can* and *can't*

The symbol /ə/ is sometimes used to represent the sound shown in this book with the symbol /ʌ/. In this book, the symbol /ə/ is reserved for the unstressed vowel known as *schwa*.

In this unit, the spelling has been changed to show students where to use the sound /ə/, because the normal spellings do not help make students aware of this sound.

Student Difficulties

Almost all students have some difficulty with the sound /ə/, even though it may not be a difficult sound for them to pronounce. Students commonly substitute a sound suggested by the spelling that /ə/ has in a word.

Many languages do not have the sound /ə/ or, in fact, any reduced vowels at all. In English, unstressed syllables are much shorter than stressed syllables and very often (but not always) have an unclear, reduced, neutral-sounding vowel, usually /ə/ or /ɪ/. In many other languages, such as Spanish, Italian, Greek, Brazilian, Portuguese, Farsi, Thai, West African languages, and Swahili, syllables that are not stressed may take as long to say as stressed syllables and have a full, clear vowel sound.

Even speakers of languages that have a reduced vowel like /ə/ may have difficulty with /ə/ in English. In other languages, the sound may not be as reduced or may not occur as frequently as in English. And in other languages, the sound /ə/ may always be spelled with the same letter (e.g., the letter *e* in German).

Students at an intermediate or advanced level often continue to have difficulty with /ə/. They may not have learned to use /ə/ from the beginning, or they may not have learned to use it as frequently as the sound occurs, and may find it difficult to change habits later on. The fact that the spelling does not show where /ə/ should be used contributes to the problem. Also, they may realize that they can get away without using /ə/. They may not always understand native speakers, but they themselves will probably be understood. And many students have the mistaken idea that the use of the schwa is sloppy or careless and that speech is more correct or more easily understood if the speaker uses full vowels.

Making the Sound

Have students read the directions for making the sound /ə/ as they listen to the audio. Emphasize that /ə/ is a very short sound. The tongue should rest relaxed in the middle of the mouth, as for the sound /ʌ/. The lips should be in a relaxed, neutral position (not rounded), with the mouth almost closed (not open wide, as for /ɑ/). Note that if the sound /ə/ is said by itself, it will automatically be stressed and will be /ʌ/ (or another vowel) and not the unstressed vowel /ə/ practiced in this unit.

Variation in the sound The vowel in many unstressed syllables varies between /ə/ and /ɪ/. Some people may pronounce the unstressed vowel in some of the words in this unit (e.g., *gui̲tar*) with an unstressed /ɪ/ sound.

A Vocabulary

Step 1 Tell students that /ə/ is the most common vowel sound in English. It is used in many unstressed syllables and unstressed words. To make it easier to refer to, it is very useful to teach the name for this sound: *schwa*.

Have students look at and repeat the words in their books. Call attention to the places where /ə/ is shown in place of the normal spelling.

Demonstrate the stress pattern of each word, for example by tapping with a ruler. Then have students tap while repeating the words again. Point out that /ə/ is never in the stressed part of a word.

To draw attention to the variety of spellings for /ə/, ask students which letters have the sound /ə/ in these words. Ask them to give an example of each spelling (e.g., *a – banana*, *e – chicken*, *o – tomatoes*, *u – lettuce*). Elicit from students that in *woman* and *women*, even though the difference in spelling is in the second syllable, the difference in pronunciation is in the first syllable: /wʊmən/ vs. /wɪmən/. The vowel in the second syllable of both words is the same: /ə/.

Note that *chocolate* is usually pronounced as two syllables in English, with stress on the first syllable. You may want to compare this with the pronunciation from the language(s) that your students speak. In other languages, *chocolate* may be three or four syllables, with stress on the third syllable. An international word like *chocolate* is useful for demonstrating differences in stress and pronunciation patterns between languages.

B /ə/ in Unstressed Syllables and Words

Background notes Words like *and, as, have, do, to,* and *from* are pronounced with a full, clear vowel when they are said alone but are normally unstressed and pronounced with the sound /ə/ in connected speech. Students usually learn these words in isolation, where the words are automatically stressed and have a full, clear vowel, and tend to carry over this strong pronunciation into their speech. This tendency is reinforced by what they see in the spelling of the words.

Learners often have difficulty hearing weak forms when said by native speakers and may perceive English speakers as "swallowing their words." Trying to reduce the stress on unstressed syllables or weak forms can be so difficult for students that they just drop the unstressed syllable or word.

Since schwa occurs so frequently and is a challenging concept for many students, it is important to teach it at an early stage, so that students get accustomed to using it and hearing it.

Explain to students that knowing about weak pronunciations will help them understand spoken English better. Make sure they realize that the use of weak pronunciations is a natural feature of ordinary English speech, not a nonstandard feature.

Step 1 Students look at the pictures and repeat the phrases, practicing the weak pronunciation of *a, of,* and *and*. Encourage students to link the words in each phrase together smoothly, connecting unstressed words to the words around them. Note that the *d* in *and* is usually silent: /ən/. The word *of*, pronounced /əv/, may be reduced to just /ə/ in relaxed speech, especially before a consonant sound.

Step 2 Working in pairs, students look at the pictures and make phrases like the ones in step 1. Make sure they do not stress the weak forms or other unstressed syllables. Tap to show stress, or write phrases on the board, showing stressed syllables and /ə/ (e.g., ə POUND əf bəNANəs).

Step 3

ANSWERS	
a cup of tea	lettuce and tomatoes
a can of soup	chicken and rice
a pound of bananas	men and women

C *can* and *can't*

Background notes The word *can,* like most other auxiliaries, has two pronunciations: a strong pronunciation and a weak pronunciation. The strong pronunciation is used when the word gets special emphasis or occurs at the end of a sentence or clause, as in short answers (e.g., *Yes, I can*). The weak pronunciation, with the unstressed sound /ə/, is normally used in the middle of a sentence. At the beginning of *Yes / No* questions, either the weak form /kən/ or the strong form /kæn/ may be used. The negative *can't* always has a strong pronunciation, with a full, clear vowel /æ/. The /t/ at the end of *can't* is often pronounced as a glottal stop (a quick stop in the breath) and can be hard to hear. Substituting a full, clear vowel sound for /ə/ in *can* may easily lead to misunderstandings, since the listener may hear this as the opposite, *can't.*

Step 1 Have students look at the pictures and repeat the sentences contrasting *can* and *can't.* Tap to show the stress. Each of the sentences with *can* has only two strong stresses. If necessary, respell the weak form on the board: "c'n."

Discuss the pronunciation rules shown in the box. Point out that the /t/ at the end of *can't* is usually a quiet sound, so that the biggest difference in pronunciation between *can* and *can't* in the middle of a sentence is the sound of the vowel – /ə/ in *can* and /æ/ in *can't*.

Encourage students to use the sound /ə/ in *a* and *the* as well as in *can*. Note that the word *the* has the sound /ə/ when the next word begins with a consonant sound.

Step 2 Check that students understand the rule that *can* has a strong pronunciation at the end of a sentence. After students repeat the questions and short answers in their books, you can continue the practice by asking more questions about the pictures in step 1 and having students ask and answer questions among themselves.

D **Test Yourself** See Overview, p. ix.
Step 1

ANSWERS

1. He can't play the piano.
2. I can stand on my head.
3. She can ride a horse.
4. She can speak Japanese, but her children can't.
5. You can't park your car here.
6. I can't meet you at three o'clock.

E **Discussion**

Step 1 Have students practice in groups of three to five people. Go over any unfamiliar vocabulary in the list of ideas. Students should take turns telling each other some things they can and can't do. Tell them to try to remember the things that the other people in their group can do.

Step 2 Ask students to report on the results for their group. Each student completes at least one of the sentences: "All of us can . . . ," "One of us can . . . ," and so on. Check that students use the unstressed vowel /ə/ in the words *of, the,* and *a*, as well as in *can*.

F **Spelling**

The great variety of spellings for the sound /ə/ naturally adds to its difficulty for students. Many common beginnings and endings for words have the sound /ə/, for example:

a- about, again, across, around

com-, con-, pro-, to- computer, compare, continue, confuse, protect, produce, today, tomorrow

-ace, -acy, -al, -ance, -ant, -graphy, -man surface, democracy, musical, special, instance, assistance, assistant, pleasant, photography, biography, policeman

-able / -ible available, possible

-en, -el, -ence, -ent, -ment open, happen, level, difference, different, excellent, excitement, arrangement, apartment

-ion, -some, -ogy question, opinion, handsome, biology

-ous famous, nervous, delicious

G **Common Expressions** See Overview, p. xii.

Further Practice

For review at a later time, write the words below on the board or on a paper handout. For each word, have students underline or put a dot under the letters pronounced as the sound /ə/. This may be done with or without reading the words aloud.

1. about
2. today
3. telephone
4. famous
5. success
6. apartment
7. complete
8. breakfast
9. polite
10. problem

Linking Pronunciation with Other Classwork

Tie pronunciation in with practice of:

1. *Can* and *can't* in asking and talking about abilities.

2. *Can* in requests, for example: "Can I have an apple / a banana / a piece of cake / a cup of tea / a bowl of soup / some chips and salsa / some chicken and rice (etc.), please?"

UNIT 9 /ər/ • letter

/ər/ in Unstressed Syllables and Words; Intonation in Choice Questions with *or*

The spelling in this unit has been changed to show students where to use the sound /ər/. The sound /ər/ practiced in this unit is the same as /ər/ in Unit 21, but in this unit it is unstressed.

Student Difficulties

Almost all learners have difficulty with the sound /ər/. Students have much the same difficulties with unstressed /ər/ as they do with /ə/ alone, replacing it with a vowel suggested by the spelling and usually adding a non-English (e.g., trilled or flapped) /r/ sound. They also often stress the vowel. For more information about student difficulties with unstressed vowels, see Unit 8. For more information about difficulties with the sound /ər/, see Unit 21.

Making the Sound

Have students read the directions for making the sound /ər/ as they listen to the audio. Students will probably need to spend some time on the mouth position for /ər/. Note that the lips should be slightly rounded. The tongue should be raised toward the hard part of the roof of the mouth (the hard palate); some students pull the tongue too far back.

Variation in the sound

1. Some English speakers say the sound /ər/ with the middle of the tongue raised toward the roof of the mouth, without curling the tongue back.

2. British and some American speakers use the sound /ə/ without a following /r/ sound in most of the words in this unit. These speakers pronounce /r/ only when a vowel comes after it.

A Vocabulary

Step 1 Students practice the sound /ər/ in the common unstressed ending *-er* / *-or*. To discourage students from putting stress on the sound /ər/ here or pronouncing it with a full, clear vowel sound, you can respell the words on the board, omitting the vowel: "waitr," "doctr," and so on. Note that the *t* in *waiter* and *reporter* sounds like a quick /d/ in North American English (see Unit 24, task A).

Ask students how the sound is normally spelled in these words. Note the different spellings for the sound in, for example, *teacher* and *doctor*.

Step 2 Students match the names of the jobs in step 1 with the pictures. You may want to have them review the weak form of *does*, introduced in Unit 7, by asking and answering the question "What does he / she do?"

After going over the answers, ask students to think of other jobs that end with the sound /ər/. Ask them if they or anyone in their family has a job that ends with the sound /ər/ (e.g., *My sister is a designer*).

ANSWERS

1. painter	5. lawyer
2. teacher	6. doctor
3. reporter	7. actor
4. waiter	8. farmer

B /ər/ in Unstressed Syllables and Words

Background notes The words *or*, *for*, and *are* are often pronounced with the sound /ər/ in connected speech. The strong pronunciation, with a full, clear vowel sound, is used at the end of a sentence: for example, *What is this for* (/fɔr/)? or *Yes, they are* (/ɑr/). At the beginning of a sentence or after a pause, either the weak or strong pronunciation may be used: for example, *Are* (/ər/ or /ɑr/) *you married?* But otherwise, especially within a phrase, the weak pronunciation is normally used: for example, *What are* (/ər/) *you doing? Do you want soup or* (/ər/) *salad?* For more on weak and strong pronunciations, see Unit 7, task E, and Unit 8.

Step 1 Students look at the pictures and repeat the short phrases, practicing the weak pronunciation of the word *or*. Encourage students to link *or* to the words around it.

Step 2 Working in pairs, students look at the pictures and make phrases with *or*. Check to make sure that they do not stress *or*. Tap to show stress, if necessary.

Step 3

C Intonation in Choice Questions with *or*

Background notes In this section, students practice intonation in choice questions, also known as *alternative questions* – questions with *or* that offer a choice between things. Questions with *or* are not always choice questions; sometimes they can be *Yes / No* questions. The difference is expressed by intonation.

Yes / No questions typically have rising intonation at the end (only): "Would you like coffee or tea?" (= "Would you like something to drink?")

In choice questions, the voice falls on the last choice offered. The voice rises on all the choices before the last one: "Would you like coffee or tea?"

Step 1 Have students repeat the examples. Show the direction of the intonation with hand gestures. Ask two students the two questions in the Student's Book. The students should answer, choosing one alternative. Then have other students ask and answer the two choice questions.

Step 2 Working in pairs, students make up choice questions about the items in task B, starting with the phrases shown or similar phrases. You may want to give an example or two to show how the phrases might be used (e.g., "Would you like soup or salad?" "Is it large or small?").

As students practice, move around the room making sure that students use the appropriate intonation and encouraging them to use weak forms.

At the end, ask each pair of students to say one of their questions. If possible, each pair should contribute a new question, without repeating questions that other pairs have said.

D Dialog

Step 1 Students repeat phrases with words that typically have a weak pronunciation in connected speech. The phrases come from the dialog that follows.

Steps 2 and 3 Play the recording of the dialog twice. You may want to pause the recording after each line, so that students can note the /ə/ and /ər/ sounds. To help keep track of the sounds, they can underline or put a dot under the letters pronounced as unstressed /ə/ or /ər/. Note that different speakers might say some of the sentences with a slightly different rhythm, so that the words with weak pronunciations might vary.

Go over the answers with the class, making a list on the board from student suggestions. Tell students not to worry if they missed some of the /ə/ and /ər/ sounds.

Summarize by making a list of some common words from the dialog that often have a weak pronunciation with /ə/ or /ər/ in the middle of a sentence: *a, and, at, can, do, for, of, or, some, to.*

Step 4 As students practice the dialog in pairs, move around the room monitoring the intonation in choice questions and making sure that students do not stress too many words. Encourage students to link words together and use natural rhythm, but do not insist that they use /ə/ and /ər/ in every possible place at this stage.

E Spelling

As with the sound /ə/, the variety of spellings for /ər/ adds to its difficulty for learners. Note that although the sound /ər/ often occurs at the ends of words, it can also occur earlier in a word, as in *forget*.

Linking Pronunciation with Other Classwork

Tie pronunciation in with practice of:

1. Quanitifiers and containers using *of: a glass of water / a bottle of juice / a container of yogurt / a box of rice / two pounds of tomatoes*, and so on. For example, students could work in pairs to make shopping lists or practice a conversation similar to the one in task D: "I'm going to the store. Do you need anything?" "Yes. Could you get me . . ."

2. Talking about occupations

Word Stress Practice

Write large and small circles on the board showing these two stress patterns:

A ● • •   B • ● •

Read the following words. Students say whether they heard stress pattern A or B.

1. reporter (B)   6. carpenter (A)
2. together (B)   7. bananas (B)
3. terrible (A)   8. designer (B)
4. apartment (B)   9. possible (A)
5. excellent (A)   10. officer (A)

UNIT 10 /ɑ/ • hot   Phrase Groups

Student Difficulties

Learners generally do not have difficulty producing a sound close to English /ɑ/, although sometimes they make the sound too short where it should be lengthened (as in *father*). This sound is often confused with the sounds /æ/ and /ʌ/, for which students often substitute /ɑ/, so that *cat* and *cut* may both be pronounced like *cot*.

Problems also arise because of spelling. In words spelled with the letter *o* and pronounced with /ɑ/ (e.g., *not*), students often substitute a sound like /ow/ or /ɔ/.

Making the Sound

Have students read the directions for making the sound /ɑ/ as they listen to the audio and look at the illustrations. Direct attention to the front view diagrams; the difference between /æ/ and /ɑ/ is clearly visible from the front. Point out the difference in the shape of the lips – open but spread for /æ/, open wider and not spread for /ɑ/. The tongue is pushed forward and visible for /æ/, with the tip of the tongue against the bottom front teeth; it is farther back, resting in the middle of the bottom of the mouth, for /ɑ/.

If students confuse /ɑ/ with /ʌ/, note that the mouth is open much wider for /ɑ/ than for /ʌ/.

Variation in the sound

1. Many British speakers use the sound /ɑ/ in some words, such as *class, bath, dance,* and *can't,* in which most North Americans use the vowel /æ/.

2. In words spelled with *o* and pronounced by most North Americans with /ɑ/, most British speakers use a different vowel sound – /ɒ/.

3. The sound /ɑ/ is longer at the end of a word or before a voiced consonant and shorter before a voiceless consonant. Compare *mob / mop, rod / rot, clogs / clocks*.

A and B Word Pairs 1 and 2   See Overview, p. viii.

Word pairs for additional practice:

/æ/ – /ɑ/: map/mop, pat/pot, tap/top, backs/box, add/odd, bland/blond, ax/ox, black/block, band/bond, ma'am/Mom, lack/lock

/ʌ/ – /ɑ/: run/Ron, done/Don, color/collar, duck/dock, luck/lock, stuck/stock, nut/not, shut/shot, come/calm, rub/rob, gulf/golf, bucks/box, muddle/model, rubber/robber, jug/jog, dull/doll

C Test Yourself   See Overview, p. ix.

Step 1

ANSWERS		
1. cut	3. cap	5. hut
2. ran	4. sock	6. Don

Step 2

D Vocabulary   See Overview, p. ix.

Step 1 Note that some North American English speakers use the vowel /ɔ/ rather than /ɑ/ in *watch* and *chocolates*.

Step 2 In the words here, /ɑ/ is followed by /r/. The mouth is open wide, but the lips are rounded a little and the tip of the tongue is curled up and back a little to make the /r/ sound.

Step 3

E Dialog   See Overview, pp. ix–x.

Step 1 Tell students that they are going to listen to a TV commercial about shopping for holiday presents. Either before or after students listen, ask questions like these about their own experiences: "Do you ever shop online?" "Have you ever watched a shopping channel on TV?" "Are there shopping channels in your native country?"

Have students cover the dialog as they listen, looking instead at the vocabulary items in task D. They should check the items in task D that are mentioned in the dialog.

Step 2 Play the recording of the dialog again and go over the answers to step 1.

Extra practice Students can practice the dialog in groups as a role play, taking turns performing in front of the class to judge which group presents the commercial most effectively. You may want to wait until students have practiced phrase groups in task F before doing this. Alternatively, have students work in pairs or with a small group to write their own commercials.

F Phrase Groups

Background notes A phrase group, sometimes called a *thought group* or *intonation group,* is a group of words connected both in grammar and pronunciation. A phrase group can be an entire short sentence or one part of a longer sentence. The end of a phrase group is usually signaled by a slight pause or a slight fall or rise in intonation. Within a phrase group, the words are usually linked together without pausing between them. One word in each phrase group is usually treated as the most important word (see Unit 5, task E). In writing, the end of a phrase group may be indicated by punctuation, for example by a comma, dash, or period.

There is often more than one way to break a long sentence up into phrase groups. If a person speaks quickly, the phrase groups are likely to be longer. In slower speech, the phrase groups will be shorter.

Read or summarize the information in the box with the class. Emphasize that dividing a sentence into phrase groups makes it easier for the listener to understand what is being said. If students have difficulty being understood, encourage them to pause more often within a sentence.

G Game

The game can be played either in groups of four or five people or with the whole class. Each student repeats what the students before them said and then adds a new item and a new person to the list, as in the example. The game ends when the list becomes too long for students to remember. Students should practice the lists of items first; explain any new vocabulary.

Check phrasing and stress. Encourage students to link the words in each phrase smoothly together. Check to make sure that students stress only the important words and not words like *a, of, for,* or *his.*

To make the game more challenging, students can play with their books closed after practicing the phrases in the list.

You might ask students which words shown in bold in box 2 do not have the sound /ɑ/ (*mother, brother, cousin, grandmother, uncle*, and for most North American speakers *aunt*). Note that some native speakers use the vowel /ɔ/ rather than /ɑ/ in the words *chocolates, watch,* and *wallet* in box 1 and *daughter* in box 2.

H Spelling

1. The spelling *o* for the sound /ɑ/ often causes confusion. Students may substitute a sound like /ow/ or /ɔ/ when they see this spelling, pronouncing *not,* for example, like *note* or *naught.* The letter *o* usually has the sound /ɑ/ when it comes before a consonant at the end of a word (especially before the sounds /p, b, t, d, k, ʃ, tʃ, dʒ, l/, as in *stop, job, not, nod, clock, posh, Scotch, dodge, doll*) or before a doubled consonant in the middle of a word (as in *bottle, shopping, possible*).

2. Note the doubling of the consonant to maintain the sound /ɑ/, rather than /ow/, in words like *shopping, stopped,* and *hotter.* Compare the pronunciation of *hopping,* with /ɑ/, and *hoping,* with /ow/.

3. The variety of sounds for the letter *a* may also cause confusion. Note that the letter *a* commonly has the sound /ɑ/ only in a few places: before *r* (as in *star*); before *lm* (with silent *l,* as in *calm*); after *w* or *qu* (as in *watch* or *quality*); at the end of a syllable (as in *Ma* or *ah!*); and in the word *father.*

Extra practice Review sounds spelled with the letter *a.* Give students a list such as the one below. Have students look at the words and decide which sound the letter *a* has in each one: Sound 1 /æ/ (*hat*), Sound 2 /ey/ (*train*), or Sound 3 /ɑ/ (*father*).

1. glasses (1)
2. bank (1)
3. station (2)
4. hard (3)
5. change (2)
6. calm (3)
7. cash (1)
8. want (3)
9. mistake (2)
10. happen (1)

I Common Expressions See Overview, p. xii.

Linking Pronunciation with Other Classwork

Tie pronunciation in with practice of:

1. Short answers with *are*: "Yes, we are." / "No, they aren't."

2. "What's the problem?" / "What's the matter?" "I have a headache / backache / stomachache," and so on. Note that this reviews vowels practiced in previous units.

3. Quantifiers and containers: *a lot of* / *a box of* / *a bottle of*, and so on. These phrases can be used for practice both of the vowel /ɑ/ and linking within a phrase group.

4. Telephone numbers: Have students compare the way numbers are grouped in phone numbers in their own countries and the way they are grouped in North America (for example, 212-691-3239) to practice phrase groups.

Word Stress Practice

One word in each group has a different stress pattern than the other words. Students say which word is different.

	1	2	3	
1.	problem	garage	concert	(2)
2.	guitar	novel	wallet	(1)
3.	bargain	complete	products	(2)
4.	popular	holiday	tomorrow	(3)
5.	example	commercial	probably	(3)
6.	apartment	possible	wonderful	(1)

Student Difficulties

Many students have difficulty with the sound /ɔ/, usually making it too short and often confusing it with /ʌ/, /ɑ/, or /ow/, which can create confusion among words like *cut, cot, caught,* and *coat.* Substituting /ɑ/ is the least serious problem, because many native speakers also use /ɑ/ rather than /ɔ/ in words like *caught.*

- Speakers of some languages, including French, German, Greek, Japanese, Russian, Spanish, and Turkish, are likely to replace both /ɔ/ and /ow/ with a pure /o/ vowel.

- Many of these speakers, as well as speakers of Arabic, Chinese, Dutch, Farsi, and Indian languages, may also confuse /ɔ/ with /ʌ/ and / or /ɑ/.

Confusion caused by spelling often contributes to problems with /ɔ/. The sound /ɔ/ is usually spelled with the letters *o, au, aw,* or *a.* In many languages, the letter *o* represents a pure /o/ sound, *au* represents either the sound /aw/ or /ow/, and the letter *a* represents a vowel similar to /ɑ/. Students may carry these habits over into English, for example, pronouncing the word *automatic* with the vowel /aw/ or /ow/.

Making the Sound

Have students read the directions for making the sound /ɔ/ as they listen to the audio and look at the illustrations. If students substitute /ʌ/ or /ɑ/ for /ɔ/, try telling them to pull their tongues back a little.

For students who substitute a pure /o/ sound, part of the problem may be length; they may make the sound too short. Try telling them to open their mouths a little and to make the sound longer. Note that the lips are only slightly rounded for /ɔ/ and more tightly rounded for /ow/. Demonstrate the sounds and the difference in mouth position, calling attention to the diagrams of the lips in Units 11 and 12.

Variation in the sound

1. Many people in the United States and Canada use the sound /ɑ/ rather than /ɔ/ in some or most of the words practiced in this unit. Speakers who do not use the sound /ɔ/

elsewhere generally use it, however, when the sound /r/ follows, as in *four* or *sports.*

2. The sound /ɔ/ is longer at the end of a word (as in *saw*) or before a voiced consonant (as in *dawn* or *four*) and shorter before a voiceless consonant (as in *caught*).

A and B **Word Pairs 1 and 2** See Overview, p. ix.

Word pairs for additional practice:

/ʌ/ – /ɔ/: cuff/cough, lung/long, sung/song, fun/fawn, lunch/launch, tuck/talk, stuck/stalk, hunt/haunt, but/bought, gun/gone

/ɑr/ – /ɔr/: farm/form, barn/born, park/pork, car/core, bar/bore, tar/tore, scar/score, mar/more, char/chore, hard/hoard, guard/gored, are/or

/ɑ/ – /ɔ/: cot/caught, Don/dawn, collar/caller, odd/awed, pond/pawned, nod/gnawed, tot/taught

C **Test Yourself** See Overview, p. ix.

Step 1

ANSWERS		
1. cut	3. caller	5. cord
2. boss	4. four	6. star

Step 2

ANSWERS
1. I'm waiting for the <u>bus</u>.
2. He <u>caught</u> the paper.
3. Is it <u>four</u>?
4. This needs a new <u>card</u>.
5. Did you get the name of the <u>color</u>?
6. Isn't it <u>dawn</u> yet?

D **Vocabulary** See Overview, p. ix.

Both the words in the list and the captions for the illustration are from the dialog that follows.

Note the stress in the compound nouns here: **air**port, **foot**ball, **score**board, **quar**terback. Words like these generally have the main stress on the first element and a lighter stress on the second. Stress in compound nouns is practiced in Unit 16, task E, and Unit 23, task E.

E Dialog See Overview, pp. ix–x.

Step 1 To introduce the situation, call attention to the illustration and the title of the dialog. If necessary, briefly discuss American football (see the illustration), contrasting it with the game known in Canada and the United States as *soccer*.

Have students read the dialog as they listen to the audio. Some of the words in the book are different from the words on the recording. Students can call out "Stop" or signal when they hear a word that is different. Pause the recording to give students time to write, or have students dictate the correction for you to write on the board. You may need to play the dialog several times for students to catch all the incorrect words.

Step 2 Play the audio again and go over the answers.

ANSWERS	
Announcer	This morning the <u>Hawks</u> returned from their game in <u>New York</u>. Laura Morgan, our sports reporter, was at the <u>airport</u> to meet them.
Laura	Good morning. I'm Laura Morgan. All the <u>football</u> players are <u>walking</u> toward me. Here's George <u>Small</u>, the halfback. Good morning, George.
George	Good morning. Are you a reporter?
Laura	Yes, I'm from Channel <u>4</u>. Can you tell our audience what you thought about the game in <u>New York</u>?
George	It was <u>awful</u>! We <u>lost</u>. The score was 4 to <u>44</u>.
Laura	Really? I thought the score was 4 to 34.
George	No, 4 to <u>44</u>. But it wasn't my fault.
Laura	Whose fault was it?
George	The quarterback's.
Laura	The quarterback's?
George	Yes, the quarterback's. He was always <u>falling</u> or dropping the ball.

F Using Stress and Intonation to Show a Contrast

Background notes In neutral English sentence stress (e.g., at the beginning of a conversation) the main stress and intonation change are usually on the last important content word in the sentence. When a person wants to emphasize something or make a contrast, however, the main stress and intonation change go on the new idea – the information that differs from what was said before.

The practice in English of varying the main stress for contrast or emphasis is difficult for many students. In some languages, contrast and emphasis are usually signaled by grammatical constructions or by changes in word order rather than by stress and intonation. In other languages, stress is used to show contrast and emphasis, but not all the features that mark stress in English (length, loudness, a clearer vowel, a change in pitch) are present as part of stress. Speakers of these languages may not make stressed syllables sound prominent enough or distinct enough from the surrounding syllables. For speakers of tone languages, such as Chinese or Vietnamese, the use of pitch (tone) as part of stress to express emphasis may be quite alien.

Step 1 Have students listen to the three short conversations. In each conversation, the word that stands out in A's line is the last content word. Speaker B, however, varies the stress to show the idea that contrasts with what A said.

Explain that in each conversation, B is surprised by something that A says. Point out that B says the same sentence in each conversation but makes a different word stand out each time. Ask students which word stands out in each of B's responses and why. They should be able to say what the word that stands out contrasts with:

In the first conversation, B thinks George played football, not baseball.

In the second conversation, B thinks George played in Boston, not New York.

In the third conversation, B thinks it was George, not Paul, who played.

Step 2 Play the audio again and have students repeat the short conversations. Then ask a few pairs of students to choose one of the three conversations and read it. Encourage students to look up when they say their sentences, rather than reading word by word from their books.

You could also ask individual students to say B's line, choosing one of the three conversations without telling anyone which conversation it is. Other students should be able to tell by the word that stands out whether the line is from conversation 1, 2, or 3.

G Conversation Practice

Step 1 Check the answers before students go on to step 2, making sure they understand why the word would stand out in each item (e.g., in the example, *football player* contrasts with *reporter*).

> **ANSWERS**
>
> 1. I thought the <u>football</u> player's name was George.
> 2. I thought <u>Boston</u> lost the game.
> 3. I thought the score was <u>4</u> to 44.
> 4. I thought he played football in the <u>morning</u>.
> 5. I thought he talked to <u>Laura</u> at the airport.
> 6. I thought it <u>was</u> George's fault.

Step 2 As students practice the short conversations, move around the room monitoring stress and intonation and the pronunciation of words with the sound /ɔ/.

H Spelling

The spellings *au* and *aw* are regular spellings for the sound /ɔ/.

Two other frequent spellings for the sound /ɔ/ – *o* and *a* – commonly spell other sounds. The letter *o* is a common spelling for the sounds /ow/ and /ɑ/. The letter *a* is a common spelling for the sounds /æ/, /ey/, and /ɑ/. Note that *a* generally has the sound /ɔ/ only before the letter *l* (as in *fall*) or after *w* or *qu* (as in *water* and *quarter*).

I Common Expressions See Overview, p. xii.

Linking Pronunciation with Other Classwork

Tie pronunciation in with practice of:

1. The greeting "Good morning."

2. Describing people and things using the words *large / small*, *tall / short*, and *long / short*. For example, ask student volunteers to go to the board and sketch items such as these: a tall glass with a little water in it; a long wall with a small door in it; a large house with four small windows and a door; a store with four tall men in it. Give each student the description of the item on a piece of paper that other students can't see. Other students then say what the picture is.

3. Telling the time using *quarter to / quarter after* (for example, *a quarter after four*).

4. Irregular past tense verbs: note the sound /ɔ/ in *thought, brought, bought, caught,* and *taught.*

Word Stress Practice

Write large and small circles on the board showing these two stress patterns:

  A ● •   B • ●

Read the following words. Students say whether they heard stress pattern A or B.

1. report (B)   5. August (A)
2. morning (A)   6. awful (A)
3. always (A)   7. before (B)
4. because (B)   8. quarter (A)

UNIT 12 /ow/ • go Linking Vowel Sounds

Student Difficulties

Students often use a pure vowel /o/ instead of English /ow/, leaving out the second, glide part of the vowel. Many students also make the vowel too short. In some cases, their pronunciation of this vowel will be noticeable as part of a nonnative accent but won't interfere with understanding. In other cases, though, confusion with other vowels may result.

■ Speakers of some languages, such as Dutch, French, German, Japanese, and Spanish, may replace both /ow/ and /ɔ/ with a pure /o/ sound, leading to confusion between pairs like *caught* and *coat.*

- Other students, including speakers of Arabic, Chinese, Greek, Italian, Swahili, and West African languages, may also (or instead) substitute a pure /o/ for the /ɑ/ in words like *not,* leading to confusion between pairs like *not* and *note.*

- Some students, especially those who make /ow/ too short, also confuse /ow/ and /ʌ/, as in *note* and *nut.* This may be a problem for speakers of Arabic, Greek, Hebrew, and Polish.

- Scandinavian speakers may also have difficulty with /ow/, sometimes confusing it with /uw/ or /ɑw/.

Making the Sound

Have students read the directions for making the sound /ow/ as they listen to the audio and look at the illustrations. Emphasize that /ow/ has two parts: /o/ and /w/. The diagrams show how the tongue and lips move from the beginning of the sound to make the /w/ glide at the end.

Demonstrate the change in mouth position in pronouncing /ow/. Show how the lips are gradually pushed into a circle as the jaw moves from the half-open position of /o/ to the nearly closed position of /w/. Some students may find it easier to think of the second part of the vowel as the sound /u/. Students can check their own pronunciation using a mirror. They can also practice making the /ow/ sound silently to feel the way their mouths move, with the lips becoming more round as they say the sound.

Practice the sound first in places where /ow/ is longest and the glide is most noticeable, as in *go* or *phone* (see *Variation in the sound* below). If any students make the second part of the sound too strong, write the /w/ as a small superscript letter: /oʷ/.

Variation in the sound

1. The sound /ow/ is longest and the glide is most noticeable in stressed syllables at the end of a word, as in *go* or *below,* or before a voiced consonant, as in *phone* or *goes.* It is shorter before a voiceless consonant, as in *coat.* In an unstressed syllable, there may be no glide at all. Compare *road / wrote, close* (verb) / *close* (adjective), *robe / rope.*

2. British speakers use the sound /əʊ/ rather than /ow/.

A Word Pairs See Overview, p. viii.

Word pairs for additional practice:

/ɔ/ – /ow/: bought/boat, called/cold, cost/coast, lawn/loan, jaw/Joe, law/low, chalk/choke, call/coal, fawn/phone, raw/row, Paul/pole, fall/foal, bald/bold

/ʌ/ – /ow/: cut/coat, nut/note, come/comb, fun/phone, must/most, but/boat, none/known, sun/sewn, does/doze, gull/goal, rub/robe, hum/home, rust/roast, dumb/dome, bun/bone, flood/flowed, suck/soak

/ɑ/ – /ow/: not/note, cot/coat, hop/hope, calm/comb, sock/soak, rod/road, rob/robe, got/goat, rot/wrote, odd/owed, holly/holy, John/Joan

If practicing the /ɑ/ – /ow/ contrast, call attention to the difference in spelling patterns for these sounds in pairs like *not / note, cot / coat, hopping / hoping.*

B Test Yourself See Overview, p. ix.

Step 1

ANSWERS	
1. D (caught, coat)	4. S (walk, walk)
2. D (saw, sew)	5. D (ball, bowl)
3. S (hole, hole)	6. S (cold, cold)

Step 2

ANSWERS
1. I fell in the <u>hall</u>.
2. Could you <u>sew</u> this for me?
3. Don't drop the <u>ball</u>!
4. I <u>walk</u> early in the morning.
5. Were you <u>cold</u>?
6. Do you know anything about the <u>coast</u>?

C Vocabulary See Overview, p. ix.

Spellings with the letter *o* can be confusing in English. The letter *o* is a common spelling for the sounds /ɑ/, /ʌ/, and /ɔ/ as well as for the sound /ow/. The combination *ow* is a common spelling for the sound /ɑw/ as well as for /ow/.

Step 1 Have students work in pairs to find the word in each column that does not have the sound /ow/. You may want to do the first column together with the class.

Step 2

D **Dialog** See Overview, pp. ix–x.

Step 1 If students do not live in an area where it snows, you may want to set the scene for the dialog by having a brief discussion. Ask, for example, "Have you ever seen snow? Where?" "What months of the year does it usually snow in New York / Montreal / Alaska / Beijing / Chile?"

Step 2 Play the recording of the dialog again and go over the answers to step 1.

E **Linking Vowel Sounds**

Background notes When a vowel that ends in a /w/ or /y/ glide, such as /ow/ or /ey/, comes before another vowel sound, the two vowels are joined by a short /w/ or /y/ sound.

Step 1 Encourage students to link the vowels together smoothly between the words, without stopping the breath. You may want to point out that the /w/ sound is pronounced even if there is no /w/ sound in the spelling, as in *go out*.

Step 2 Have students work individually or in pairs to mark the linked words.

Step 3

8. Is there snow on the ground?
9. Joe isn't home.
10. No, are you cold?

F **Scrambled Conversations**

Step 1 Working in pairs, students find the best response on the right to each sentence on the left. Go over the example. You may want to have student A cover B's sentences and student B cover A's sentences while they practice.

Encourage students to link words together where possible. If necessary, direct their attention to the linking marked in the same sentences in task E.

Step 2

G **Spelling**

The spelling patterns for the sounds /ɑ/ and /ow/ often cause confusion. Compare common spellings for these sounds using the letter *o*. Note that before two consonants, *o* normally has the sound /ɑ/. But *o* before two consonants is also a common spelling for /ow/: before *l* + another consonant (as in *cold* or *soldier*) or before *ll* at the end of a word (*roll*). (See the notes in Unit 10, task H, for more on spelling the sound /ɑ/.)

Extra practice For review, give students a list of words such as the one on page 33. Students indicate whether the *o* spelling in each word has the sound /ow/ (Sound 1) or /ɑ/ (Sound 2).

1. told (1)
2. clock (2)
3. joking (1)
4. don't (1)
5. college (2)
6. only (1)
7. woke (1)
8. bottle (2)
9. popular (2)
10. open (1)

H **Common Expressions** See Overview, p. xii.

Further Practice

Practice rhyming words that are spelled with the letter *o*. Give students the list of words below. Explain that some of the words have the sound /ow/ and some have other vowel sounds. Students work with a partner, drawing a line to connect pairs of words that rhyme (e.g., *phone* and *groan*).

phone	now	groan	no
done	come	home	some
snow	one	how	comb

ANSWERS		
phone – groan	snow – no	come – some
done – one	now – how	home – comb

Linking Pronunciation with Other Classwork

Tie pronunciation in with practice of:

1. Negative short answers: "No, I don't. / No, I won't."

2. Rejoinders expressing opinion: "I hope so / I think so / I suppose so / I hope not / I don't think so."

3. Asking questions about where people are going, with present or future meaning. For example, use a short dialog such as this:

   A Hello! Where are you going? Are you going home?
   B No. I'm going _____.
   A Oh.
   B Where are *you* going? Are *you* going home?
   A No. I'm going _____.

Students substitute phrases in the blanks, for example: *to the post office / to the movies / to the mall / to Joe's house / to the store / for a walk / bowling / shopping*

Word Stress Practice

Write large and small circles on the board showing these two stress patterns:

A ● •   B • ●

Read the following words. Students say whether they heard stress pattern A or B.

1. window (A)
2. only (A)
3. ago (B)
4. joking (A)
5. hello (B)
6. alone (B)
7. over (A)
8. problem (A)

UNIT 13 /uw/ • too   Stress and Pronouns

Student Difficulties

Many learners confuse the sounds /uw/ and /ʊ/ (see Unit 14). Although most students replace both sounds with a pure vowel /u/ that sounds more like /uw/, speakers of some languages, such as Greek, Polish, Russian, and Turkish, may use a shorter or more relaxed vowel that resembles /ʊ/. Japanese speakers tend to pronounce /uw/ without rounding the lips, which gives it a different sound. Speakers of Scandinavian languages also sometimes have difficulty with /uw/.

Making the Sound

Have students read the directions for making the sound /uw/ as they listen to the audio and look at the illustrations. The lips start by being rounded and continue rounding into a tighter circle. To emphasize the length and the rounding of the lips, it may be helpful to tell students to say /uw/ twice or to round their lips twice. Emphasize that /uw/ is a long sound: "tooo," "sooon," "foood."

Variation in the sound

1. Dialect variation: In a few words, including *room, broom, groom, roof, hoof, root,* and *soot,* the spelling *oo* is pronounced with the sound /uw/ by some people and /ʊ/ by others.

2. The sound /uw/ is longest when it is stressed and at the end of a word, as in *too,* or followed by a voiced consonant. It is shorter, and the /w/ glide sound is less noticeable, before a voiceless consonant. Compare *lose / loose, use* (verb)/ *use* (noun), *prove / proof, sued / suit, rude / root.*

A Vocabulary

Students repeat words and phrases from the dialog that have the sound /uw/. Note that when "What do you do?" is said with neutral stress, the word *you* normally has a weak pronunciation with the sound /ə/ (see Unit 8), not /uw/. For more about the pronunciation of *you,* see task C.

B Dialog See Overview, pp. ix–x.

Step 1 Introduce the dialog, directing students' attention to the title. You could ask which day of the year people say "Happy New Year."

Tell students that they are going to read some short conversations between people at a New Year's Eve party. Have students work with a partner to fill in the missing lines in the short conversations.

Step 2 After students listen to the conversations, you could ask follow-up questions, such as "Which people probably know each other?" "Which people are meeting for the first time?"

ANSWERS

A Happy New Year!
B Happy New Year to you, too!

A This is Lou. He's from Peru.
B Nice to meet you, Lou.

A What's new?
B Just the usual. What's new with you?

A Do you like this music?
B Yes. Do you like it?

A Let me introduce you to my roommate, Sue.
B Is she a student, too?

A What do you do?
B I work with computers. What about you? What do you do?

A I like your blue shoes.
B Thank you. They're new.

A Are you doing anything on Tuesday?
B No, are you?
A Do you want to see a movie?

A Excuse me. I want to get some food.

A I have to leave soon.
B Me, too.

A Nice to meet you, Sue!
B Nice to meet you, too!

A See you on Tuesday, Lou.
B Happy New Year!

Extra practice

1. To build fluency, it is helpful for students to learn the rhythm of some common expressions. See the Unit 13 Web Site Worksheet (at www.cambridge.org/pp/student) to practice some of the sentences here.

2. Talk about ways of celebrating New Year's Eve and New Year's Day in different countries. You may want to discuss different customs associated with New Year's, such as making New Year's resolutions, making predictions about the coming year, or eating special foods. Ask students how they usually spend New Year's Eve or New Year's Day ("I usually . . .").

C Stress and Pronouns

Background notes Pronouns typically have a weak pronunciation in sentences with neutral stress (e.g., at the beginning of a conversation). The pronoun *you* is often reduced to /yə/, especially when it is not at the end of a sentence. The words *do you* in a question are commonly pronounced /də yə/ or, at the beginning of a sentence in very rapid speech, /dyə/. But the stress changes when a second speaker repeats a sentence, using *you* to refer to the other person. In that case, *you* is stressed for contrast and has the pronunciation /yuw/.

Steps 1 and 2 Tap or clap to show the rhythm of the sentences, if necessary, as students listen and repeat. Note that *do* keeps its weak pronunciation /də/ in B's sentence. Only *you* changes to show the contrast in meaning.

D Conversation Practice

Step 1 Working in pairs, students make up a question or other sentence for A that could be followed by B's response. They should cover the conversations in task B, working from memory or using their own ideas.

Step 2 After students have had a chance to practice with their partners, call on pairs of students to say some of their short conversations. Check that B stresses the pronoun *you* in conversations 1, 3, 4, 6, and 8, but that other pronouns are generally not stressed.

Alternatively, divide the class into "A" students and "B" students and have them mingle. "A" students say the first line in one of the conversations in step 1. "B" students say the response that follows that line.

E Spelling

The letter *u* as a spelling for /uw/ sometimes includes the sound /y/ (/yuw/), as in *use, music,* or *confused.* For more information, see the notes for Unit 36, task G.

For practice of spellings with *u* and *oo,* see the notes for Unit 14, task H.

F Common Expressions See Overview, p. xii.

Linking Pronunciation with Other Classwork

Tie pronunciation in with practice of:

1. Introductions and small talk, "Nice to meet you." "What do you do?"

2. Compliments, for example:

   A I like your shoes / glasses / boots / coat / bag / sweater.
   B Thank you.
   A Are they / Is it new?

   Note that compliments often have a rather high intonation before the fall at the end.

3. *too*: for example, *I do, too.*

Word Stress Practice

Students listen to the following pairs and say whether the stress pattern for the two words or phrases is the same or different.

1. introduce / afternoon (S)
2. thank you / Peru (D)
3. excuse / music (D)
4. student / movie (S)
5. Tuesday / confuse (D)
6. computer / usual (D)
7. introduce / New Year's Eve (S)
8. Happy New Year / conversation (S)

UNIT 14 /ʊ/ • book Negative Contractions

Student Difficulties

Many students have difficulty distinguishing the sounds /uw/ (as in *boot*) and /ʊ/ (as in *foot*).

■ Students likely to have particular difficulty include speakers of Chinese, Korean, Farsi, French, Italian, Portuguese, Spanish, and African languages. These languages have only one vowel sound in the area of /uw/ and /ʊ/ – a pure vowel /u/ without the extra glide sound at the end. Students tend to substitute this pure /u/ vowel for both /uw/ and /ʊ/, causing confusion between words like *pool* and *pull.*

■ Speakers of Dutch, Japanese, and Scandinavian languages may also have difficulty; they may confuse /ʊ/ with /uw/ or with other vowels, such as /ʌ/.

■ Japanese speakers may pronounce /ʊ/ as a very quiet, whispered sound in some words, often giving the impression that they are dropping the sound altogether.

The combination /wʊ/, as in *would,* can be especially difficult for some students. They may omit the /w/ or pronounce it as a different sound, such as /v/ or /g/. To say /wʊ/, the lips are tightly rounded and then quickly relaxed and unrounded just a little.

Making the Sound

Have students read the directions for making the sound /ʊ/ as they listen to the audio and look at the illustrations. Demonstrate and model the two vowels /uw/ and /ʊ/. The tongue is a little lower in the mouth for /ʊ/ than for /uw/. The lips are a little more relaxed and not as tightly rounded.

Variation in the sound

1. See the note on dialect variation in Unit 13, *Variation in the sound*.

2. The sound /ʊ/ is longer before a voiced consonant, as in *stood*, and shorter before a voiceless consonant, as in *put*.

A Word Pairs See Overview, p. viii.

There are very few pairs of common words that contrast the sounds /uw/ and /ʊ/. Instead of relying on word pairs, you may want to contrast the sounds in phrases that use both vowels, for example: *too full, two books, new wool*.

Word pairs for additional practice:

/uw/ – /ʊ/: who'd/hood, cooed/could, shoed/should
/ʌ/ – /ʊ/:   luck/look, buck/book, tuck/took, putt/put
/ɔ/ – /ʊ/:   fall/full, ball/bull, wall/wool, talk/took, fought/foot, Paul/pull, hawk/hook

B Test Yourself See Overview, p. ix.

Step 1

> **ANSWERS**
>
> | | | | | |
> |---|---|---|---|---|
> | 1. | S | (pool, pool) | 4. S | (stewed, stewed) |
> | 2. | D | (look, Luke) | 5. S | (foot, foot) |
> | 3. | D | (fool, full) | 6. D | (suit, soot) |

Step 2 Note that *food/foot* and *fool/full*, used to contrast the two sounds, are not exact word pairs.

> **ANSWERS**
>
> 1. The sign on the door says "Pull".
> 2. Luke, I want you to come here.
> 3. Where did that black suit come from?
> 4. I think he's full.
> 5. I stewed the vegetables in the pot.
> 6. She stepped on my foot.

C Vocabulary See Overview, p. ix.

Step 1 Students work in pairs to find the word in each column that does not have the sound /ʊ/. You may want to do the first column together with the class. If necessary, remind students to focus on the sound and not the spelling.

Step 2 The sound /ʊ/ has the same basic spelling patterns as /uw/, which of course increases students' confusion between the two sounds. Note that /ʊ/ is not spelled with *u* at the beginning of words *(under, use)*. And it is not spelled with *ou*, except before *l* in words like *could* and *would*.

> **ANSWERS**
>
> The words *enough, use, food,* and *under* do not have the sound /ʊ/.

D Dialog See Overview, pp. ix–x.

Step 1 Students can work alone or with a partner to fill in the blanks. If they work with a partner, encourage them to say the words aloud as they fill them in. You may want to check their pronunciation of the words *should, shouldn't,* and so on, before they begin (e.g., to check for silent *l*). Note that the words *should, could,* and *would* have the sound /ʊ/ when they are said in isolation, but often have the weak vowel /ə/ when they are said within a sentence.

To check understanding, you may want to ask at the end: "Who was eating the cookies?"

Step 2 Play the recording of the dialog again and go over the answers to step 1.

> **ANSWERS**
>
> **Julia** Luke, <u>could</u> you help me look for my book? I'm not sure where I put it.
>
> **Luke** Which book?
>
> **Julia** My new cookbook – *Good Cooking*.
>
> **Luke** <u>Should</u> I look in the bookcase?
>
> **Julia** No, the bookcase is full. It <u>wouldn't</u> be there.
>
> **Luke** Maybe you <u>should</u> look in the living room.
>
> **Julia** I looked everywhere, even under the cushions.
>
> **Luke** <u>Couldn't</u> you use another cookbook?
>
> **Julia** No, the cookbook I'm looking for is a sugar-free, fat-free –
>
> **Luke** *(interrupting)* – food-free cookbook?
>
> **Julia** Very funny. You eat too much junk food. It isn't good for you.
>
> **Luke** But it tastes good!
>
> **Julia** Well, you <u>shouldn't</u> eat so much sugar. Hmm . . . I think you took that book and put it somewhere so I <u>couldn't</u> use it.
>
> **Luke** I didn't put it anywhere! *(pause)* I think you <u>should</u> look under that box of cookies.
>
> **Julia** *(picking up the cookies)* Oops.

E Negative Contractions

Background notes Students sometimes think it is more "correct" to use full forms, but native speakers generally use contractions where possible. Using the full forms is likely to sound overly formal or emphatic. In formal or academic writing, however, the full forms are usually used.

Learners often have difficulty pronouncing negative contractions like *couldn't, wouldn't,* and *shouldn't,* where *-n't* comes after a /d/ sound. They tend to either omit the /d/ or add a vowel sound between the /d/ and /n/. The /n/ here is a syllabic /n/ (see Unit 45, task E), with no vowel sound before it – for example, /kʊdnt/. To make the sound, the tongue goes to the roof of the mouth for /d/, without releasing air, and stays in the same place to make /n/. The air for both sounds escapes through the nose as /n/ is pronounced.

Step 1 Point out the different rhythms in the negative and affirmative sentences. Note that the negative contractions are stressed, but the affirmative forms are not.

Steps 2 and 3

ANSWERS

1. I <u>could</u> get a job as a cook.
2. I <u>wouldn't</u> wear a suit to school.
3. You <u>couldn't</u> learn to cook from a book.
4. You <u>should</u> eat a lot of fruit.
5. You <u>shouldn't</u> drink a lot of juice.
6. You <u>couldn't</u> make good cookies without sugar.

F Conversation Practice

Step 1 Students practice in pairs. One person says each sentence, choosing a word from the word pair. The other person points to the word that was said. Then students should switch roles.

Before students practice, you may want to review the contrast between /uw/ and /ʊ/. Ask them which words in the sentences have the sound /ʊ/ *(could/couldn't, would/wouldn't, should/shouldn't, cook, book, good, cookies, sugar)* and which words have the sound /uw/ *(suit, school, fruit, juice).* (The strong pronunciation of *you* would also have the sound /uw/.) Remind students to make a clear difference between the two vowels.

Step 2 Have students practice in small groups, taking turns completing each of the sentences in their books. Encourage each person to complete

each sentence in a different way. When students have finished practicing, you may want to have them say some of their sentences to the class.

G Rhythm Chant

Step 1 Play the recording of the rhythm chant. Then play it again, this time accompanied by the teacher clapping or tapping (e.g., with a ruler).

ANSWERS

The words *shouldn't, cookies, sugar, good, book,* and *look* have the sound /ʊ/.

Step 2 Play the chant again, either pausing after each line for students to repeat or having students say the chant along with the recording. Encourage them to tap on their desks or clap. After students practice the chant chorally, you may want to ask a few individuals to say it while the rest of the class claps or taps.

Extra practice Ask students to complete these lines with their own words:

You shouldn't eat too many _____.
You shouldn't eat too much _____.

H Spelling

Confusion between the sounds /ʊ/ and /uw/ is no doubt increased by the spelling, since both sounds are usually written with the letters *oo* or *u*. The spelling *oo* may look to students as if it should be a long sound, encouraging them to substitute /uw/ in words that have /ʊ/. Note, too, that in many languages the letter *u* is the spelling for a pure tense vowel /u/, which students may use in place of both /ʊ/ and /uw/ in English. The letter *u* is also a common spelling in English for the sound /ʌ/, which students sometimes confuse with /ʊ/.

Students may find it helpful to know that /ʊ/ is not a very common vowel in English. The spelling *oo* is likely to be pronounced /ʊ/ before the letters *d, t,* and *k,* as in *good, foot,* and *look.* (This rule is not foolproof; exceptions include *food, blood,* and *boot.*) The spelling *u* is likely to be pronounced /ʊ/ before *ll* and *sh,* as in *pull* and *push* (exceptions include *dull* and *rush*).

Extra practice Review spellings with the letters *u* and *oo*. Give students a list of words such as the following: *good, food, cook, blood, soon, look, student, put, full, June, just, introduce, study.* Have students group the words according to the vowel sound: /ʊ/ *(book),* /uw/ *(boot),* or /ʌ/ *(cup).*

I Common Expressions See Overview, p. xii.

Further Practice

1. Students can practice this tongue twister for fun: "How much wood would a woodchuck chuck if a woodchuck could chuck wood?"

2. Have students practice short dialogs that use the sounds /ʊ/ and /uw/, for example:

> **A** Excuse me. Do you know a good place to get (1)_____?
>
> **B** Yes. The store next to the (2)_____ is a good place to get (1)_____. I'm going there, too.

Substitute words from group 1 in blanks marked 1 and words from group 2 in blanks marked 2.

> 1: shoes / boots / wool / cookies / toothpaste / cookbooks / fruit / juice / sugar
>
> 2: supermarket / bookstore / movie theater / shoe store / newspaper stand / school / swimming pool

Linking Pronunciation with Other Classwork

Tie pronunciation in with practice of:

1. Modal auxiliaries *could / couldn't, should / shouldn't, would / wouldn't.*

2. Negative questions or tag questions using *should, would,* and *could.*

3. Expressions using the word *good,* such as "Good morning / afternoon / night." "Have a good weekend / time / trip / vacation / day."

Word Stress Practice

Practice compounds that have a strong stress on the first part and a lighter stress on the second part:

- ● • football, bookshelf, cookbook, bedroom, junk food

- ● • • living room, dining room, everywhere, anywhere

UNIT 15 Review /ʌ/, /ɑ/, /ɔ/, /ow/, /uw/, /ʊ/, and /ə/

This unit provides additional practice and review of the vowels /ʌ/, /ɑ/, /ɔ/, /ow/, /uw/, /ʊ/, and /ə/.

A Test Yourself

The set of words with contrasting vowels is not on the audio program. Before proceeding, you may want to have students listen to and repeat some or all of these words, reading across or reading first down and then across. They can use dictionaries to check the meaning of unfamiliar words, but they do not have to understand every word to do the task.

Play the audio. Students write or say aloud the number of the vowel they hear in each word, using the numbers at the top of each column in the table. Explain that they do not need to write the word – just the number.

B Vocabulary

Step 1 Each of the phrases includes a word that usually has a weak pronunciation with the unstressed sound /ə/. The phrases are taken from the dialog that follows. Working individually or with a partner, students underline the word that they expect to have the sound /ə/.

Step 2 Check that students do not put stress on the weak forms when they repeat the phrases.

C **Dialog** See Overview, pp. ix–x.

Step 1 Students cover the dialog in their books and listen to the audio. You may want to give them questions to direct their listening. For example, tell them to listen to the dialog and mark each sentence below *T* for *true* or *F* for *false*. They should correct the sentences that are false.

Paul's mother thinks:

1. _____ The apartment has a good view. (T)
2. _____ The sofa should be under the window. (F – opposite the window)
3. _____ They should move the bookcase. (T)
4. _____ The photo should go over the sofa. (F – on top of the bookcase)

Step 2 Note that some of the words below may belong in different columns, depending on the speaker's dialect. Words like *are* that would normally be unstressed and pronounced with /ə/ or /ər/ are not shown. Also, only one form of a word is listed – for example, *move,* but not *moved* or *moving.*

D **Puzzle**

Students circle or say the word in each group that does not have the same vowel sound as the other words. Go over the example. If necessary, remind students to focus on sounds, not spellings. Students can work alone or with a partner.

To check the answers at the end, use the numbers for the sounds from the table in task A: "Which vowel sound does *put* have?" (6) "Which vowel sound do the other words have?" (1) If students need the practice, have them listen to and repeat the words when checking answers.

Spelling Review

Give students a list of words, on paper or on the board, with the sounds practiced in Units 7–14. Have students sort the words by sound, grouping words with the same vowel sound together. Alternatively, write each word on a card, preparing more than one set of cards for larger classes, and have students work in groups to sort them.

Sample list of words to be given in scrambled order:

/ʌ/	love, nothing, cousin, doesn't, funny
/ɑ/	job, shopping, father, problem, holiday
/ɔ/	fall, thought, awful, lost, walk
/ow/	cold, won't, throw, coat, over
/uw/	movie, music, Tuesday, suit, shoes
/ʊ/	shouldn't, woman, took, push, good

Word Stress Practice

Write large and small circles on the board showing these two stress patterns:

A ● •   B • ●

Read the following words. Students say whether they heard stress pattern A or B.

1. nonsense (A)   5. before (B)

2. sometimes (A)   6. always (A)

3. because (B)   7. photo (A)

4. nothing (A)   8. review (B)

Student Difficulties

Most students do not have much difficulty with the sound /ɑy/.

■ Some students, for example speakers of Russian, Spanish, and Scandinavian languages, may make the second part of the diphthong too strong, giving the two parts of the sound equal weight. For these students, it may be helpful to write the symbol for the sound on the board as /ɑ^y/, with the /y/ shown as a small superscript letter.

■ French and Italian speakers may either make the second element too strong or drop it altogether.

■ Chinese speakers may make both parts of the diphthong too short and indistinct.

■ Other students who may have difficulty with the sound /ɑy/ include speakers of Arabic, Swahili, and Thai. Students who have difficulty commonly substitute the first vowel alone or confuse /ɑy/ with /ey/ or /ɔy/.

■ Vietnamese speakers may drop final consonants after this or other diphthongs.

Making the Sound

Have students read the directions for making /ɑy/ as they listen to the audio and look at the illustrations. The sound /ɑy/ is a diphthong – a vowel sound made with movement from one position to another. It starts from a position similar to English /ɑ/ and ends at the position for /y/.

Variation in the sound

1. The exact sounds making up the diphthong /ɑy/ may vary. Some people say the first part as a sound between /ɑ/ and /æ/. Some speakers, especially Canadians and people from the northern United States, pronounce the first part of this sound more like /ʌ/ before a voiceless consonant (/p, t, k, s, ʃ, tʃ, f, θ/), as in *like* /lʌyk/.

2. Many speakers in the southern U.S. tend to drop the second part of this diphthong, especially before a consonant.

3. The sound /ɑy/ is longest when it is stressed and at the end of a word, as in *hi*, or followed by a voiced consonant, as in *fine*. It is shorter before a voiceless consonant. Compare *ride /right, eyes /ice, hide /height, live* (adj.)*/life*.

A Word Pairs See Overview, p. viii.

Word pairs for additional practice:

/æ/ – /ɑy/: had/hide, sad/side, laugh/life, man/mine, fan/fine, am/I'm, sand/signed, rat/right, bat/bite, fat/fight, mat/might, lamb/lime, as/eyes, dad/died, sat/sight, add/I'd, lack/like, tap/type, dam/dime, clam/climb, pan/pine, flat/flight

/ey/ – /ɑy/: A/I, lake/like, late/light, May/my, tray/try, wait/white, bake/bike

B Test Yourself See Overview, p. ix.

Step 1

ANSWERS					
1.	van	3.	pints	5.	kite
2.	hat	4.	bike	6.	sad

Step 2

ANSWERS
1. Carry it on your <u>back</u>.
2. Is this your <u>height</u>?
3. My <u>cat</u> got stuck in a tree.
4. They don't sell <u>pants</u>.
5. There's a <u>vine</u> next to the house.
6. They <u>had</u> the money.

C Vocabulary

Step 1 Note that all of the words here are stressed on the first syllable: **hik**ing, **bike** riding, **kay**aking, and so on. Most of the words are compound nouns, which are practiced in task E, so you may want to hold off on practicing stress until you get to that task.

Step 2 Students work in pairs to match the words in step 1 with the illustrations in step 2. You may want to go over the first item with the class.

D Dialog See Overview, pp. ix–x.

Step 1 Students listen to the dialog and check the activities in task C that Liza invites Mike to do. They should look at the vocabulary words in task C, and not at the dialog, as they listen.

Background notes

1. When /ay/ comes before another vowel sound, the /y/ sound in /ay/ is used to link the two vowels together: try it.

2. The word *I* is often pronounced just as the vowel /a/, especially when it is unstressed or used in contractions like *I'm* or *I'll*.

Step 2 Play the recording of the dialog again and go over the answers to step 1.

E Stress in Compound Nouns

Background notes When two words – often, but not always, two nouns – are used together in English to form a compound noun, the first part of the compound usually has the main (or primary) stress and the second part has lighter (or secondary) stress. This stress pattern is used whether the compound is written as one word *(skydiving)* or as two words *(ice cream)*. Not all compound nouns follow this stress rule, but it is a very common pattern in English.

Extra practice Have students practice the conversation below with a partner. Student A replaces the underlined items with an activity from task C. Student B chooses one of the responses in the example below. Read the dialog, either by yourself or with a student, as a model. Then students practice in pairs, switching roles.

A Do you like <u>horseback riding</u>?
B I've never tried it. Why? / Sometimes. Why? / I like <u>horseback riding</u> a lot. Why?

A I'm going <u>horseback riding</u> on Friday. Would you like to come?
B Oh, I'm busy on Friday. Maybe some other time.

F Survey

To do this activity, students will need to walk around the room and ask questions. If possible, they should write each name only once.

Model the example questions in the Student's Book. Note that the first question is always the same ("Have you tried _____?"), but the question that follows depends on the other person's answer to the first question.

You may want to set a time limit for the survey (for example, 10 minutes). After the class has finished the activity, you can ask follow-up questions to find out what they learned, for example, "Did you find out anything surprising?"

G Spelling

The spelling patterns for the sounds /ɪ/ and /ay/ often cause confusion. Compare these word pairs to call attention to the different spellings for these sounds using the letter *i*:

bit/bite, hid/hide, fin/fine, pin/pine, dim/dime, rid/ride

lit/light, fit/fight

dinner/diner, filling/filing

You may also want to review the basic spelling rules for adding *-ing* to verbs (see the Unit 16 Web Site Worksheet at www.cambridge.org/pp/student for practice).

1. Verbs that end in silent *e* drop the *e* before adding *-ing:* ride – riding.

2. Verbs that end in a single stressed vowel letter followed by a single consonant letter double the consonant before adding *-ing:* swim – swimming, begin – beginning (exceptions: the consonants *x* and *v* are not usually doubled).

3. Verbs that end in *ie* change the *ie* to *y* before adding *-ing:* lie – lying.

4. Other verbs do not change before adding *-ing:* fly – flying, climb – climbing.

Call attention to the difference in spelling between *-ing* verbs pronounced with the sounds /ay/ and /ɪ/. If a word has two consonants after the vowel, the letter *i* usually has the sound /ɪ/. If the word has a single stressed *i* followed by a single consonant and *-ing*, *i* has the sound /ay/.

Common Expressions See Overview, p. xii.

Linking Pronunciation with Other Classwork

Tie pronunciation in with practice of:

1. Talking about likes and dislikes: for example, "I like / don't like ice cream / pineapple / rice / fried rice / wine / pie / wide ties / mice / doing exercise."

2. Offering things using *Would you like:* for example, "Would you like some ice cream?"

3. Using the present progressive to talk about the future: for example, "What are you doing tonight / on Friday / Saturday night?" "I'm going to the library / going hiking" etc.

Word Stress Practice

Read the following words. Have students mark the stressed syllable in each word, either by underlining the syllable or drawing a circle over the stressed vowel.

1. hiking
2. sometimes
3. library
4. invite
5. Friday
6. maybe
7. tonight
8. e-mail
9. skydiving
10. kayaking

UNIT 17 /ɔy/ • boy   Sentence Rhythm and Timing

Student Difficulties

Many students do not have difficulty with the sound /ɔy/.

- Students who may have difficulty include speakers of Arabic, Farsi, French, Swahili, Thai, and Indian languages. These learners commonly substitute either the first part of the diphthong alone (/ɔ/) or the sound /ay/, for example, saying *all* or *isle* in place of *oil.* Many students find /ɔy/ hardest to pronounce when it is followed by /l/, as in *boil.*

- Speakers of some languages, such as Dutch, Italian, Spanish, and Scandinavian languages, may have a tendency to make the second part of the sound too strong. For these students, it may be helpful to write the symbol for the sound on the board as /ɔʸ/, showing the /y/ as a small superscript letter.

- Other students, such as Lao, Vietnamese, and to a lesser extent Khmer speakers, tend to drop final consonants after a diphthong like /ɔy/.

Making the Sound

The sound /ɔy/ is a diphthong – a vowel sound made with movement from one position to another. Have students read the directions for making the sound as they listen to the audio and look at the illustrations.

Variation in the sound

1. Some people, particularly in the southern part of the United States, tend to drop the second part of this diphthong, especially before a consonant.

2. The sound /ɔy/ is longest when it is stressed and at the end of a word, as in *enjoy,* or followed by a voiced consonant, as in *noise.* It is shorter before a voiceless consonant, as in *voice.*

A **Word Pairs** See Overview, p. viii.

Word pairs for additional practice:

/ay/ – /ɔy/: tile/toil, liar/lawyer, fire/foyer, kind/ coined, lied/Lloyd, vice/voice, pies/poise, lighter/loiter, rye/Roy, rise/Roy's

/ɔ/ – /ɔy/: all/oil, ball/boil, bald/boiled, tall/toil, fall/foil, call/coil, jaw/joy, raw/Roy, saw/ soy, pause/poise

B **Test Yourself** See Overview, p. ix.
Step 1

ANSWERS			
1. S (boy, boy)		4. S (aisle, aisle)	
2. D (ties, toys)		5. S (foil, foil)	
3. D (point, pint)		6. D (liar, lawyer)	

Step 2 You may need to explain the phrase *a good buy* in sentence number 4. Something that is a good buy is something that is worth more than the price you pay for it.

C Vocabulary

Some students may pronounce the letter s in words such as *boys, noise,* and *noisy* as the sound /s/ instead of /z/.

If students pronounce the *-ed* in *annoyed* or *spoiled* as an extra syllable, write these words on the board and erase or draw a line through the *e* to show that it is not pronounced. Then write the words *enjoyed* and *destroyed* and have students try to pronounce them. (The pronunciation of *-ed* endings is practiced in Unit 25, task E.)

D Dialog   See Overview, pp. ix–x.

Step 1 Students often have difficulty with the unstressed endings of words. If learners speak a language that does not allow a consonant at the end of a word, they may tend to drop final consonants in English. The task here focuses attention on the endings of words and the grammatical meaning these endings communicate.

Have students work with a partner to circle the correct words in parentheses. Encourage them to say the words aloud as they circle them.

Step 2 After students listen and check their answers, you may want to have a class discussion about toys, asking questions such as these: "What were your favorite toys when you were a child?" and "Did you like noisy toys or quiet toys?"

Joy   Why are you so annoyed, Roy? They're just enjoying themselves.

Roy   But the noise is very annoying.

Joy   They're little boys – of course they'll make noise.

Roy   I'm sure I wasn't that noisy when I was a little boy. *(raising his voice)* Boys!

Boys   *(continue making noise)*

Roy   They don't listen. They're spoiled. They destroy all the toys I buy them. And they're the noisiest boys I've ever heard.

Joy   Well, maybe you shouldn't buy them such noisy toys.

Roy   It's not the toys that are noisy – it's the boys!

E Sentence Rhythm and Timing

Background notes   There is a greater difference between stressed and unstressed syllables in English than in many other languages. English is also a "stress-timed" language. This means that stressed syllables tend to occur at regularly spaced intervals, regardless of the number of unstressed syllables between them. The amount of time it takes to say a sentence depends mostly on the number of stressed syllables it has rather than on its total number of syllables. The more unstressed syllables there are between stressed syllables, the more rapidly they tend to be said.

Many learners have difficulty both with reducing vowels and with stress timing. Many languages, including Spanish, Italian, Chinese, Korean, and Indian languages, are "syllable-timed." In syllable-timed languages, all syllables take about the same amount of time to say and tend to follow each other at more or less regular intervals. There is no squashing together of unstressed syllables between much more prominent stressed syllables.

When speakers of syllable-timed languages transfer their native language rhythms to English, it can create problems both in being understood and, especially, in understanding others. These speakers tend to pronounce words that should be unstressed and reduced with stress and full vowels. And they may have difficulty hearing these words at all when they are said by a native English speaker in their unstressed, reduced form.

Step 1 Remind students that in English, only the important words in a sentence are stressed (see Unit 4, task E). The unimportant words, typically structure words like articles *(a, the),* prepositions *(in, of, to,* etc.), and auxiliary verbs *(have, been, will,* etc.), are usually not stressed. Stressed syllables in English are not just louder, they also take longer to say. Unstressed syllables are not just quieter, they are also shorter and often have a reduced (unclear) vowel sound, especially /ə/.

Play the recording of the sentences on the left. Then play the sentences again, clapping or tapping to show the rhythm.

Step 2 Play the recording again. Either pause after each line for students to repeat or have students say the sentences at the same time as the recording. Encourage students to tap on their desks or clap. If they have difficulty with the rhythm, draw different sized dots on the blackboard to represent the rhythm of each sentence, or write the sentence on the board, using large capital letters for stressed syllables and small, squashed-together lowercase letters for unstressed syllables. The rhythm can also be practiced using nonsense syllables: DAH DAH DAH. də DAH DAH DAH. də DAH də DAH DAH.

Step 3 Have students say the sentences on the right chorally. Alternatively, students can practice this with a partner or in a small group, monitoring each others' rhythm and timing.

Extra practice Write a simple sentence consisting of two or three stressed words on the board. Students then try progressively adding structure words to make a set of sentences for rhythm practice.

F Spelling

The spelling of /ɔy/ is relatively straightforward:

1. At the end of words, /ɔy/ is spelled *oy*.

2. At the beginning or in the middle of words, it can be spelled either *oi* or *oy*, though *oi* is more common.

G Common Expressions See Overview, p. xii.

Linking Pronunciation with Other Classwork

Tie pronunciation in with practice in:

Talking about what students enjoy, don't enjoy, or avoid doing, for example: "I enjoy / don't enjoy / avoid hiking / walking / sports / drawing / cooking / driving / noisy parties."

Word Stress Practice

Use the Vocabulary words and other words from the unit to practice word stress.

Write large and small circles on the board showing these three stress patterns:

A ● •   B • ●   C • ● •

Read the following words. Students say whether they heard stress pattern A, B, or C.

1. annoy (B)   5. destroy (B)
2. themselves (B)   6. annoyed (B)
3. noisy (A)   7. annoying (C)
4. enjoying (C)   8. enjoy (B)

/aw/ • house   Stress and Linking in Phrasal Verbs

Student Difficulties

Many students have little difficulty with the sound /aw/. The most common errors are to omit the second part of the diphthong, substituting a sound close to /a/, or to make the first part of the diphthong too short and the second part too strong. The latter is a common tendency among speakers of French, Italian, Russian, and Spanish. Chinese speakers may make both sounds too short and indistinct.

Making the Sound

Have students read the directions for making /aw/ as they listen to the audio and look at the illustrations. The sound /aw/ is a diphthong, starting from a position similar to English /æ/ and ending at the position for /w/ or /uw/.

If students omit the second sound, have them watch the way your lips change position as you say /aw/ and encourage them to use a mirror when practicing it themselves. If students make the second sound too strong, tell them to say the second sound quietly. You could also write the first part of the symbol larger or the second part smaller (e.g., /ɑʷ/, with a small superscript /w/).

Variation in the sound

1. The first vowel in the diphthong /aw/ may vary in sound. Some people say it more like /æ/, some more like /ɑ/, and many speakers use a vowel that is somewhere between these two vowels in quality.

2. Canadians often pronounce this diphthong as /ʌw/ before voiceless consonants (/p, t, k, s, ʃ, tʃ, f, θ/), as in *house* /hʌws/ or *about* /əbʌwt/.

3. Speakers in the southern United States may tend to drop the second part of the diphthong, pronouncing it as a long /ɑ/ or /æ/ sound.

4. As with other vowels, the sound /aw/ is longest when it is stressed and at the end of a word, as in *how,* or followed by a voiced consonant, as in *down.* It is shorter before a voiceless consonant, as in *shout.* Compare *bowed / bout, house* (verb) / *house* (noun), *mouth* (verb) / *mouth* (noun).

A **Word Pairs** See Overview, p. viii.

Some native speakers say *moss* (in the Student's Book) and *moth* (below) with the sound /ɔ/ rather than /ɑ/.

Word pairs for additional practice:

/ɑ/ – /aw/: Scot/scout, dot/doubt, spot/spout, fond/found, moth/mouth

/ow/ – /aw/: oh!/ow!, no/now, phoned/found, load/ loud, tone/town, a boat/about

B **Test Yourself** See Overview, p. ix.

Step 1

ANSWERS		
1. pond	3. hour	5. mouse
2. shout	4. Don	6. how

Step 2

ANSWERS
1. Did you see the <u>moss</u> in the garden?
2. Is it one <u>R</u> or two?
3. Are you going <u>down</u>?
4. The <u>shouts</u> woke me.
5. How many <u>pounds</u> are there?
6. "<u>Ha!</u>" he said in surprise.

C **Vocabulary**

Step 1 Students can work individually or with a partner to find the word that does not have the sound /aw/.

Step 2 Note that many native speakers add the sound /ə/ between /aw/ and a following /r/, whether or not it is shown in the spelling, as in *hour* /awər/ or *shower* /ʃawər/.

ANSWER
The word *saw* does not have the sound /aw/.

D **Dialog** See Overview, pp. ix–x.

Step 1 Have students work with a partner to fill in the blanks. Encourage them to say the words aloud as they fill them in.

Step 2

ANSWERS	
Holly	*(shouting loudly)* There's a mouse in the house!
Howard	Ow! Not so loud! Calm <u>down</u>! Please stop shouting and sit <u>down</u>.
Holly	*(sitting down)* I found a mouse!
Howard	A mouse?
Holly	Yes! I was lying <u>down</u> on the couch and I heard a sound.
Howard	It was probably something outside. Or maybe the shower. I was taking a shower.
Holly	No, I saw the mouse! It was a little brown mouse, and it was running <u>around</u>.
Howard	Where is it now?
Holly	It's under the couch.
Howard	Well, let's get it <u>out</u>!
Holly	How?
Howard	*(shouting)* Move the couch <u>around</u>. Turn it upside <u>down</u>. We have to get it <u>out</u> somehow. We can't have a mouse in the house. We have company coming from <u>out</u> of town. They'll be here in an hour!
Holly	Calm <u>down</u>, Howard! Please stop shouting and sit <u>down</u>! It's just a little brown mouse.

E Stress and Linking in Phrasal Verbs

Background notes Phrasal verbs, sometimes called two-word verbs, are made up of a verb and a particle (a preposition or adverb). Unlike other prepositions, the particle in a phrasal verb is usually stressed; compare, for example, *He's **work**ing on it* and *He turned it **on***. The particle often has the main stress when the phrasal verb does not have an object (e.g., *He's sitting **down***) or when it has a pronoun object (e.g., *Throw it **out***). If the object is a noun, the main stress sometimes shifts to the noun, depending on the rhythm of the sentence (e.g., *Cross out the **word**.*).

The words in a phrasal verb, along with its object (if there is one), are usually linked together and pronounced as a single unit.

Step 1 Read or summarize the information in the box about phrasal verbs. Note that sometimes the meaning of a phrasal verb is easy to guess from the individual words, as in many of the phrasal verbs in step 1 (e.g., *sit down, turn around*). But sometimes the meaning is less obvious, as in a phrasal verb like *work out*.

The phrasal verbs in step 1 do not have an object. Both the verb and the particle are stressed. Tap or clap to show the stress if necessary.

Step 2

ANSWERS	
1. He's **ly**ing **down**.	4. He's **go**ing **out**.
2. He's **turn**ing a**round**.	5. He's **sit**ting **down**.
3. He's **work**ing **out**.	6. He's **run**ning a**round**.

Step 3 The phrasal verbs in step 3 have a pronoun object. This object is not stressed. All three words in each phrase are linked together: **Throw** it **out**. Note that when /t/ is linked to a following vowel, (as in *Throw it out*), the /t/ is "flapped" and sounds like a quick /d/ (see Unit 24, task C).

Step 4

ANSWERS	
1. **Cross** it **out**.	4. **Put** it **down**.
2. **Fig**ure it **out**.	5. **Throw** it **out**.
3. **Turn** it **down**.	6. **Write** it **down**.

At the end of the task, ask students to look at the dialog again. Ask them to find a phrasal verb that means:

1. to become calmer or quieter (*calm down*)

2. to cause something to leave (*get it out*)

Extra practice Have students take turns acting out one of the phrasal verbs without saying anything. The others guess what that student is doing, for example: "You're writing something down."

F Spelling

1. At the end of a word, the sound /aw/ is spelled *ow*.

2. At the beginning or in the middle of a word, /aw/ can be spelled either with *ou* or *ow*.

3. Note that *ow* is also a common spelling for the sound /ow/ (see Unit 12, task G).

G Common Expressions See Overview, p. xii.

Linking Pronunciation with Other Coursework

Tie pronunciation in with practice of:

1. Questions beginning with the word *how*: For example, write questions like the following on the board:

   How far is it from your house to _____?

   How long does it take to get to _____?

   Encourage students to ask the questions using places they know. At first the teacher answers "about two miles," "about an hour," and so on. Then have students ask and answer the questions.

2. Questions like "How are you?" "How's your sister?"

3. Questions with *How often* (e.g., "How often do you eat out / work out?") or *How much / How many*.

4. Phrasal verbs.

Review   /ay/, /ɔy/, and /aw/

This unit provides additional practice and review of the diphthongs /ay/, /ɔy/, and /aw/.

A Test Yourself

The set of words with contrasting vowels is not on the audio program. Before proceeding, you may want to have students listen to and repeat some or all of these words, reading across or reading first down and then across. They can use dictionaries to check the meaning of unfamiliar words, but they do not have to understand every word to do the task.

Play the audio. Students write or say aloud the number of the vowel they hear in each word, using the numbers at the top of each column in the table. Explain that they do not need to write the word – just the number.

ANSWERS		
1. 2 (boy)	4. 3 (bow)	7. 3 (loud)
2. 1 (lied)	5. 1 (tile)	8. 1 (aisle)
3. 2 (toil)	6. 2 (oil)	9. 3 (towel)

B Linking Practice

Step 1 Students listen to the sentences and draw linking lines between /ay/, /ɔy/, /aw/ and a following vowel. You may want to go over the two examples.

With the diphthongs here, the linking sound is apparent from the spellings. But note that linking between vowels also occurs when the /y/ or /w/ sound is not shown in the spelling, as in *high up*.

Step 2

ANSWERS
1. Did you buy it? /y/
2. Now I see. /w/
3. Why don't you try it? /y/
4. You might enjoy it. /y/
5. How are you doing? /w/
6. Is the boy on the ground? /y/
7. Why is there a cloud? /y/

C Dialog   See Overview, pp. ix–x.

Step 1 Students, working alone or with a partner, read the dialog and add more words from the dialog to each column of the table.

Step 2 Play the recording of the dialog. Have students dictate words for each sound. Write them on the board for students to check their answers.

If it would be helpful for your students, have them practice the dialog with a partner at the end.

ANSWERS	
1. /ay/	Kyle, all right, I (I'm, I've), trying, sky, why, try (tried), buy, might, like, my, nice, behind
2. /ɔy/	Troy, oil (oils), enjoy, pointing
3. /aw/	how, ground, now, sounds, brown, cloud, mountain

D Puzzle

Students circle or say the word in each group that does not have the same vowel sound as the other words. Go over the example. Students can work alone or with a partner.

If students need the practice, have them listen to and repeat the words to check their answers.

ANSWERS		
1. win	3. throw	5. give
2. hole	4. show	6. going

Spelling Review

Give students a list of words, on paper or on the board, that have the sounds practiced in Units 16, 17, 18, and 12. Students sort the words by sound, grouping words with the same vowel sound together. Alternatively, write each word on a card, preparing more than one set of cards for larger classes, and have students sort them in groups.

Sample list of words to be given in scrambled order:

/ay/   high, buy, pint, eye, fly
/ɔy/   point, destroy, choice, annoying, noisy
/aw/   loud, crowd, thousand, flower, brown
/ow/   grow, though, sew, snow, know

UNIT 20 Review   The Unstressed Vowels /ə/ and /ər/

This unit provides additional practice and review of the vowels /ə/ and /ər/ in unstressed syllables and words.

Student Difficulties

Many students have difficulty with both word stress and reduced vowels in English.

- In many languages, including Czech, Farsi, French, and Hungarian, word stress is predictable, always falling on the same syllable (e.g., the first or the last) in words. To students who speak these languages, English stress may seem chaotic and unpredictable.

- In some languages, such as French, the stress patterns of individual words may be modified when the words occur in a phrase. The stress pattern of an English word does not usually change when it occurs in a phrase or sentence.

- In some languages, such as Chinese, Japanese, and Swahili, all or most syllables may be pronounced with almost equal stress – or they may sound as if they are to an English speaker, because the features that indicate stress in English (greater force, a longer vowel, a change in pitch) are not all used to indicate stress in these other languages.

- Long words in English often have more than one stress – a stronger stress and a lighter stress. Other languages, such as Greek and Russian, may have only one stress per word. Speakers of these languages may seem to slur over the syllables with weaker stress in words like *conversation* or *photograph*.

- In many languages, even syllables that are unstressed are pronounced with a full, clear vowel sound. In English, unstressed syllables usually have an indistinct, reduced vowel – usually /ə/ or /ɪ/. Students who pronounce unstressed syllables with clear vowels may sound to native English speakers as if they are stressing those syllables. In English, stressed syllables sound more prominent and unstressed syllables less prominent than in most other languages. The use of reduced vowels contributes greatly to this effect.

See Unit 8 for more about difficulties with /ə/.

A Test Yourself

Students practice predicting and listening for words pronounced with their weak forms – both useful skills for understanding native speakers. Although learners do not need to use a lot of weak pronunciations in their own speech – and, indeed, these may sound unnatural if their speech is slow – they need to recognize these forms to understand native speakers. Practice in saying the forms is helpful in raising awareness of these pronunciations.

Step 1 Students read the sentences and predict the word that goes in each blank.

Step 2 Play the audio and have students check their answers. The missing words all have weak pronunciations. Note that in the middle of a sentence, the /h/ sound is often dropped in the weak pronunciation of *her* and the vowel after it is linked to the preceding word: She closed ȟer eyes. For more on dropped /h/, see Unit 40, task E.

Then play the audio again and have students repeat the sentences. Encourage them to link words together and to slow down for the stressed words rather than simply rushing through the unstressed words. Have them repeat the sentences until they can say them at a natural speed. It can be helpful for students to say the sentences at the same time as the recording.

ANSWERS

She closed her eyes.
She looked at the clock.
She packed a pair of binoculars.
Her brother and sister were laughing at her.
"I'd love to go to South America."

B Stressed Syllables in Words

Background notes The stress pattern of a word is an essential part of its pronunciation. Since unstressed syllables often have reduced vowels, knowing which syllable is stressed and which syllables are unstressed also help indicate how the vowels should be pronounced. If stress is put on the wrong syllable, the vowels may also be given the wrong sound, and the word may be incomprehensible to an English listener.

Although word stress is often unpredictable in English, there are some rules that can help learners stress words correctly (see also Unit 1, task C). Note that many of the words in steps 1 and 2 begin with a short prefix like *a-, be-, de-, for-,* or *re-*. These word beginnings, along with others, such as *com-* (*complete*), *im-* (*important*), *pre-* (*prepare*), *pro-* (*pronounce*), and *to-* (*tomorrow*), are usually unstressed, especially at the beginning of a verb or adjective.

The vowel in an unstressed syllable is usually reduced, but the exact sound of the vowel may vary. Often it is reduced to schwa, but in words like *begin, decide,* or *repeat,* it usually sounds more like /ɪ/.

If the stress in any of the words in steps 1, 2, or 3 causes difficulty, indicate their stress pattern on the board. If students do not put enough stress on syllables, tell them to make the stressed syllables stronger or more important. Show them that the stressed vowel is lengthened. Make sure that students slow down for the stressed syllables, so that they sound clearly different from unstressed syllables. Discuss the rules for predicting stress, according to the level of the class.

Step 1 Elicit, or remind students, that two-syllable verbs (*decide, forget, repeat*) often have stress on the second syllable (see Unit 1, task C). Reflexive pronouns (*herself*) also have stress on the second syllable.

Step 2 Note that words ending in *-ion* (e.g., *conversation*) generally have stress on the syllable before the last; this pattern is practiced in Unit 32, task C.

Step 3 Elicit, or remind students, that most nouns with two syllables (*sister, answer, morning, breakfast*) have stress on the first syllable (see Unit 1, task C). Note that *camera* looks like it would have three syllables, but it is usually pronounced as two syllables, with the *e* silent.

Endings like *-able* (*comfortable*), *-ly* (*quietly*), and *-ful* (*beautiful*) are normally unstressed. (For more on stress in words with various endings, see Unit 48, task E.)

Extra practice Write additional words, such as those below, on the board. Ask students to indicate whether each word belongs with the words in step 1, 2, or 3.

brother	careful	water	deliver
about	below	myself	wonderful
picture	asleep	review	pronunciation

C Puzzle

Students circle or say the word in each group that does not have the same stress pattern as the other words. Some of the words in the puzzle are also in task B; others are similar to words in task B, for example, because they have the same prefix or ending. You may want to explain, or remind students, that words with the same prefix or ending often have the same stress pattern.

Go over the example. Students can work alone or with a partner.

Check the answers at the end. If students need the practice, have them listen to and repeat the words when checking answers.

ANSWERS

1. yourself	3. began	5. afternoon
2. open	4. photograph	6. decide

D Reading

Step 1 Tell students they are going to listen to a story about Maria and her trip to South America. Students should look at the sentences in task A, and not at the reading, as they listen. Play the recording. Students number the sentences in task A in the order that they occur in the story.

Either before or after students listen, check their understanding of the title "A dream vacation." Usually a dream vacation would mean the best vacation you could imagine, but it could also mean a vacation that takes place in a dream you have while sleeping. Ask students which meaning it has here.

ANSWERS

"I'd love to go to South America."
She closed her eyes.
She packed a pair of binoculars.
She decided to have some breakfast.
She looked at the clock.
Her brother and sister were laughing at her.

Step 2 Play the recording of the story again. Students listen and read along in their books.

Step 3 Have students try reading the story, or part of the story, aloud. They can do this in small groups, taking turns reading and monitoring each others' pronunciation. Alternatively, they could try recording their own voice. In either case, tell students not to worry about pronouncing every /ə/ sound shown in their books.

Student Difficulties

The sound /ər/ is difficult for almost all learners. They may confuse it with almost any other vowel, often depending on how it is spelled. Students are likely to pronounce it with the vowel suggested by the spelling, for example in *person, bird, work,* or *nurse,* often adding a non-English (e.g., trilled or flapped) /r/ sound. Many students have particular difficulty with /ər/ after the sound /w/, as in *work* or *worst,* or before or after /l/, as in *girl* or *clerk.*

Some students, especially speakers of Japanese, also confuse the sound /ər/ with /ɑr/ or /ʌ/, so that *burn* may sound like *barn* or *bun.* Other students, including speakers of Dutch, French, and Scandinavian languages, may pronounce the vowel with the lips pushed forward and rounded.

Making the Sound

Have students read the directions for making the sound /ər/ as they listen to the audio and look at the illustrations. Students should spend some time on the mouth position for /ər/. The lips should be slightly rounded. The tongue should be raised toward the hard part of the roof of the mouth (the hard palate). You can use hand gestures, holding your hand flat with the palm up and then curling your fingers up slightly to show how the tip of the tongue is curled up. The body of the tongue moves back only slightly; some students pull their tongues too far back.

The tongue position for the sound /ər/ is basically the same as for the English consonant /r/. If students can produce an English /r/, try respelling words on the board omitting the vowel letter, for example "brd" for *bird* or "prson" for *person.* Even if students haven't mastered English /r/, these respellings will call attention to the fact that there is no distinct, separate vowel sound in the sound /ər/.

In teaching this sound, emphasize the fact that /ər/ has many different spellings, all with the same sound.

Variation in the sound

1. Some English speakers say the sound /ər/ with the middle of the tongue raised or bunched up toward the roof of the mouth, without curling the tip of the tongue back.

2. British speakers do not have an /r/ sound at the end of this vowel.

3. The sound /ər/ is longer at the end of a word or before a voiced consonant and shorter before a voiceless consonant. Compare *heard / hurt.*

A, B, and C **Word Pairs 1, 2, and 3** See Overview, p. viii.

Word pairs for additional practice:

/ɔr/ – /ər/: wore/were, born/burn, warm/worm, board/bird, blackboard/blackbird, ward/ word, course/curse, form/firm, Norse/ nurse, walk(/ɔ/)/work

/ɑr/ – /ər/: hard/heard, farm/firm, carton/curtain, dart/dirt, Carl/curl

/ʌ/ – /ər/: huts/hurts, fun/fern, study/sturdy, cut/ curt, but/Burt, pus/purse

D **Test Yourself** See Overview, p. ix.

Step 1

ANSWERS		
1. four	3. shut	5. torn
2. stir	4. bird	6. barn

Step 2

ANSWERS
1. Is it <u>far</u>?
2. They were wearing black <u>shorts</u>.
3. Do you see the <u>birds</u> on the tree?
4. Can you <u>walk</u> faster?
5. Those <u>burns</u> don't look good to me.
6. There were two <u>gulls</u> on the beach.

E **Vocabulary** See Overview, p. ix.

To draw attention to the variety of spellings for /ər/, ask students which letters have the sound /ər/ in these words. Ask them to give an example of each spelling (e.g., *ur – nurse, ear – heard, or – work, ir – first, er – certainly*).

F **Dialog** See Overview, pp. ix–x.

Step 1 Have students work with a partner to fill in the blanks. Encourage them to say the words aloud as they fill them in.

Step 2

Bert Nurse! Nurse! I'm thirsty!

Earl Nurse! My head <u>hurts</u>!

Bert (*turning to Earl*) Pearl is the <u>worst</u> nurse, isn't she?

Earl Personally, I think Kurt is worse.

Bert Mmm. He always leaves work <u>early</u>.

Earl And he always wears a <u>dirty</u> shirt.

Bert I heard he <u>earns</u> thirty dollars an hour.

Earl He <u>certainly</u> doesn't deserve it.

Bert He and Pearl weren't at work on Thursday, <u>were</u> they?

Earl They're the worst nurses on the floor, aren't they?

Bert No – they're the worst nurses in the <u>world</u>!

Extra practice Read aloud the following words from the dialog: *hour, thirsty, turning, wears, worse, floor, aren't, they're, personally, deserve*. Ask students to indicate which words have the sound /ər/.

thirsty, turning, worse, personally, deserve

G Tag Questions with Falling Intonation

Background notes This unit practices tag questions with falling intonation. Some students tend to use rising intonation on all tag questions, either because question tags in their own language use that intonation or because the question form leads them to think rising intonation should be used. Tag questions in English are said with rising intonation when the speaker is asking a real question or is less sure that the other person will agree. Often, however, the speaker strongly expects or hopes that the other person will agree with or confirm what was said. The speaker is not really asking a question, but doing something more like making a comment or giving an opinion and expects confirmation or agreement. Question tags of this type have falling intonation. People often use tag questions this way to keep a conversation going.

Note that tag questions have two intonation groups, each with its own main stress. In the first part of the sentence, the main stress is typically on the last important (content) word. In the tag, the main stress is on the auxiliary verb.

Play the audio and have students listen and repeat the two tag questions chorally. You can use hand gestures to indicate the correct intonation. If it would be helpful for your students, point out that the affirmative statement has a negative tag (*isn't he?*) and the negative statement has an affirmative tag (*were they?*).

H Conversation Practice

Students ask and answer questions in pairs, using the examples as a model. Go over the examples first, modeling the short conversations. If the grammar of tag questions is challenging for your students, you can do this activity with the whole class.

I Spelling

Point out the variety of spellings for the sound /ər/. The only vowel letter that is *not* used to represent this sound (at least not by itself) is *a*.

Extra practice For review, give students, on paper or the board, pairs of words like those below. Ask students to indicate which word has the sound /ər/.

1. worse	horse	6. short	word
2. heard	heart	7. earn	near
3. fire	first	8. sorry	worry
4. were	there	9. turn	torn
5. ear	early	10. verb	very

J Common Expressions See Overview, p. xii.

Extra practice Teach students one or both of these proverbs:

The early bird catches the worm.
A bird in the hand is worth two in the bush.

Discuss the meaning of the proverb at a level appropriate to the students – for example, "People who get up early in the morning are more successful or make more money" for the first proverb. Have students practice saying the proverb.

Linking Pronunciation with Other Classwork

Tie pronunciation in with practice of:

1. Tag questions using *were / weren't*.

2. Short answers using *were / weren't*.

3. Talking about a daily work routine, for example:

   I work in a . . .
   I start work at . . . in the morning.
   I walk / don't walk to work.

Word Stress Practice

Write large and small circles on the board showing these two stress patterns:

A ● •   B • ●

Read the following words. Students say whether they heard stress pattern A or B. Or have students try this before listening and then have them listen to check their answers.

1. circle (A)   6. person (A)
2. dirty (A)   7. perfect (adj.) (A)
3. thirsty (A)   8. occur (B)
4. prefer (B)   9. early (A)
5. nervous (A)   10. Thursday (A)

B Consonants

The introduction to Section B in the Student's Book presents the vocabulary that students will need in order to follow the directions for making the consonant sound that begin each unit. It also familiarizes students with the parts of the mouth, the types of mouth movements they will use to produce English consonant sounds, and the use of the breath (air) and voice in producing consonant sounds.

Work through the unit with students. It would be helpful for students to use mirrors to watch their own mouths as they follow the directions in the book.

UNIT 22 /p/ • pop   Intonation in Lists

Student Difficulties

Students may have the following difficulties with the sound /p/:

- Arabic and sometimes Vietnamese speakers tend to substitute the sound /b/ for /p/, so that *pie*, for example, sounds like *buy*.

- Speakers of some Asian languages, such as, Korean and Tagalog, may confuse /p/ and /f/, usually substituting /p/ for /f/ , but occasionally doing the reverse and substituting /f/ for /p/.

- Many students, including speakers of Greek, Italian, Spanish, French, Dutch, Japanese, Indian languages, and Slavic languages, may fail to aspirate the sound /p/ at the beginning of a word or stressed syllable. Without the puff of air, the sound may be heard as a /b/ by native speakers of English.

Many students have difficulty hearing the sound /p/ at the end of a word, where it is often not released in English. This may be a particular problem for students who speak languages such as Spanish, Italian, and many Asian languages, in which words do not commonly end with consonants. Some of these students may omit final /p/ when speaking, while others pronounce final /p/ too strongly, sometimes adding an extra vowel after it.

Making the Sound

Have students read the directions for making the sound /p/ as they listen to the audio and look at the illustrations. The directions describe the production of aspirated /p/ – the pronunciation of /p/ with a puff of air that occurs before a stressed vowel.

The sounds /p/, /b/, /t/, /d/, /k/, and /g/ are known as *stops*. To make each of these sounds, part of the mouth is completely closed and then the air is quickly released.

Variation in the sound See notes on the different pronunciations of /p/ under task A, below.

A Vocabulary

Step 1 In the words in step 1, /p/ is aspirated – accompanied by a puff of air. The sound /p/ is strongly aspirated before a stressed vowel, as in a *pen, pictures,* or *a piece of pie*, and less strongly aspirated before /l/ or /r/, as in a *plastic bag* or *presents*.

Demonstrate the pronunciation by holding a light piece of paper, a feather, or a lighted match in front of your mouth as you say words like pen and pie. Have students try this, too. The puff of air should make the paper or feather move or the flame flicker. It may help some students to think of the aspiration as an /h/ sound following the /p/. Try respelling words on the board – for example, "p̓en," "p̓ie."

Step 2 The sound /p/ is not aspirated in the words here. To demonstrate the difference between aspirated /p/ and unaspirated /p/, hold the piece of paper, feather, or lighted match in front of your mouth and compare saying words like *pen* and *spoon, pot* and *spot, pie* and *spy*. The paper or flame should move for *pen, pot,* or *pie*, but not for *spoon, spot,* or *spy*.

The sound /p/ is very quiet at the end of a word. At the end of a word, as in *map*, or before another consonant, as in *napkins*, /p/ may not be released at all, or the release may be inaudible. The mouth forms a /p/ sound, but the lips stay closed and the air is not let out.

Step 3

> **ANSWERS**
>
> a p̲urse, a p̲ostcard, p̲ennies

B Dialog See Overview, pp. ix–x.

Step 1 Students listen to the dialog and check the items in task A that Peter and Pam mention. Have students cover the dialog. They should look at the vocabulary words in task A, and not at the dialog, as they listen.

Step 2 Play the recording of the dialog again. You may want to have students compare answers with a partner.

> **ANSWERS**
>
> a pen, a pencil, pictures, presents, a paper plate, a plastic bag, a newspaper, a map, a cup, an envelope, a spoon, a purse, a postcard, stamps, pennies, an apple

C Intonation in Lists

Background notes Two of the functions of intonation are to help divide sentences into phrase groups and to show whether a sentence is finished or not.

In making a list, each item is usually pronounced as a separate phrase group, with a change of intonation in each. A common pattern, practiced in this unit, is for the intonation to rise on each item except the last. To show that the list is complete, the intonation falls to a low pitch on the last item. It is also possible for the intonation to fall slightly on each item before the last and then fall to a low pitch on the last item. If the list is not complete, the intonation on the last item is the same as in previous items – slightly rising or slightly falling.

Steps 1 and 2 Students listen first to lists that are not complete and then to a list that is complete.

You can use hand gestures to show how the intonation rises on each item and then falls at the end of the list that is finished. Say lists with the two different intonation patterns and check to see if students can say which lists are complete and which are not.

D Conversation Practice

Students talk about the things they usually pack when they travel. Set a time limit of four or five minutes for this. As students practice, move around the room checking their intonation and pronunciation of words with the sound /p/. At the end, you may want to ask some follow-up questions, for example: "Which items do both you and your partner usually pack?"

E Game

Each student repeats what the students before them said and then adds a new item to the list, as in the example. If a student cannot remember the list, he or she is out of the game. Students should practice the lists of items first. Remember to explain any new vocabulary.

Check stress and intonation. If necessary, remind students to make the intonation on the last item fall to a low note. To make the game more challenging, students can play with their books closed, after practicing the words in the list.

Alternatively, introduce the game with students' books closed. Say, for example, "We're having a picnic and I'm bringing pretzels. (Student's name), what are you bringing?" If the student suggests an item that has the sound /p/, indicate that it's OK. If the item does not have the sound /p/, it isn't OK. Ask various students what they plan to bring. Only items with the sound /p/ are acceptable. (Note: Instead of using this activity here, it could be adapted to practice or review a different sound.)

F Spelling

1. Note the double *p* after the vowels /æ, ɛ, ɪ, ʌ/ and after /ɑ/ spelled with the letter *o*: *happy, pepper, slippers, supper, dropped* (compare, for example, *super* and *supper*). Call attention to the doubling of the *p* when endings like -*ing* and -*ed* are added to words with these vowel sounds, as in *shopping* or *slipped*. Compare, for example, *hopping*/*hoping*. (This note applies to other consonants, as well.)

2. You may want to demonstrate the pronunciation of words with silent *p*. Many

students tend to pronounce all the letters in a word. They may have difficulty with the idea that some letters are silent, especially if they speak languages in which spelling corresponds closely to pronunciation.

3. Note that the spelling *ph,* as in *telephone,* has the sound /f/ rather than /p/.

G **Common Expressions** See Overview, p. xii.

When two /p/ sounds come together, as in a phrase like *stop pushing*, the two /p/ sounds are linked together and pronounced as one long /p/, with the first /p/ held and not released until the second /p/ is pronounced.

Further Practice

1. Have students practice this well-known English tongue twister:

   Peter Piper picked a peck of pickled peppers.

Then have students, either for homework or in class, make up their own tongue twisters using the sound /p/ and practice saying them. They can use ideas from the dialog or their own ideas.

Examples: Peter put the passports in the back pocket of his pants.

Pam packed the paper plates in the purple plastic bag.

Pick a partner and practice pronunciation in pairs.

2. See Unit 23, *Further Practice*, for practice of linking /p/ and /b/.

Linking Pronunciation with Other Classwork

Tie pronunciation in with practice of:

1. Making requests using *please* or *Could you help me. . . .*

2. Discussing future plans, using *hope to, plan to, promise to.*

Word Stress Practice

Write large and small circles on the board showing these four stress patterns:

A ● •   B • ●   C ● • •   D • ● •

Read the following words. Students say whether they heard stress pattern A, B, C, or D.

1. envelope (C)	7. upstairs (B)
2. police (B)	8. passengers (C)
3. presents (A)	9. impatient (D)
4. picnic (A)	10. pictures (A)
5. important (D)	11. plastic (A)
6. potato (D)	12. probably (C)*

*The word *probably* is sometimes pronounced as two syllables: /ˈprɑ•bliy/.

UNIT 23 /b/ • baby   Stress in Compound Nouns and Phrases

Student Difficulties

Difficulties with the sound /b/ include the following:

■ Speakers of Arabic may confuse /p/ and /b/, often replacing /p/ with /b/, but sometimes doing the reverse and replacing /b/ with /p/.

■ Spanish and Portuguese speakers tend to pronounce /b/ as a sound that resembles /v/ in some positions, especially in the middle of words.

■ In some languages, most voiced consonants are pronounced as their voiceless equivalents

at the end of a word. Students likely to replace voiced /b/ with voiceless /p/ at the end of a word include speakers of Dutch, German, Danish, Turkish, Russian, Chinese, West African languages, and sometimes Spanish.

■ Some students tend to drop stop consonants like /b/ when they are at the end of a word.

Making the Sound

Have students read the directions for making the sound /b/ as they listen to the audio and look at the illustrations. To help students who substitute voiceless /p/, focus on voicing. Have them put their hands gently on their throats, and say a long /s/ or /h/ sound. Then have them say a long vowel sound (e.g., /ɑ/). They should feel a vibration in their throat with the vowel but not with the other sound. Then have them repeat these steps with /p/ and /b/. They should feel a vibration for /b/, but not for /p/.

If learners substitute a sound more like /v/, emphasize that /b/ is a stop sound (see Unit 22, *Making the Sound*) – a very short sound that cannot be prolonged. The lips are completely closed for /b/, stopping the air in the mouth.

Variation in the sound The sound /b/ is strongly voiced between two vowels, as in *about*. In other positions, it may be partially voiceless.

Note This applies to all voiced consonants other than /y, w, m, n, ŋ, l, r/.

A Word Pairs See Overview, pp. viii.

Note that the vowel sound is longer before a voiced consonant like /b/ (as in *robe*) than before a voiceless consonant like /p/ (as in *rope*).

Word pairs for additional practice:
/p/ – /b/: path/bath, peas/bees, pack/back, pig/big, peach/beach, pat/bat, pull/bull, pole/bowl, pen/Ben, cup/cub, rip/rib, mop/mob, lap/lab, simple/symbol

B Test Yourself See Overview, p. ix.

Step 1

ANSWERS	
1. D (bear, pear)	4. S (cap, cap)
2. S (buy, buy)	5. D (rope, robe)
3. S (pill, pill)	6. D (pig, big)

Step 2

ANSWERS
1. She threw away her old pills.
2. It was a little big.
3. What color was the cab?
4. There are bears in the garden.
5. I put the rope in the closet.
6. Could you tell me where the path is?

C Vocabulary

Step 1 Play the audio and have students repeat the words. Most of the items are compound nouns

or noun phrases, which are practiced in task E. You may want to hold off on correcting stress until you get to that task.

Step 2

ANSWERS		
1. blue beads	6. a bookshelf
2. paintbrushes	7. a beautiful bracelet
3. a cookbook	8. October
4. a black box	9. a backpack
5. a birthday cake	

Step 3 Make sure that students lengthen the vowel before /b/ at the end of a word. If they do not lengthen the vowel before a final /b/, it may sound like a /p/ to native English speakers. Since final stop consonants are often not released, the main difference between /b/ and /p/ at the end of a word is often that the vowel before /b/ is longer.

D Dialog See Overview, pp. ix–x.

Step 1 Play the audio. Students read the dialog and listen. Some of the words in the book are different from the words on the recording. Students can call out "Stop" or signal when they hear a word that is different. Pause the recording to give students time to write, or have students dictate the correction for you to write on the board. You may need to play the dialog several times for students to catch all the incorrect words.

Step 2 Play the audio again and go over the answers.

ANSWERS	
Bob	Hi, Barbara. You look happy.
Barbara	(*pause*) Well . . . you know, today's my birthday.
Bob	Oh, right, October 7th. Your birthday! Happy birthday!
Barbara	Thanks, Bob. Look at this bracelet Abby gave me. I can't believe she made it.
Bob	Yeah, those blue beads are beautiful. (*pause*) Is that a new backpack? Was that a birthday present, too?
Barbara	The backpack? No, I bought it myself.
Bob	What did your parents give you for your birthday?
Barbara	A set of paintbrushes. And my Mom baked a birthday cake.

Bob	What about your brother? Did he give you anything?
Barbara	Yes, he built a <u>bookshelf</u> for my bedroom. And, uh, somebody gave me a <u>cookbook</u>.
Bob	I'm really sorry, Barbara, but I totally forgot about your birthday. I've been so busy with my <u>job</u>.
Barbara	Well, my birthday isn't over yet. . . .
Bob	Right! Let's go out and celebrate. How about taking a cab to that new <u>club</u>?

Extra practice Have a discussion about birthdays, asking questions such as these:

"How do you usually celebrate your birthday? How did you celebrate your birthday as a child?"

"How do people usually celebrate birthdays in (student's native country)? Do they send cards? Have parties? Have surprise parties? Bake birthday cakes?"

"Do you buy people presents for their birthdays? Who do you buy presents for? What's the best birthday present you've ever gotten?" "Have you ever gotten a birthday present you didn't like?"

E Stress in Compound Nouns and Phrases

Background notes When two words – both often, but not always, nouns – are used together to form a compound noun, the first part of the compound usually has the main stress and the second part has lighter stress. This stress pattern is used whether the words are written together as one word (like *bookshelf*) or as two words (like *shopping bag*). Many students have difficulty with this stress pattern, especially as it contrasts with adjective + noun stress. In an ordinary noun phrase containing an adjective + a noun, both the adjective and the noun are stressed, but the main stress is on the last word – the noun. Compare the stress in the compound nouns *a **black**bird* (referring to a particular kind of bird) and *a **green**house* (a glass building for growing plants) with the stress in the adjective + noun phrases *a black **bird*** (a bird that is black in color) and *a green **house*** (a house that is green in color).

Play the audio. Have students repeat the compound nouns and noun phrases. Ask them to find more compound nouns in the dialog (*birthday, a backpack, a birthday present, paintbrushes, bedroom*).

F Conversation Practice

Step 1 Students work in pairs to make a compound noun or a noun phrase that describes each picture. Go over the example with the class. Note that some of the answers will be a single word, like *cookbook*, and some will have more than one word.

Step 2

ANSWERS	
1. a <u>cookbook</u>	5. a funny <u>book</u>
2. a <u>teapot</u>	6. cowboy <u>boots</u>
3. a black <u>bag</u>	7. a sleeping <u>bag</u>
4. a big <u>pot</u>	8. rubber <u>boots</u>

Step 3 Students practice the conversation in pairs, as in the example, substituting compound nouns or noun phrases from the unit.

Depending on the level of the students, you may want to have them suggest other compound nouns and phrases from the unit (e.g., from the dialog) before they begin practicing. Or you may want to broaden the task, allowing them to add compound nouns or noun phrases with the sound /b/ that do not occur in this unit. As students practice, move around the room checking stress and their pronunciation of words with the sound /b/.

Extra practice

1. Working in small groups, have students choose birthday presents for other students, using words, compounds, or phrases with the sounds /p/ or /b/. Suggest or elicit useful phrases for discussing this, such as "How about _____?" "Or maybe _____?" At the end, see if their classmates agree with the choices.

2. Most names for types of stores are compound nouns. Elicit or provide a few examples, such as *drugstore, bookstore, department store*. Students can then practice, as in the following example, using items from task F:

   Example: **A** Where did you get the black bag?
   B At a department store.

G Spelling

1. The letter *b* always has the sound /b/, except for a few words in which it is silent. It never has a different sound.

2. For notes on doubling of consonants (as in *rubber*) and silent letters, see Unit 22, task F.

Common Expressions See Overview, p. xii.

Further Practice

Linking /p/ and /b/ sounds: When two /p/ sounds, two /b/ sounds, or a /p/ and /b/ sound are linked between words, they are pronounced as one long sound, with the first sound held and not released until the second one is pronounced: *stop pushing; rob banks; stop barking.*

   Students can practice the following sentences, substituting words beginning with /p/ or /b/ using words on the board, pictures, or real objects as prompts:

   I bought some cheap: paper / books / bread / pictures / boxes / bags / plates.

   Stop / Keep: pushing / pulling / banging / playing / pointing / painting / begging / bragging / barking / breathing.

Linking Pronunciation with Other Classwork

Tie pronunciation in with practice of:

1. Wishing people a happy birthday.

2. Sentences with *but.*

3. Talking about jobs.

Word Stress Practice

1. Talk about what people are wearing, either in class or in a picture, to contrast stress in compound nouns and ordinary adjective + noun phrases:

   He's / She's / I'm wearing (or carrying) . . .

   compound nouns: a raincoat, a winter coat, a sports jacket, a T-shirt, sunglasses, cowboy boots, a handbag, a shoulder bag, and so on.

   adjective + noun: a wool coat, a green jacket, a striped shirt, a long skirt, a sleeveless dress, a leather bag, and so on.

2. Practice compound noun stress in discussing items used in a kitchen or on a table, as in buying things for a new house or requesting items in a restaurant: for example, tablespoon, teaspoon, water glass, soup bowl, butter knife, steak knife, teapot, sugar bowl, salt shaker, pepper mill, cake pan, mixing bowl, frying pan.

UNIT 24 /t/ • two   Linking a Final Consonant

Student Difficulties

Most learners do not have difficulty producing a sound approximately like English /t/, but their exact articulation may be different. Many students use a dental /t/, made with the tongue against the top teeth, instead of English alveolar /t/, made with the tongue in back of, and not touching, the teeth.

- Japanese speakers may pronounce /t/ as /tʃ/ before the vowels /iy/ or /ɪ/ and as /ts/ before /uw/ or /ʊ/.

- Portuguese students may also substitute /tʃ/ before /iy/ or /ɪ/.

- Speakers of Indian languages often substitute a retroflex /t/, made with the tip of the tongue curled back.

Many students find the different pronunciations of /t/ in English confusing. Some students may not aspirate /t/ at the beginning of a word or syllable, as in *time* or *return*, causing it to sound more like /d/ to English speakers. Students may also have difficulty with /t/ at the end of words, where it is often not released. Many students find the voiced flap sound that occurs in North American English in words like *city* or *little* confusing. Unlike /t/ elsewhere in words, this sound is voiced. To some students (e.g., speakers of Spanish or Italian), it may sound more like an /r/ sound in their own language than a /t/. Although it is not necessary for students to use the flap /t/ when they speak, it is important for them to recognize this sound as /t/ when they hear it; otherwise they may mistake it for /d/ or /r/.

Making the Sound

Have students read the directions for making the sound /t/ as they listen to the audio and look at the illustrations. The directions in the Student's Book describe how to say aspirated /t/, as it is pronounced before a stressed vowel (as in *time* or *hotel*).

Variation in the sound For the different pronunciations of /t/, see the notes under task A, below. Each step practices a different pronunciation of /t/.

A Vocabulary

Step 1 In the words in step 1, /t/ is aspirated, or pronounced with a puff of air. The sound /t/ is strongly aspirated before a stressed vowel (as in *tall*) and less strongly aspirated before /w/ or /r/ (as in *twelve* or *train*). Before /r/, many English speakers pronounce the sound /t/ with the tongue farther back than usual; the resulting sound often resembles /tʃ/, so that *train* sounds like "chrain."

Note that many North Americans do not pronounce the second /t/ in *twenty*: /twɛniy/.

Step 2 The sound /t/ is not aspirated after /s/. Word pairs that illustrate the contrast of aspirated and unaspirated /t/ include: *top / stop, tore / store, tears / stairs, team / steam, tone / stone*.

Many students have difficulty with the consonant cluster /st/, as in *store*. Practicing by making the initial /s/ extra long may help: ssss – ssstore – store. See Unit 29 for more practice of /st/ clusters.

Step 3 The sound /t/ is unreleased, and very quiet, in the words here. The mouth forms a /t/ sound, but the tongue stays on the roof of the mouth and air does not escape. Students may have difficulty hearing this sound and may omit the /t/ when speaking or they may pronounce it too strongly.

Step 4 In the words here, the sound /t/ is pronounced as a voiced flap in North American English. This sound occurs when /t/ comes after a vowel or /r/ and before an unstressed vowel or syllabic /l/, as in *city, party,* or *little*. It also occurs between words, when /t/ is followed by either a stressed or unstressed vowel, as in *get up* or *What are you doing?* To make this sound, the tip of the tongue lightly taps the tooth ridge, or alveolar ridge, just behind the upper front teeth and moves quickly away (or, before /l/, does not move away

but lets air escape over the side of the tongue to make /l/). Point out to students that /t/ has a different sound here – more like a quick English /d/. Demonstrate the pronunciation.

Even if students will not be expected to use this sound when they speak, it is useful to give them some practice saying it in order to familiarize them with the sound.

B Dialog See Overview, pp. ix–x.

Step 1 Introduce the dialog, directing attention to the map. Before students listen, have them read the question and the names of the places. Explain that they will listen for the directions to these places in the dialog. Students should look at the map, and not at the dialog, while they listen.

Step 2 Play the recording of the dialog again and go over the answers to step 1.

ANSWERS

train station (3)
Taste of Thailand restaurant (4)
taxi stand (2)
City Lights Hotel (1)
post office (5)
The Times Tower is not on the map.

C Linking a Final Consonant

Background notes Awareness of linking is important for understanding natural speech and for being understood, as well as for building fluency. In English, words within a phrase group are normally linked together, with no breaks where spaces are shown in writing. This can make it hard for learners to tell where one word ends and another begins. Their own speech can often sound choppy, especially if they add extra sounds, for example interrupting the breath to add a glottal stop before a vowel sound, or if they drop final consonants.

The way a final consonant is linked to the next word depends on the sound that follows it.

Step 1 Play the audio. Students repeat phrases in which a final /t/ is linked to a vowel at the beginning of the next word.

Step 2 Note that in the phrases here, the /t/ is between two vowel sounds. It is pronounced the same way as when it is between two vowels within a word – as the voiced flap that sounds like a quick /d/.

Step 3 When two /t/ sounds are linked between words, they are pronounced as one long /t/ sound, with the first /t/ held and not released until the second one is pronounced.

Step 4 Groups of consonants between words are often difficult for students to say. In the phrases here, the final /t/ is quiet. The /t/ sound is not released before going directly to the next consonant sound. It can sometimes help to tell students to say both consonants at the same time. Make sure that students do not add a vowel sound between the consonants. In *your best bet*, the sequence of three consonants /st b/ can be simplified by leaving out the /t/: bes~~t~~ bet.

D Conversation Practice

Step 1 Have students read the dialog again. You may also want to have them listen to the dialog again, to help with the phrasing and intonation of the questions in step 2.

Step 2 Model the example questions and have students repeat chorally. To help with rhythm and intonation, it can be useful to have them say the questions at the same time that you say them. Note that the intonation in polite questions like these often starts high, jumps down on the important word, and then rises at the end of the question. This intonation pattern is practiced in Unit 49, task E.

   Working in pairs, students practice asking for directions and answering, using the map on page 93. Explain the task. One person asks directions from the train station to the places listed. The other person answers. Students should switch roles. Move around the room while students practice, checking the pronunciation of the sound /t/ and encouraging students to link words together.

E Spelling

1. Note the doubling of *t* after the vowels /æ, ɛ, ɪ, ʌ/, and /ɑ/ spelled with the letter *o*, especially when endings like *-er* and *-ing* are added after a stressed vowel: hot – hotter, sit – sitting, get – getting.
   The spelling *tt* also often occurs in the middle of a word after an unstressed vowel when *r* or a stressed vowel follows, as in *attract, attempt*, or *attack*.

2. Students often have difficulty with silent letters. Give them practice, according to the level of the class, in saying the words with silent *t* that they will be expected to know.

F Common Expressions See Overview, p. xii.

Further Practice

Final /t/: If students have difficulty with final /t/, especially if they tend to drop it, have them practice word pairs that contrast words lacking a final consonant and words ending in an unreleased /t/; for example, *way / wait, tie / tight, star / start, see / seat, pass / past, bell / belt, men / meant*. See the Unit 24 Web Site Worksheet (at www.cambridge.org/pp/student) for an exercise that practices some of these pairs.

Linking Pronunciation with Other Classwork

Tie pronunciation in with practice of:

1. Asking for and telling the time. Use a clock to practice, for example:
   A Could you tell me the time / What time it is?
   B It's ten after twelve.
      twenty to ten.

2. Asking for and giving directions.

3. Exclamations: Look at that / What a(n) / Isn't that a(n) . . .
   (beautiful / pretty / interesting / dirty / short, etc.) (table / shirt / hat / story, etc.)!

Word Stress Practice

Write large and small circles on the board showing these four stress patterns:

A ● •   B • ●   C ● • •   D • ● •

Read the following words. Students say whether they heard stress pattern A, B, C, or D.

1. visitor (C)   6. computer (D)
2. hospital (C)   7. restaurant (C) or (A)
3. hotel (B)   8. teenager (C)
4. traffic (A)   9. station (A)
5. exactly (D)   10. minute (A)

Student Difficulties

Learners may have the following difficulties with the sound /d/:

- Speakers of Chinese, Portuguese, and Swahili may confuse the sounds /t/ and /d/.

- Speakers of some languages, including Russian, Thai, Turkish, German, Dutch, Danish, and West African languages, tend to pronounce /d/ as its voiceless equivalent /t/ at the end of words. For example, *ride* might sound like *write*.

- Japanese and Portuguese speakers may pronounce /d/ close to /dʒ/, especially before the vowels /iy/ and /ɪ/; for example, *deep* can sound like *jeep*. Japanese speakers may pronounce /d/ more like /dz/ before the vowels /uw/ and /ʊ/; for example, *do* might sound more like "dzoo."

- Spanish and Portuguese speakers tend to pronounce /d/ more like /ð/ in the middle of a word, so that *ladder* may sound like *lather*. At the end of a word, Spanish speakers may pronounce /d/ as a very weak /ð/ or as /t/, or they may drop the sound entirely.

- Many learners use a dental /d/, made with the tongue against the top teeth, instead of English alveolar /d/, made with the tongue in back of, but not touching, the teeth. Speakers of Indian languages may substitute a retroflex /d/, made with the tip of the tongue curled back. Although a dental /d/ and retroflex /d/ contribute to a nonnative accent, they do not lead to misunderstandings.

- Many students do not lengthen the vowel before final voiced consonants like /d/, which can lead to confusion between words ending in voiceless /t/ and voiced /d/.

Making the Sound

Have students read the directions for making the sound /d/ as they listen to the audio and look at the illustrations. Demonstrate and model the sound. Show students that /d/ is made the same way as /t/, except that it is voiced (made using the voice).

Variation in the sound

1. The sound /d/ has the same flap sound as /t/ when it occurs after a vowel or /r/ and before another vowel or a syllabic /l/ sound: *adding, harder, middle*. Learners sometimes mistake this sound for an /r/, for example hearing *Judy* as *jury*.

2. Before the sound /r/, as in *dry*, the position of the tongue for /d/ is a little farther back than usual. The sound often resembles a /dʒ/ sound.

A Word Pairs See Overview, p. viii.

Word pairs for additional practice:

/t/ – /d/: two/do, town/down, tear/dare, tear/dear, tie/die, trip/drip, train/drain, true/drew, bat/bad, light/lied, seat/seed, neat/need, coat/code, sat/sad, debt/dead, bet/bed, beat/bead, let/led, hit/hid, built/build, plant/planned, white/wide

/dʒ/ – /d/: G/D, J/day, jeep/deep, jeer/dear, gym/dim, jeans/deans, jam/dam, just/dust, Jane/Dane, jet/debt, June/dune, Jew/do, page/paid, age/aid, stage/stayed, badge/bad, range/rained

B Test Yourself See Overview, p. ix.

Step 1

ANSWERS		
1. door	3. try	5. cart
2. time	4. ride	6. seeds

Step 2

ANSWERS
1. Do you have the <u>time</u>?
2. I want to <u>dry</u> this shirt.
3. I'll give you my <u>card</u>.
4. She <u>writes</u> very well.
5. Are there any <u>seats</u> left?
6. We <u>send</u> all the packages on Monday.

Step 3 In contrasting the sounds /t/ and /d/ at the end of words, make sure that students make the vowel longer before /d/.

C Vocabulary

Encourage students to link the words in the phrases together. See Unit 24, task C, for notes on linking a final consonant to the next word.

The phrases can be used later as part of a dictation to check students' ability to hear the linked words.

D Dialog   See Overview, pp. ix–x.

Step 1 Students listen to the dialog and check the things in task C that Diana did yesterday. They should look at the vocabulary words in task C, and not at the dialog, as they listen.

Step 2 Play the recording of the dialog again and go over the answers to step 1.

ANSWERS

Diana studied, listened to CDs, watched a DVD, decided to stay home, heated up some food.

E -ed Endings

Background notes Many students have difficulty with the three different pronunciations of the -ed past tense ending. The difference between the /d/ and /t/ pronunciations is not very significant, and can be hard to hear in connected speech, but the difference between these pronunciations and the /əd/ pronunciation is important. Students often add an extra syllable for the -ed where they shouldn't or fail to add an extra syllable where they should. These pronunciation problems are likely to sound like mistakes in grammar.

Step 1 Students repeat past tense verbs with each of the three pronunciations of the -ed ending: /t/, /d/, and /əd/. Have students count the number of syllables in the present and past tense forms of these verbs. They should see that the number of syllables stays the same in the present and past for *wash / washed, cook / cooked, listen / listened, study / studied*, but that an extra syllable is added in *wait / waited, decide / decided*.

If students add an extra syllable where they shouldn't, draw a line through the e in -ed, or respell the word on the board, for example writing *listened* as "listend."

Write the past tense verbs from the first two columns on the board. Underline the sound/letters before the -ed. Have students say the sound, placing their fingers on their throats to see whether they use their voice in saying it. Help

students formulate rules similar to the rules on page 98 in the Student's Book.

Step 2 Students listen to more verbs and add them to the table, sorting them according to the pronunciation of the -ed ending. If necessary, remind students that the pronunciation of the -ed ending depends on the sound that comes before it.

Step 3

ANSWERS

-ed = /t/: watched, talked, worked, missed, stopped

-ed = /d/: called, played, tried, cleaned, answered, stayed

-ed = /əd/: wanted, visited, needed, started

Step 4

ANSWERS

The –ed ending is pronounced as an extra syllable /əd/ after the sound /t/ or /d/.

The –ed ending is pronounced /d/ after sounds made using the voice (/b, g, z, ʒ, dʒ, v, ð, m, n, ŋ, l, r/, and vowels).

The –ed ending is pronounced /t/ after sounds made *without* using the voice (/p, k, s, ʃ, tʃ, f, θ/).

Extra practice Introduce or review spelling rules for the -ed past tense:

1. If the verb ends in -e, just add d: *dance – danced, decide – decided*.

2. If the verb ends in a consonant + y, change the y to i and add -ed: *study – studied, try – tried*.

3. If the verb ends in a single consonant after a stressed vowel spelled with a single letter, double the consonant and add -ed: *stop – stopped, plan – planned, occur – occurred*. *Exception*: The letter x is not doubled: *fix – fixed*.

4. For other verbs, add -ed: *rain – rained, play – played, call – called, answer – answered*.

F Game

Explain the task. Before students get into groups, you may want to have them practice saying the word *didn't*, which causes difficulty for many students (see Unit 45, task E, for notes on pronouncing the syllabic /n/ in *didn't*).

Encourage students to say rather than read their sentences. The game ends when everyone has had a turn.

Move around the room as students practice, monitoring pronunciation of the -ed ending. Rather than correcting errors on the spot, you may want to keep a list of verbs that caused problems. Write the verbs on the board. After students finish the game, have them use the table in task E to identify the correct pronunciation of the -ed ending in each verb.

G Spelling

The spelling dd is used in the middle or at the end of words after the vowels /æ, ɛ, ɪ, ʌ/ and /ɑ/ spelled with the letter o: *middle, suddenly, add, odd* (see Unit 22, task F). It is also used before r, l, or a stressed vowel: *address, riddle*.

H Common Expressions See Overview, p. xii.

Further Practice

1. Linking /d/ sounds between words: On the board, write one column of adjectives ending in /d/ and another of nouns beginning with /d/. Students use these words to make phrases. Write one or two phrases to show linking; for example, a *hard day*. The linked /d/ sounds are pronounced as one long /d/ rather than as two separate /d/ sounds, with the first /d/ held and not released until the second /d/ is pronounced.

a	bad	dog
	good	day
	hard	dress
	cold	desk
	wide	doctor
	red	door
an	old	decision

2. Some students tend to omit the -ed ending when they speak. They may also have difficulty hearing it. Listening to pairs of sentences that contrast the present and past tense may be helpful. See the Unit 25 Web Site Worksheet (at www.cambridge.org/pp/student) for sentences that practice this contrast.

Linking Pronunciation with Other Classwork

Tie pronunciation in with practice of:

1. Simple past tense: For example, tell students to imagine that yesterday they had a bad day. What happened? Why was it a bad day? Provide an example such as this:

> Yesterday I had a bad day. I failed a test. I missed my train. My goldfish died.

After some practice with this, switch to "a good day."

2. Past perfect tense.

3. *would like / would rather*.

Word Stress Practice

Write large and small circles on the board showing these four stress patterns:

A ● •   B • ●   C ● • •   D • ● •

Read the following words. Students say whether they heard stress pattern A, B, C, or D.

1. today (B)   6. remembered (D)
2. damaged (A)   7. studied (A)
3. decided (D)   8. visited (C)
4. repaired (B)   9. answered (A)
5. listened (A)   10. nobody (C)

UNIT 26 /k/ • key Stresses in Noun Phrases with Compounds

Student Difficulties

Many learners, including speakers of Spanish, Portuguese, Greek, Russian, Dutch, and Indian languages, do not aspirate the sound /k/ at the beginning of words. Without the puff of air, /k/ may sound like /g/ to English speakers – for example, making *coat* sound more like *goat*.

Aside from this, the sound /k/ is not difficult for most students, although Turkish speakers may have some difficulty with /k/ before the sounds /iy/ or /ɪ/ and some Arabic speakers may confuse /k/ and /g/ in all positions.

Making the Sound

Have students read the directions for making the sound /k/ as they listen to the audio and look at the illustrations. The directions describe the production of aspirated /k/ – the pronunciation of /k/ with a puff of air that occurs before a stressed vowel.

The exact position of the tongue for /k/ varies depending on the sound that comes after it. The tongue is farther forward in the mouth when /k/ is followed by a front vowel (a vowel made with the high part of the tongue toward the front of the mouth) like /iy/, as in *key*, and farther back when it is followed by a back vowel like /uw/, as in *cool*.

Variation in the sound See notes on the different pronunciations of /k/ under task A, below.

A Vocabulary See Overview, p. ix.

Step 1 At the beginning of a word or stressed syllable, /k/, like the other voiceless stop consonants /p/ and /t/, is aspirated – pronounced with a puff of air. It is more strongly aspirated before a stressed vowel, as in *kitchen*, and less strongly aspirated before a consonant sound, as in *clock*. See the teaching suggestions for aspirated /p/ in Unit 22, task A, though the aspiration for /k/ is likely to be less strong and less visible using a piece of paper or a match than the aspiration for /p/. The contrast of aspirated and unaspirated /k/ can be demonstrated with such pairs as *key / ski*, *care / scare*, and *cool / school*.

Note the stress in the compound nouns **cuck**oo *clock*, **book**case, and (in step 2) **com**ic *books*, with the main stress on the first element.

Step 2 The sound /k/ is not aspirated in the words in step 2. When /k/ is in final position, as in *look*, or before another consonant, as in *electric*, it is often not released; the mouth forms a /k/ sound, but no air is let out.

Step 3 Many students have difficulty with /k/ in consonant clusters, even if they don't otherwise have trouble with the sound /k/. The tongue actually moves very little as it passes from one consonant sound to the next. It may be helpful to tell students to try saying the two sounds, for example /kt/, at the same time.

Note the "invisible" /k/ sound in *six, expensive*, and so on. Ask students which letter has the sound /k/ in those words. (The letter *x* is pronounced /ks/ here.)

B Dialog See Overview, pp. ix–x.

Step 1 Introduce the situation. Talk about the meaning of the title, and the difference between *junk* (things that don't have much value) and

keepsakes (objects that are special because they help you remember someone or something). If appropriate for your students, ask them how many of them have an attic or basement or storage room in their houses and what kinds of things they keep there.

Have students work with a partner to fill in the blanks. Encourage them to say the words aloud as they fill them in.

Step 2

ANSWERS	
Chris	(*climbing up to the attic*) Yikes! <u>Look</u> at all this junk. What's in that box? Can you check?
Kate	Just a second. . . . Cool, my old <u>comic</u> <u>books</u>!
Chris	OK, they can go in recycling.
Kate	Recycling? No, I can sell them. People <u>collect</u> old comic books.
Chris	Can you take a look at that rocking chair? It looks like the back is <u>broken</u>.
Kate	I can fix it, I think. We could use an extra –
Chris	Excuse me, what's that <u>next</u> to the bookcase? Is that a clock?
Kate	It's a cuckoo clock. I got it in <u>Canada</u>.
Chris	Can I ask you a <u>question</u>? Why are you keeping a plastic cuckoo clock?
Kate	It isn't plastic. It's oak. Actually, it was kind of <u>expensive</u>.
Chris	Does it work? It's exactly <u>six</u> o'clock now, and it's very quiet.
Kate	Of course it works. Here, let me connect it. It's <u>electric</u>. (CUCKOO CUCKOO CUCKOO CUCKOO CUCKOO)
Kate	It would be perfect for the <u>kitchen</u>, don't you think?
Chris	Are you kidding? Listen to that while I cook? I'd go crazy! (CUCKOO!)
Chris	Hey, where are you taking all that <u>junk</u>? Bring it back to the attic!
Kate	Junk? You call this junk? These are keepsakes!

C Stress in Noun Phrases with Compounds

The phrases on the left in the Student's Book use ordinary adjective + noun stress. Both the adjective and the noun are stressed, but the main stress is on the noun. The phrases on the right illustrate adjective + compound noun stress, which combines the adjective + noun pattern with the stress pattern for compound nouns. The main stress in these phrases goes on the first part of the compound noun.

D Scrambled Phrases

Step 1 Working in pairs, and switching roles during the activity, students unscramble phrases with an adjective + compound noun. Go over the meaning and pronunciation of any unfamiliar vocabulary first (e.g., *expired* = no longer good or able to be used). Check the answers before students proceed with step 2.

ANSWERS

1. a plastic key ring
2. a black coffee cup
3. an empty cola can
4. an expired credit card
5. an electric can opener
6. a pink ski jacket
7. a broken music box
8. some old concert tickets
9. an expensive picture book

Step 2 Still working in pairs, students match the phrases with the pictures. If some pairs finish either step 1 or step 2 early, ask them to try to make similar phrases for other students to unscramble. If necessary, suggest some additional compound nouns that they might include in their phrases – for example, *ice skates, address book, birthday card, desk lamp, rock collection*.

E Spelling

1. Some of the letters used to spell /k/ are also commonly used for other sounds:

    c has the sound /s/ before the letters *e, i,* and *y*;

    ch is usually pronounced /tʃ/;

    x is sometimes pronounced /gz/ (see Unit 27, task G).

2. Note the silent *k* in words like *know*.

F Common Expressions See Overview, p. xii.

Further Practice

1. Final cluster /kt/: List these or other activities using past tense verbs ending in /k/ + *-ed* on the board:

    cooked breakfast
    baked a cake
    walked to school / work
    worked / worked for exactly six hours
    talked to a cousin / an uncle / a doctor
    looked at pictures / in the mirror
    parked a car / a truck
    fixed something broken

    Ask one or two students which of these things they did, specifying a time such as yesterday or over the weekend. Students then practice in pairs or small groups, telling each other which things they did. Then ask a few students to report back to the class.

2. Linking /k/ sounds between words: See Unit 27, *Further Practice*.

Linking Pronunciation with Other Classwork

Tie pronunciation in with practice of:

1. Saying "Excuse me," "Thank you," "Thanks," and "You're welcome."

2. Telling the time using the words *o'clock, quarter*, and *six*.

3. Third-person singular present tense verbs ending with the sound /k/ such as *likes, looks, makes, asks, speaks, takes, walks, works, drinks, cooks,* and *thinks*.

4. Order of modifiers in noun phrases.

Word Stress Practice

To review the difference in stress between ordinary adjective + noun phrases and compound nouns, read the following words and ask students to say whether they heard an ordinary noun phrase (A) or a compound noun (B).

1. a key ring (B)
2. a good book (A)
3. an old coat (A)
4. a bank clerk (B)
5. a wool skirt (A)
6. a raincoat (B)
7. a rock band (B)
8. a gold ring (A)
9. a clean knife (A)
10. a steak knife (B)

UNIT 27 /g/ • good Gonna (*going to*)

Student Difficulties

Difficulties with the sound /g/ include the following:

- Thai and Vietnamese speakers may have difficulty with /g/ at the beginning of a word. Thai speakers sometimes replace it with /k/, and Vietnamese speakers may use a more guttural sound.

- Some speakers of Arabic have difficulty with /g/ and substitute either /k/ or /dʒ/.

- Some speakers of Japanese may pronounce /g/ as /ŋ/ between vowels.

- Dutch speakers tend to replace /g/ with the sound /k/ or /x/ (the non-English sound at the end of *Bach*).

- Greek and Spanish speakers may use a softer non-English sound rather than the hard stop sound /g/ in some words.

- At the end of words, speakers of Danish, German, Russian, Turkish, and some West African languages may pronounce /g/ as /k/, its voiceless equivalent, for example, pronouncing *dug* as *duck*. Some students, including speakers of Chinese and Spanish, have difficulty in general with consonants at the ends of words and may either drop a final /g/ or pronounce it as voiceless /k/.

- Many students do not lengthen the vowel before final voiced consonants like /g/, leading to possible confusion between words ending in voiceless /k/ and voiced /g/.

Making the Sound

Have students read the directions for making the sound /g/ as they listen to the audio and look at the illustrations. For students who substitute /k/ for /g/, show that the voice is used for /g/. For students who substitute a softer, non-English sound, demonstrate that /g/ is a stop consonant – a short sound made by completely stopping the air in the mouth before releasing it.

Variation in the sound Notes on the position of the tongue for /k/ (see Unit 26, *Making the Sound*) also apply to /g/.

A Word Pairs See Overview, p. viii.

Word pairs for additional practice:

/k/ – /g/: cold/gold, could/good, coast/ghost, cot/got, came/game, cave/gave, clue/glue, crab/grab, crow/grow, card/guard, come/gum, picky/piggy, pick/pig, rack/rag, duck/dug, Dick/dig, peck/peg, buck/bug, lock/log, dock/dog

B Test Yourself See Overview, p. ix.

Step 1

ANSWERS		
1. goat	3. girl	5. clock
2. glass	4. cold	6. bag

Step 2

ANSWERS
1. Is that really <u>gold</u>?
2. There's a fly on your <u>back</u>.
3. He has a white <u>goat</u>.
4. Does the store sell <u>clogs</u>?
5. Those <u>curls</u> look nice.
6. How many <u>classes</u> do you have?

Step 3 Remind students, if necessary, to make the vowel sound longer before /g/ than before /k/ in word pairs like *back* / *bag*.

C Vocabulary

Step 1 Working in pairs, students circle the word in each column that does not have the sound /g/. Go over the example. Make sure that students understand that they should focus on the sound, not the spelling.

Step 2 Have students repeat the words and check their answers. There is no /g/ sound in words like *long, coming,* and *sang*; the *ng* spelling in these words has the sound /ŋ/. *England* (like the word *English*) does have a /g/ sound: /ɪŋglənd/.

Note that at the end of a word, as in *big* or *dog*, stop sounds like /g/ are often unreleased. The mouth forms a /g/ sound, but the air is not released.

The words *long, coming, message,* and *sang* do not have the sound /g/.

D Dialog See Overview, pp. ix–x.

Step 1 Before students listen, have them read the sentences they will complete. Explain that they will listen for the correct words to complete each sentence. Tell students to circle all the words that are true; there may be more than one correct word or phrase in parentheses in a sentence.

Students should not look at the dialog in their books when they listen.

Step 2 Play the recording of the dialog again and go over the answers to step 1.

1. Gary and Grace live in Chicago.
2. Their guests, Maggie and Greg, live in England.
3. Gary and Grace plan to go jogging, go to a baseball game, and play golf with their guests.
4. After they visit Chicago, Maggie and Greg are going to Canada.

E Gonna (*going to*)

Background notes *Going to* can be pronounced two ways when it is used with another verb to show the future. It can be pronounced as the two separate words /gowɪŋ tə/ or it can have the reduced pronunciation "gonna" /gʌnə/ or /gɔnə/. Reduced pronunciations like "gonna" are very common in the relaxed speech of native speakers. Sometimes people even spell this as "gonna" in very informal writing. This pronunciation is not used when *going* is a main verb followed by the preposition *to*.

Although students do not need to use this pronunciation in their own speech, they should learn to recognize it when they hear it and understand how it is used.

Read or summarize the information in the box with the class. Have students repeat the three sentences in their books. Make sure they don't add an extra *to* in the sentences with "gonna." If necessary, explain that "gonna" includes the word *to*.

Extra practice Have students listen to and read the dialog in task D again. Ask them to circle *going to* when it is pronounced "gonna."

F Conversation Practice

Step 1 Students listen to the model conversations. Check that they understand why the first two lines would not use "gonna."

The last two lines of the conversation use "gonna": "What are you gonna do in England? I'm gonna go to art galleries."

Step 2 Students practice the conversation in pairs. Go over any unfamiliar vocabulary or place names first. You may want to demonstrate with a student before they practice, making sure that students understand that they choose a place name in line 2, use the same place name in line 3, and name an activity in line 4. Set a time limit for practice of about three or four minutes.

Step 3 Students who finish step 2 early can talk about which activities in step 2 they like doing.

Extra practice "Hush Little Baby" is a traditional children's song with lyrics that repeat "gonna."

G Spelling

Note that the letters *ng* at the end of a word do not have the sound /g/.

H Common Expressions See Overview, p. xii.

Further Practice

1. Final clusters /ks/ and /gz/: Have students practice "X likes . . ." substituting words such as *dogs / eggs / clocks / lakes / rugs / frogs / snakes / long walks*, using prompts on the board or pictures as cues. For *X*, substitute the name of an imaginary person, a famous person, or someone in the class.

2. Linking /k/ and /g/ between words: When two stop sounds made in the same place in the mouth, like /k/ and /g/, link two words, the two sounds are pronounced as one long sound. The sound is held briefly and then released: a big garden; a sick cat. The first /k/ is quieter; the second /k/ is louder. Linking /k/ and /g/ can be practiced by having students ask and answer the question "Do you like . . . ?" completing it with words such as these: cooking / cleaning / cats / cards / coffee / carrots / cake / quiet places / quiet people / games / golf / gardening / grapes / gray hair / going to parties / big classes.

Linking Pronunciation with Other Classwork

Tie pronunciation in with practice of:

1. *Go + -ing* verb: for example, "Let's go jogging / dancing / shopping together" or "Would you like to go jogging / swimming / skating / etc.?"

2. Requests beginning "Could you give me . . . ?" or "Could you get me . . . ?"

Word Stress Practice

Write large and small circles on the board showing these four stress patterns:

A ● •   B • ●   C ● • •   D • ● •

Read the following words. Students say whether they heard stress pattern A, B, C, or D.

1. again (B)
2. guitar (B)
3. forget (B)
4. together (D)
5. August (A)

6. message (A)
7. photograph (C)
8. England (A)
9. beginning (D)
10. exactly (D)

UNIT 28 Review /p/, /b/, /t/, /d/, /k/, and /g/

This unit provides additional practice and review of the stop consonants /p/, /b/, /t/, /d/, /k/, and /g/. When you say a stop consonant, you stop the air completely and then quickly let it out of your mouth.

A Test Yourself See Overview, p. ix.

Step 1 Play the audio. Students circle the words they hear. They can check the meaning of unfamiliar words, but they do not have to understand every word to do the task.

> **ANSWERS**
>
> 1. back
> 2. pig
> 3. gold
> 4. plant
> 5. card
> 6. tap
> 7. bet
> 8. goat
> 9. duck
> 10. pad
> 11. bug
> 12. cap

Step 2 If students have trouble completing the rules, play the audio again or say selected words in step 1 for them.

> **ANSWERS**
>
> The consonant sounds /p/, /t/, and /k/ are pronounced with a strong puff of air at the beginning of a word or stressed syllable.
>
> Vowel sounds are longer when they come before the consonant sound /b/, /d/, or /g/ at the end of a word.

Extra practice

1. Have individual students say the words in step 1, choosing a word from each numbered item. Other students write down the word they heard. This can be done with the whole class or in small groups.

2. For additional practice of final stop consonants and the lengthening of the vowel before a voiced consonant, see the Unit 27 Web Site Worksheet (at www.cambridge.org/pp/student).

B Vocabulary

Steps 1 and 2 Students mark the syllable with the strongest stress in individual words (*kitchen*), compound nouns (*potato chips, baking pan, cake plates*), adjective + noun phrases (*cold drinks, plastic cups, an extra table, her electric guitar*), and noun phrases with compounds (*chocolate ice cream, a paper tablecloth*). If students stress any of the items incorrectly, ask or tell them what type of word or phrase it was to help correct the error.

> **ANSWERS**
>
> 1. kitchen
> 2. potato chips
> 3. cold drinks
> 4. plastic cups
> 5. a baking pan
> 6. cake plates
> 7. chocolate ice cream
> 8. a paper table cloth
> 9. an extra table
> 10. her electric guitar

Steps 3 and 4 Students listen to, and then practice reading, the *To Do List*. Use hand gestures, if necessary, to indicate the intonation for the list of items to buy (see Unit 22, task C).

Step 5 Students write their own To Do lists. Check their understanding of *To Do List* or elicit suggestions for the kind of events or projects for which they might write such a list (e.g., a party, a trip, dinner, a meeting, a test, or household chores). When they read their lists aloud, monitor the pronunciation of stop consonants and the intonation of items in a list.

C Puzzle

Students circle or say the past tense verb in each group in which the *-ed* ending has a different pronunciation from the other verbs. Go over the example. If necessary, remind students that the *-ed* ending has three pronunciations. Students can work alone or with a partner.

Check the answers at the end. If students need the practice, have them listen to and repeat the words when checking answers. Note that most of the items here focus on whether the *-ed* ending adds an extra syllable or not, since that is the most important feature for students to master.

ANSWERS		
1. called	3. rented	5. decided
2. asked	4. painted	6. pushed

Further Practice

Linking: Remind students that when two stop sounds made in the same place in the mouth (/p/ + /p/ or /b/; /t/ + /t/ or /d/; or /k/ + /k/ or /g/) link two words, the two sounds are pronounced as one long sound.

Examples: I like cooking.   I don't like golf.

Have students make phrases, filling in the spaces in the items below with these adjectives: *big, cheap, good, black, hot.* They should choose an adjective that ends with a sound made in the same place in the mouth as the sound that begins the next word.

1. __big__ classes   6. _____ tea
2. a _____ doctor   7. a _____ kitchen
3. a _____ garden   8. a _____ day
4. _____ paper   9. a _____ cat
5. _____ gloves   10. _____ books

ANSWERS	
1. big classes	6. hot (or good) tea
2. a good doctor	7. a big kitchen
3. a big garden	8. a good (or hot) day
4. cheap paper	9. a black (or big) cat
5. black (or big) gloves	10. cheap books

UNIT 29 /s/ • sun   Linking a Final Consonant Cluster

Student Difficulties

Most students can pronounce the sound /s/.

- Speakers of Greek, Italian, and Spanish may replace /s/ with /z/ before /m/ or other voiced consonants, for example saying "zmall" for *small*.

- German speakers may substitute /z/ before a vowel, for example saying "zo" for *so*. Following the sound-spelling patterns of German, they may also pronounce /s/ as /ʃ/ in initial consonant clusters, so that *spoon* sounds like /ʃpuwn/.

- Some students confuse /s/ and /ʃ/ (see Unit 31, *Student Difficulties*). Speakers of European Spanish and Portuguese, for example, may pronounce /s/ so that it sounds like /ʃ/ in some words.

- Japanese speakers may replace /s/ with /ʃ/ before /iy/ and /ɪ/, for example saying "she" for *see*.

Many students have difficulty with consonant clusters containing /s/. Students likely to have difficulty include speakers of Spanish, Portuguese, Chinese, Japanese, Korean, Arabic, Turkish, Farsi, Thai, Vietnamese, Swahili, and many other Asian and African languages. Here are some common problems and ways to help students:

1. Initial clusters with /s/: At the beginning of a word, students commonly insert a vowel either before the cluster or after the /s/, resulting in pronunciations like /ɛspuwn/ or /sɪpuwn/ for *spoon*. Some learners, including speakers of Vietnamese and some other Asian languages, may drop the /s/, saying /puwn/ for *spoon*.

Clusters with three consonants, as in *spring* or *street*, are especially difficult for learners.

It can be helpful to have students start by lengthening the /s/, for example: ssss – ssssstay – stay. In a word like *speak*, tell students to make the /s/ very long and then close their lips for /p/ while still saying /s/.

If students add a vowel before initial clusters, it may also be helpful to contrast words that begin with a cluster and words that begin with a vowel + a cluster: *state / estate, sleep / asleep, spot / a spot, school / a school.*

2. In the middle of a word, students often drop one of the consonants in a cluster, for example saying "esplain" for *explain*. Respelling the word can be helpful; for example, "eksplain."

3. Final clusters with /s/: In final clusters, students may insert a vowel or, more commonly, drop one of the consonants (usually the last one), saying "des" for *desk* or "ness" for *next*. Clusters with more than two consonants are a particular problem.

In final clusters of consonant + /s/, as in plural endings (e.g., *cats*), many students drop the final /s/, though some students may insert a vowel either after the cluster or between the consonants, saying /kætsə/ or /kætɪs/ for *cats*. Forward and backward buildup may be helpful: let – let's; s – ts – let's.

Note that native English speakers also find certain consonant clusters difficult and sometimes simplify them by dropping a middle consonant, as in /æst/ for *asked*, /fɪfs/ for *fifths*, or /tɛksbʊk/ for *textbook*. Native speakers do not, however, simplify clusters by leaving out the sound that represents an *-s* or *-ed* ending.

Making the Sound

Have students read the directions for making the sound /s/ as they listen to the audio and look at the illustrations.

A Vocabulary See Overview, p. ix.

Step 1 Students first practice the sound /s/ at the beginning of a word, where it is easiest for most learners. If any students substitute a different sound, explain that the letter *s* at the beginning of a word always has the sound /s/, except in the spelling *sh*.

Step 2 Students practice /s/ in consonant clusters at the beginning of a word or syllable. If students

have difficulty, have them begin by making the /s/ sound extra long – for example, ssssskating. In a word like *swimming*, tell students to make the /s/ sound long and then round their lips for /w/ while still staying /s/.

After steps 1 and 2, you may want to ask students what they think the dialog will be about.

Step 3 Note that some of the words here have "invisible" clusters spelled with *x*. The letter *x* often represents the sounds /ks/, as in *six* or *expensive*. Respelling the words to show the sounds may help students know what pronunciation they should be aiming at – for example, "ekspensiv" (*expensive*).

ANSWERS

Excellent, sports, exciting, that's, six, and *expensive* have the consonant clusters listed.

Extra practice With books closed, ask students to name as many sports or activities as they can that include the sound /s/. They can include activities from task A as well as their own ideas. Make a list on the board. Then ask questions about them, for example "Which activities can you do in the sea?"

Activities from task A are: sailing, surfing, swimming, waterskiing, skating, sports. Other activities include: soccer, skiing, baseball, softball, tennis, basketball, scuba diving, snorkeling, bicycling (or cycling), dance, aerobics, gymnastics, exercise.

B Dialog See Overview, pp. ix–x.

Step 1 Have students cover the dialog (e.g., with a piece of paper). They should not cover the questions in step 1. Before students listen to the dialog, have them read the sentences they will complete. Explain that they will listen for the correct words to complete each sentence.

Step 2 Play the recording of the dialog again and go over the answers to step 1.

ANSWERS

1. Stacy likes <u>waterskiing</u>.
2. Steve wants to <u>save</u> money.
3. Stacy wants to stay over <u>Saturday</u> night.
4. Stacy thinks sleeping outside is <u>exciting</u>.

C Linking a Final Consonant Cluster

Background notes Many students have difficulty linking /s/ sounds smoothly between words. Clusters across word boundaries are especially likely to present problems; students may add extra vowels in phrases like *this street* or *Six Star Hotel*. Sometimes native speakers may drop a middle stop consonant to simplify a long cluster: Let's *just̸* sit on the sand. Native speakers do not, however, drop a final *-s* in a word.

Step 1 If the next word begins with a vowel, the final consonant cluster can be simplified by dividing it between the words: for example, "Let seat" (for *Let's eat*).

Step 2 Two linked /s/ sounds between words are pronounced as one long sound. Students should make the /s/ sound long. Check that they do not add an extra vowel sound between the words.

D Scrambled Conversations

Step 1 Working in pairs, students find the best response on the right to each sentence on the left. Go over the example. You may want to tell student A to cover B's sentences, and student B to cover A's sentences while they practice.

Remind students to link words together where possible.

Step 2

ANSWERS	
A	**B**
Let's sit in the sun.	Let's sit in the shade instead.
Let's eat steak.	Let's eat pizza instead.
Let's stay in a hotel.	Let's sleep outside instead.
Let's spend all the money.	Let's save some money instead.
Let's swim in the ocean.	Let's swim in the pool instead.
Let's see a movie on Sunday.	Let's study on Sunday instead.
Let's ask Stacy.	Let's ask Steve instead.
Let's speak Spanish.	Let's speak English instead.

E Interview

Step 1 Review the intonation in choice questions with *or* (see Unit 9, task C). Questions with *or* that ask the listener to make a choice have rising intonation on the first choice and falling intonation on the last choice.

Step 2 Explain that students will interview each other for a test about whether they like to take

risks or not. This is a made-up test, intended for fun. Go over any unfamiliar vocabulary before they begin.

Students should ask and answer questions, as in the example in step 1. The person asking questions keeps track of the scores for the other person's answers. Students should switch roles so that both partners are interviewed.

While students practice, move around the room monitoring the pronunciation of words with the sound /s/ and intonation in choice questions. Note that many of the words here have consonant clusters with /s/.

Step 3 After students finish, ask them if they agree with their scores.

F Spelling

The fact that /s/ has so many spellings may be confusing to students. Point out that most of the spellings contain the letter *s* or the letter *c* (followed by *e, i,* or *y*). Note that the letter *s*, especially between two vowels, is also a common spelling for the sound /z/ (see Unit 30, task G). At the beginning of a word, however, *s* always has the sound /s/, except in the spelling *sh*.

Extra practice For review, give students a list of words such as the one below. Students indicate whether the *c* spelling in each word has the sound /s/ or /k/. When checking answers, refer to the spelling rules in the Student's Book, if necessary: *c* has the sound /s/ before the letters *e, i,* or *y*.

1. receive
2. medicine
3. recognize
4. emergency
5. exercise
6. ceiling
7. occasion
8. plastic
9. recycling
10. accident

G Common Expressions   See Overview, p. xii.

Linking Pronunciation with Other Classwork

Tie pronunciation in with practice of:

1. Suggestions beginning with *Let's.*

2. Present tense verbs having the sound /s/ in the third-person singular: *asks, breaks, cooks, counts, drinks, drops, eats, forgets, gets, keeps, likes, looks, makes, puts, shuts, sits, sleeps, speaks, stops, takes, waits, walks, wants, works, writes.*

3. Nouns having the sound /s/ in the plural: For example, have students practice sentences using the prompts below, as in the example. For *X*, substitute the name of an imaginary person, a famous person, or someone in the class.

   Example: I like cats. *X* likes cats, too.
   I like cats / hate hats / get headaches / eat lots of carrots / take good photographs / collect stamps / want some interesting books.

Word Stress Practice

Write large and small circles on the board showing these two stress patterns:

A ● • •   B • ● •

Read the following words. Students say whether they heard stress pattern A or B.

1. excellent (A)	5. Saturday (A)
2. excitement (B)	6. sensible (A)
3. expensive (B)	7. relaxing (B)
4. serious (A)	8. interesting (A)

UNIT 30 /z/ • ZOO   -*s* Endings

Student Difficulties

Many learners, including speakers of Spanish, Italian, Portuguese, Chinese, Vietnamese, Thai, Turkish, German, Dutch, and Scandinavian, West African, and Indian languages, have difficulty with the sound /z/. The most common error is to replace this sound with /s/, especially at the end of a word, so that *eyes* sounds like *ice*. Many students also do not make the vowel before a final /z/ long enough, causing confusion with /s/.

■ Spanish, Chinese, Thai, and Scandinavian speakers tend to have difficulty with /z/ in all positions in words.

■ Japanese speakers may replace /z/ with /dz/ or, before the vowels /iy/ and /ɪ/, with /dʒ/, so that *zoo* sounds like "dzoo" or *zip* sounds like "jip." Speakers of some Indian and other Asian languages, including Korean, may also confuse /z/ and /dʒ/.

Many students have difficulty with /z/ in final consonant clusters. Most commonly, they omit the final /z/ or add a vowel between the preceding consonant and /z/. They are especially likely to add a vowel sound if there is a vowel in the spelling, as in *loves*. Clusters ending in /z/ often occur when the ending -*s* or *'s* is added to form a noun plural, possessive, contraction, or third person singular present tense verb. Try using backward buildup (see Unit 29, *Student Difficulties*) to practice these clusters. Respelling the word with a final *z* instead of an *s* is also helpful: "dogz."

Making the Sound

Have students read the directions for making the sound /z/ as they listen to the audio and look at the illustrations.

If students confuse /s/ and /z/, practice of the sound in isolation is helpful. Point out that the voice is used when making the sound /z/ but not when making /s/. Demonstrate by placing your hand on your throat and moving it to show the vibration as you say /z/. Students should be able to feel the vibration with their hands placed over their ears or on their throats as they say /z/. Note that voicing may not be as strong when /z/ occurs in a word, especially at the beginning or end of a word.

If students replace /z/ with /dʒ/, show that /z/ can be a long sound: /zzzz/.

A Word Pairs   See Overview, p. viii.

Word pairs for additional practice:

/s/ – /z/: C/Z, sink/zinc, seal/zeal, racer/razor, ice/eyes, race/raise, peace/peas, niece/knees, place/plays, loose/lose, rice/rise, since/sins

B Test Yourself   See Overview, p. ix.

Step 1

ANSWERS					
1. Sue		3. bus		5. prize	
2. Z		4. sip		6. lacy	

Step 2

Step 3 In contrasting the sounds /s/ and /z/ at the end of words, make sure that students make the vowel longer before /z/.

C Vocabulary

Step 1 Working in pairs, students circle the four words that do not have the sound /z/. Go over the example.

Step 2 Have students repeat the words and check their answers. Elicit or point out that the sound /z/ is often spelled with the letter *s*.

D Dialog   See Overview, pp. ix–x.

Step 1 Have students work with a partner to fill in the blanks. Encourage them to say the words aloud as they fill them in.

Step 2 The dialog provides practice of the sound /s/ as well as the sound /z/. If students practice reading the dialog aloud, make sure that they clearly distinguish between the two sounds. For example, in the words *smells*, make sure that students do not substitute /z/ for /s/ at the beginning or /s/ for /z/ at the end. Other words with the sound /s/ include: *post office, this, box, say, six, mice, listen, what's, it's, strange, sound, case, sack, snakes,* and *hissing.* You may want to wait until students have done task E before practicing the dialog aloud.

Liz   It <u>says</u>: This contains six mice.

Zoe   Yikes!

Liz   Listen! What's in this sack?

Zoe   It's making a strange <u>hissing</u> sound.

Sack   Ssssssssssssss!

Liz   Zoe! It sounds like snakes!

Zoe   Oh, it does! I wonder what's in this case, Liz.

Liz   It's making a <u>buzzing</u> noise.

Box   <u>Zzzzzzzzzzzzzz</u>!

Liz   <u>These</u> are bees!

Zoe   A box of mice! And a sack of snakes! And a case of bees!

Liz   This is very <u>surprising</u>.

Zoe   It's amazing. This <u>isn't</u> a post office, Liz. It's a zoo!

E *-s* Endings

Background notes Many students have difficulty with final *-s* endings. They not only have to remember to add the sound /s/ or /z/, but also have the challenge in many words of pronouncing a final consonant cluster ending in /s/ or /z/. Particularly if students drop the final /s/ or /z/ sound, pronunciation difficulties will sound like grammar mistakes, whether or not they actually are.

Step 1 Students repeat plural nouns with the three pronunciations of the *-s* ending: /s/, /z/, and /əz/. Then have students practice saying words from the first two columns. Underline the letter/sound before the *-s* ending in a few words and have students say it. Ask them whether or not each sound is made using the voice; ask the same question about the sounds /s/ and /z/ that head each column. They should see that after a voiceless sound like /t/ or /k/, the *-s* ending is pronounced /s/, and after a voiced sound like /g/, /l/, or a vowel, it has the sound /z/. If students add an extra syllable where the word ends in *-es*, as in *snakes*, draw a line through the *e* to show that it is not pronounced.

For words in the third column, write the singular form of the noun and underline the final letter / sound. Point out that the letter *x* in *box* is pronounced /ks/. Students say the words and then the final sound alone. With their help, make a list of the sounds (/s, z, ʃ, ʒ, tʃ, dʒ/) that are followed by -es pronounced as an extra syllable /əz/. These are all sibilant ("hissing") sounds or sounds that contain a sibilant (like /tʃ/). Note that the plural ending is always spelled -es, rather than just -s, after these sounds.

Step 2 Students listen to third-person singular present tense verbs and sort them according to the pronunciation of the -s ending. These follow the same pronunciation rules as plural nouns. If necessary, remind students that the pronunciation of the -s ending depends on the sound that comes before it.

Step 3

> **ANSWERS**
>
> -s = /s/: likes, hates, laughs, collects
>
> -s = /z/: loves, owns, wears, knows, says
>
> -es = /əz/: washes, watches, loses

Step 4

> **ANSWERS**
>
> The -s ending is pronounced as the sound /z/ after other sounds made using the voice (/b, d, g, v, ð, m, n, ŋ, l, r/, and vowels).
>
> The –s ending is pronounced as the sound /s/ after sounds made *without* using the voice (/p, t, k, f, θ/).

Extra practice Add examples of other words used in the unit or otherwise familiar to students. Give the singular form of the noun or the base form of the verb. Students pronounce the word with -(e)s added and say which column it belongs in.

F Conversation Practice

Step 1 Explain the task. Students fill in the blanks with the name of a person who fits the description in each sentence. Go over any unfamiliar vocabulary before they begin.

Step 2 Students check their information by asking each other questions, for example: "Sofia, do you like dogs?" They will probably need to move around the room to do this. Check that they know what questions to ask.

You may want to set a time limit of 5–10 minutes. If some students finish early, encourage them to ask the people on their lists follow-up

questions (e.g., "What kind of flowers do you grow?"). After students finish, ask questions about what they found out, for example, "Did you find someone who collects stamps?" "What was the most surprising thing you learned?"

G Spelling

Spellings for the sound /z/ that use the letter s often cause difficulty. Although there is no foolproof way to predict whether the spelling s will have the sound /s/ or /z/, there are some guidelines that can help:

1. The letter s has the sound /s/ at the beginning of a word. It also usually has the sound /s/ when it is next to a voiceless sound, when it is doubled (ss), or when it is in the prefix dis- (as in disappoint, disagree, and so on).

2. The letter s commonly has the sound /z/ when it comes between two voiced sounds (e.g., two vowels, as in visit) or between a vowel and a final e (as in because).

Extra practice For review, give students a list of words such as the one below. Students indicate whether the letter s has the sound /s/ or /z/.

1. busy	6. visit
2. lose	7. disappoint
3. serious	8. easy
4. present	9. small
5. person	10. surprise

H Common Expressions See Overview, p. xii.

Further Practice

1. Linking: The sound /z/ at the end of a word becomes /s/ when the next word begins with /s/. Compare:

Whose is it? /z/   Whose seat is it? /s/

This linking occurs frequently, especially after such common words as *these, those, is, whose,* and *his*. You can practice this, for example, by having students all change seats at random and then choosing two students to practice the following dialog:

   A Whose seat are you in?
   B Y's seat.
   A Who's sitting in your seat?
   B Z's sitting in my seat.

Note the contrast of the vowels /iy/ and /ɪ/ here, in addition to the linking /s/.

Alternatively, practice linking /s/ using the present progressive to describe students or pictures, for example: "He's sleeping." "She's swimming." "Who's smiling?"

2. Practice pairs of nouns and verbs that contrast the sounds /s/ and /z/, for example: *advice / advise, choice / choose, use* (noun) / *use* (verb), *excuse* (noun) / *excuse* (verb).

Linking Pronunciation with Other Classwork

Tie pronunciation in with practice of:

1. Final /z/ in plurals: For example, list headings such as these on the board: Families; Animals; Times; Parts of the body; Clothes; Things in houses; Things with wheels.
   Write words, such as the following, on flash cards, to be shown in random order. Students read the word aloud and say which group it belongs to.
   (Families) mothers, fathers, sisters, brothers, uncles, boys, girls, babies
   (Animals) dogs, horses, llamas, lions, bears, wolves, camels, monkeys
   (Times) days, hours, years, mornings, afternoons, evenings
   (Parts of the body) fingers, hands, arms, heads, eyes, ears, legs, toes

(Clothes) jeans, sweaters, slippers, shoes, gloves
(Things in houses) chairs, tables, sofas, beds, walls, floors, ceilings
(Things with wheels) cars, trains, buses, cabs, airplanes, bicycles
A more challenging variation would be to have groups of students compete to see who can come up with the most items for each category. Only plural forms would be accepted.

2. Simple present tense verbs having the sound /z/ in the third-person singular – for example, *buys, calls, comes, drives, earns, gives, goes, grows, leaves, lives, loves, owns, plays, reads, sells, sends, smiles, spends, wears.*

Word Stress Practice

Write large and small circles on the board showing these three stress patterns:

A ● •   B • ●   C • ● •

Read the following words. Students say whether they heard stress pattern A, B, or C.

1. easy (A)
2. surprises (C)
3. always (A)
4. because (B)
5. contains (B)
6. office (A)
7. busy (A)
8. amazing (C)

UNIT 31   /ʃ/ • shoe   Linking Words with /ʃ/

Student Difficulties

Students may have the following difficulties with the sound /ʃ/:

■ The sounds /s/ and /ʃ/ are confused by speakers of Greek and by some speakers of Korean, Dutch, Swahili, European Spanish, and Indian languages.

■ Chinese speakers may have difficulty with the sound /ʃ/, too, confusing it with /s/ or pronouncing it in a way that sounds foreign to native English speakers. Japanese and Chinese speakers may confuse /ʃ/ and /h/ before the vowels /iy/ or /ɪ/, which often creates problems in distinguishing words like *he* and *she*.

■ Speakers of Thai, Vietnamese, and especially Spanish may substitute /tʃ/ for /ʃ/.

Making the Sound

Have students read the directions for making the sound /ʃ/ as they listen to the audio and look at the illustrations.

For students who find /ʃ/ difficult, spend some time on the mouth position and practice of the sound in isolation. Tell students who confuse /s/ and /ʃ/ to make their lips round and slowly move their tongues back as they make the sound /s/. It may help for them to exaggerate rounding their lips at first. The hissing sound for /ʃ/ is quieter than for /s/; /ʃ/ is the sound used in English to tell someone to be quiet: *shhhh.*

For those who replace /ʃ/ with /tʃ/, demonstrate that /ʃ/ can be a long sound (/ʃʃʃʃ/) and /tʃ/ cannot. Also point out that for /tʃ/ the tip of the tongue touches the roof of the mouth (for the /t/ part of the sound), while for /ʃ/ it does not.

A Word Pairs See Overview, p. viii.

Word pairs for additional practice:

/s/ – /ʃ/: sea (or see)/she, save/shave, sip/ship, sew/show, sort/short, suit/shoot, said/shed, same/shame, self/shelf, sock/shock, fasten/fashion, iris/Irish, class/clash, mass/mash, Russ/rush

/h/ – /ʃ/: he/she, he's/she's, heat/sheet, hip/ship, heap/sheep, hear/sheer, he'd/she'd, he'll (or heel)/she'll

B Test Yourself See Overview, p. ix.
Step 1

ANSWERS

1. S (shell, shell)
2. D (Sue, shoe)
3. D (shine, sign)
4. S (seats, seats)
5. D (lease, leash)
6. D (save, shave)

Step 2

ANSWERS

1. Are they Sue's?
2. We need more sheets for the guests.
3. Could you sign this, please?
4. Did you shell all the peas?
5. I can't find the leash.
6. He needs to save more.

C Vocabulary See Overview, p. ix.
Step 2

ANSWERS

The letters sh (shake), s (sure), ci (special), ch (machine), and ti (information) have the sound /ʃ/ here.

Extra practice Have students identify the stressed syllable in some or all of these words: *shouldn't, washes, special, English, Danish, Swedish, finished, washing machine, information, demonstration.*

D Dialog See Overview, pp. ix–x.

Step 1 Tell students they are going to listen to a conversation that takes place in a store. Have students work with a partner to fill in the blanks. Encourage them to say the words aloud as they fill them in.

Step 2 Students who tend to confuse /s/ and /ʃ/ may have difficulty pronouncing words like *sale, sell,* and *salesman*. To practice these sounds, ask questions such as the following: "What is the woman shopping for?" "What does the man do?" (What is his job?)

ANSWERS

Shannon	Do you sell washing machines?
Salesman	Yes. We're having a special sale on this washing machine here.
Shannon	Could you give me some information about it? Was it made in Denmark? The name looks Danish.
Salesman	No, it's from Sweden. It's a Swedish machine. Would you like a demonstration?
Shannon	Sure. I'd like to see how it washes.
Salesman	It's very simple to operate. I'll demonstrate. Here are some sheets and shirts. You put them in the machine, add soap, and shut the door. Then you just push this button.
Shannon	The machine shouldn't shake like that, should it?
Salesman	Washing machines always shake. (*pause*) Ah! It's finished.
Shannon	But the sheets have shrunk. And look at how short these shirts are!
Salesman	Oh, those are English sheets. English sheets always shrink a little. And those shirts were short before we washed them.
Shannon	Well, I'm not sure. Could you show me another washing machine?
Salesman	Certainly. But this is the only machine we have at the special sale price. (*pause*) We also have this dishwasher on sale. Would you like a demonstration?

E Linking Words with /ʃ/

Background notes Two /ʃ/ sounds (as in *English sheets*), or a /s/ and a /ʃ/ sound (as in *Swiss shops*), are linked and pronounced as a single long /ʃ/ sound. The same linking also often occurs when a final /z/ sound is followed by /ʃ/, as in *is she* (/ɪʃiy/).

Step 1 Check that students link the words smoothly, using a long /ʃ/ sound to link them. Note that both words are stressed in phrases like *English sheets* and *Spanish shoes*, with the main stress on the second word.

Step 2 Students practice the short conversation, as in the model. This may be done in pairs, with students switching roles, or in a larger group as a chain drill. If necessary, remind students to link the words together.

Step 3

ANSWERS

1. Danish ships
2. Spanish shoes
3. Japanese shells
4. Swedish shampoo
5. Turkish sugar
6. Chinese shirts
7. Polish sheep
8. Swiss shops

F Tongue Twisters

Introduce the idea of a tongue twister – a phrase or sentence that is difficult to say, even for native speakers, because it repeats the same sound or sounds several times.

Model the tongue twister in the Student's Book. Have students repeat, starting slowly and then increasing their speed. For fun, you may want to ask students to say tongue twisters from their native language.

Then have students write their own tongue twisters, using words from the unit or other words they know with the sound /ʃ/. They can do this either individually (e.g., for homework) or working in pairs or groups in class. Have students practice their tongue twisters until they can say them quickly and smoothly. Students should choose one tongue twister to say to the class. To make the activity more competitive, you can have them judge who has the funniest or most natural-sounding tongue twister or see who can say their tongue twister the fastest without making any errors. Since tongue twisters are by their nature hard to say, don't worry too much about correcting errors in pronunciation. This activity is intended to be fun.

G Spelling

The variety of spellings in addition to *sh* for the sound /ʃ/ may cause confusion. Point out that many of the other spellings tend to occur in certain endings (e.g., *-ion*, *-ial*, and *-ious*). In other places, these spellings (e.g., *ti* and *ci*) are pronounced as the ordinary consonant one would expect + a vowel. Some of the other spellings, such as *ce* and *ch*, occur only rarely with the sound /ʃ/. For example, the spelling *ch* occurs mainly in words borrowed from French.

H Common Expressions See Overview, p. xii.

Further Practice

Practice names of nationalities with the sound /ʃ/, such as Spanish, English, Irish, Scottish, British, Swedish, Danish, Turkish, Polish, Finnish, Russian, for example:

1. Do a chain drill. The teacher or a student begins by saying "I think she's (Danish)." The next person says "Are you sure? I think she's (Polish)." Students continue, using as many nationalities with the sound /ʃ/ as they can think of.

2. Using students' suggestions, make a list of famous people of the nationalities listed above. Then practice questions and answers: "What nationality is (*or* was) X?" "He's / She's / He was / She was . . ."

   Examples: Pablo Picasso, Miguel de Cervantes (Spanish), Alfred Nobel, Ingmar Bergman (Swedish), J. K. Rowling, David Beckham (English / British)

Linking Pronunciation with Other Classwork

Tie pronunciation in with practice of:

should / shouldn't : For example, have students complete sentences like the following with the words *should* or *shouldn't* to make rules about appropriate behavior in their native countries: "You _____ shake hands with someone you've just met." "You _____ take your shoes off when you visit someone's house."

Word Stress Practice

Have students underline or put a circle over the stressed syllable in these nouns ending in *-tion*:

conversation, demonstration, information, pronunciation, education

(conver<u>sa</u>tion, demon<u>stra</u>tion, infor<u>ma</u>tion, pronunci<u>a</u>tion, edu<u>ca</u>tion)

Ask them to formulate a rule about the main stress in these words. They should see that the main stress goes on the syllable just before the -tion ending.

See the Unit 31 Web Site Worksheet (at www.cambridge.org/pp/student) for practice of stress in verbs ending in -ate and nouns ending in -ation. For further practice, give students verbs that have related nouns that follow this pattern and ask them to form the noun – for example, *graduate, concentrate, celebrate, illustrate, continue, reserve.*

UNIT 32 /ʒ/ • television   Stress in Words with *-ion*

Student Difficulties

Many learners find the sound /ʒ/ difficult, including speakers of Greek, Italian, German, Dutch, Japanese, Thai, Chinese, Korean, Indian languages, Scandinavian languages, and sometimes Arabic. Many Spanish speakers also have difficulty with this sound, although some South Americans do not, since it occurs in words spelled with *ll* in some dialects.

Students tend to replace the sound /ʒ/ with sounds close to /dʒ/, /ʃ/, or /z/, or sometimes with /zy/, under the influence of the spelling (e.g., in *measure*).

Making the Sound

Have students read the directions for making the sound /ʒ/ as they listen to the audio and look at the illustrations.

If students substitute /dʒ/ for /ʒ/, demonstrate that /ʒ/ can be prolonged (/ʒʒʒ/) while /dʒ/ cannot. If they substitute /ʃ/, focus on the fact that /ʒ/ is voiced and /ʃ/ is not. If students confuse /ʒ/ with /z/, it may be helpful to exaggerate the rounding of the lips for /ʒ/.

A Vocabulary   See Overview, p. ix.

Background notes The sound /ʒ/ is not a common sound in English. Note that it rarely occurs at the beginning of words in English, occurring there only in words borrowed from other languages, especially French (e.g., *genre*). It is also not very common at the end of words, where it is spelled *ge* (e.g., in *beige, rouge, garage*). Note that some North American speakers say the sound at the end of *garage* as /dʒ/ rather than /ʒ/. The sound /ʒ/ occurs in English mostly before a few word endings, such as *-ion* (*decision, occasion,*

television), *-ual* (*casual, usual*), *-ure* (*pleasure, measure*), and *-ia(n)* (*Asian*).

Note that word pairs are not practiced in this unit. There are not many pairs that contrast /ʒ/ and other sounds, and the ones that exist tend to include uncommon words – for example, *legion / lesion, pledger / pleasure, Caesar / seizure, bays / beige.*

Step 1 Discuss any unfamiliar vocabulary. For example, *casual clothes* are informal or relaxed in style – the opposite of *formal.*

Step 2 Students repeat the names of the television shows in the schedule. The titles practice the sounds /s/ (*it's, what's, twice, de<u>s</u>tination*), /z/ (*new<u>s</u>, Martian<u>s</u>*), and /ʃ/ (*chic, trash, destina<u>ti</u>on, Mar<u>ti</u>ans*), as well as /ʒ/.

Step 3 Working in pairs, students decide which television program is shown in each picture. Tell students that they will check their answers when they hear the dialog.

B Announcement

Students listen to the announcement and check their answers to task A, step 3. Have students cover the announcement. They should look at the TV schedule and pictures in steps 2 and 3 of task A, and not at the announcement, as they listen.

ANSWERS
1. *What's the Occasion?*
2. *Destination: Asia*
3. *It's a Pleasure*
4. News: An unusual collision
5. *Invasion of the Martians*
6. *Trash to Treasure*

7. *Treasure Island*
8. *Measure Twice*
9. *Casual Chic*

After students listen to the announcement, talk about the television shows. For example, ask students questions such as the following:

Which shows would you like to watch?

What kind of TV shows do you usually watch?

Do you ever watch a channel like the Leisure Channel?

Do you usually watch the news on television?

What do you usually watch on (Tuesdays)?

Have you read the book *Treasure Island* or seen a movie version of it?

(Note: The book *Treasure Island* was written by Robert Louis Stevenson. There have been several film and TV versions of the story.)

C Stress in Words with *-ion*

Background notes Various changes in pronunciation may occur when suffixes (word endings) are added in English. In the words practiced here, the sound /d/ at the end of a verb changes to /ʒ/ when the ending *-ion* is added to form a noun. The stress in the verbs and nouns here follow typical patterns: stress on the second syllable in two-syllable verbs (especially verbs beginning with a short prefix such as *in-, de-,* or *ex-*) and stress on the syllable before the *-ion* ending in nouns. The word *television*, with stress on the first syllable, is a common exception to the usual pattern of stress in *-ion* nouns.

Step 1 Students repeat pairs of words: a verb ending in the sound /d/ and a related noun ending in *-ion*. Call attention to the change in stress and the change in consonant sound. Underline the letter *d* at the end of the verbs and *s* in the nouns, and ask students what sounds these letters have here. Note that in the pairs *decide – decision, divide – division,* and *collide – collision,* the vowel sound also changes from /ay/ to /ɪ/ (e.g., *divide* /dɪ•ˈvayd/ – *division* /dɪ•ˈvɪʒ•ən/).

Step 2 Working alone or with a partner, students fill in the blanks with an *-ion* noun formed from the underlined verb. If students work with a partner, they should take turns reading the news stories aloud.

Step 3

ANSWERS		
1. collision	2. decision	3. explosion

Extra practice Other pairs of verbs and nouns that follow similar patterns include:

/d/ – /ʒ/: persuade – persuasion, conclude – conclusion, include – inclusion, exclude – exclusion, delude – delusion, provide – provision, erode – erosion

/z/– /ʒ/: confuse – confusion, revise – revision, supervise – supervision

D Survey

Step 1 *Usually* is a very common word with the sound /ʒ/. Some native speakers pronounce this as /ˈyuw•ʒə•wə•liy/ or /ˈyuw•ʒwə•liy/; the sequence /ʒwə/ in the second pronunciation is particularly difficult for learners to say. Many native speakers fortunately simplify the pronunciation to /ˈyuw•ʒə•liy/, which is, of course, easier for students to say.

Step 2 Practicing in small groups, students take turns completing the sentences in different ways. There are many ways that these sentences can be completed. In addition to the models given in the Student's Book, a sentence beginning like *I usually watch television* could be completed, for example, with a phrase like *with my sister* or *after work* or *when I'm too tired to read.*

Extra practice Ask questions with *usually* about students' native countries, for example: "What time do people usually eat dinner?" "When do stores usually open / close?" "How many hours a day do children usually go to school?" "How many hours a week do people usually work?" "How much vacation time do people usually get?" or "What do people usually wear to work, for example in an office?"

E Spelling

The spellings for the sound /ʒ/ may cause difficulty, since they are all regular spellings for other, more common sounds. Note that the letter *s* has the sound /ʒ/ only before the letter *i* or *u*.

F Common Expressions See Overview, p. xii.

Linking Pronunciation with Other Classwork

Tie pronunciation in with practice of:

1. Descriptions of daily routines using the word *usually*.

2. The response "My pleasure," or "It was my pleasure," used when somebody has thanked you for doing something.

Word Stress Practice

Give students a list of words ending in *-ual* or *-ial*; for example: *casual, unusual, special, commercial, official*. Have them underline or put a circle over the stressed syllable (**cas**ual, un**u**sual, **spe**cial, com**mer**cial, of**fi**cial). Encourage students to formulate a rule about stress: Words that end in *-ual* or *-ial* usually have stress on the syllable just before the *-ual* or *-ial* ending.

UNIT 33 /tʃ/ • chips Silent Syllables

Student Difficulties

Learners may have some of the following difficulties with the sound /tʃ/:

■ French, Portuguese, Dutch, Greek, Scandinavian, and some Vietnamese speakers have difficulty with the sound /tʃ/. Many of these students replace it with /ʃ/. Greek students often replace it with /ts/, and Scandinavians may pronounce it as /ty/.

■ Chinese speakers may use a foreign-sounding pronunciation of the sound /tʃ/. Some students, including speakers of Thai, Lao, and Khmer, may have some difficulty with the sound at the end of words, often replacing it with /t/.

■ Italians do not have trouble pronouncing /tʃ/, but may make mistakes because of spelling, pronouncing the spelling *c* or *cc* before *e* or *i* (as in *accent* or *city*) as /tʃ/ or pronouncing the spelling *ch* as the sound /k/.

■ Spanish speakers do not have difficulty with /tʃ/, but need practice in learning to discriminate /tʃ/ from /ʃ/, since they often substitute /tʃ/ for /ʃ/.

Making the Sound

Have students read the directions for making the sound /tʃ/ as they listen to the audio and look at the illustrations. For students who substitute /ʃ/ for /tʃ/, focus on adding a short /t/ sound before the /ʃ/. If students substitute /ts/ for /tʃ/, tell them to move their tongues back just a little and make their lips round to say /tʃ/.

A Word Pairs See Overview, p. viii.

Word pairs for additional practice:

/ʃ/ – /tʃ/: shoes/choose, shows/chose, share/chair, she's/cheese, sheet/cheat, sherry/cherry, shin/chin, shore/chore, wish/witch (*or* which), mash/match, dish/ditch, crush/crutch, marsh/march

/ts/ – /tʃ/: eats/each, cats/catch, mats/match, eights/H, coats/coach, what's/watch, beats/beach, pizzas/peaches

B Test Yourself See Overview, p. ix.

Step 1

ANSWERS		
1. sheep	3. shopping	5. catch
2. chips	4. wash	6. chose

Step 2

ANSWERS
1. I don't like <u>chips</u>.
2. Are those <u>sheep</u>?
3. He <u>chose</u> a lot of paintings.
4. I've done all the <u>chopping</u> for dinner.
5. Could you <u>wash</u> the car for me?
6. I tried to <u>cash</u> the check.

C Vocabulary See Overview, p. ix.

Step 1 Students listen and repeat the names of foods with the sound /tʃ/.

Step 2 Students work in pairs to match the words in step 1 with the illustrations in step 2. You may want to go over the first item with the class.

Extra practice Ask questions to be answered with the vocabulary words, for example: "Are there any foods here that you've never tried?" "Which foods do you like?" "Which ones don't you like?" "Which foods are popular in your country?"

D Dialog   See Overview, pp. ix–x.

Step 1 Introduce the situation, for example asking students if they ever watch cooking shows on TV. Check their understanding of the word *chef* (a cook, especially the main cook, at a restaurant).

Students listen to the dialog and answer the questions. Have them read the questions before they listen. They should look at the vocabulary words in task C, and not at the dialog, as they listen.

Step 2 Play the recording of the dialog again and go over the answers to step 1.

E Silent Syllables

Background notes In English, unlike many other languages, the written form of a word does not always indicate the number of spoken syllables. Many words have vowel letters that are not pronounced by most people in ordinary conversational speech. When the vowel is dropped, the word has fewer syllables when spoken than it appears to have in writing. For example, *chocolate* looks as if it would have three (or even four) syllables, but it is usually said with only two syllables: "chocØlate."

Some of the words in task E have more than one possible pronunciation. For example, while many people say *interesting* with three syllables, some native speakers pronounce all the vowel sounds and say it with four syllables.

Step 1 Students listen and count the number of syllables they hear in each word. Tapping out the syllables may help them with counting. Remind them to think about the pronunciation, not the spelling, of the word. Go over the example. You may want to have students compare the two-syllable pronunciation of *chocolate* in English with the pronunciation this word (or its equivalent) has in their native language. In other languages, *chocolate* is usually pronounced as three or four syllables. (The location of the stress usually differs from English, too.)

Step 2 Check the answers at the end, making sure that students do not add extra syllables when they repeat the words. Students can also be asked to draw a slash through the silent syllable in each word. *Actually* is another word from the dialog that often has a silent syllable.

Step 3

F Discussion

In groups, students plan an imaginary meal. Before they get into groups, you may want to write a list of foods that have the sounds /ʃ/ and /tʃ/ on the board, using suggestions from students. In addition to the foods listed in task C, foods with these sounds include: peaches, French fries, cheddar cheese, chops, nachos, anchovies, chickpeas, chives, chestnuts; fish, shrimp, sugar, mashed potatoes, squash, mushrooms, shallots, pistachio nuts, cashews, marshmallows.

Have each group describe their meal to the rest of the class.

Extra practice Students dictate a recipe for a dish in their imaginary dinner.

G Spelling

Students often find the spelling *t* for the sound /tʃ/ confusing. Direct students' attention to the examples in the Student's Book. Then write a few more examples on the board, or elicit more examples from students (e.g., *mixture, future, furniture, natural, actually, century, literature, culture*); have students try pronouncing the words. Review the *t* spelling as used for different sounds. Give students a list of words such as the ones below. They say which sound *t* has in each word: /t/, /ʃ/ (as in *show*), or /tʃ/ (as in *chair*), for example:

1. picture	6. return
2. question	7. initial
3. conversation	8. vacation
4. practice	9. naturally
5. furniture	10. future

H Common Expressions See Overview, p. xii.

Further Practice

1. To review the sounds /ʃ/ and /tʃ/ at a later time, give students the following words, either on the board or on a handout. Ask them to circle the four words that have the sound /ʃ/ and not /tʃ/.

watching	chosen	special
lunch	chef	kitchen

naturally	mixture	temperature
delicious	rich	commercial

Answers: *delicious, chef, special,* and *commercial* have the sound /ʃ/.

2. Linking sounds: See Unit 34, *Further Practice*.

Linking Pronunciation with Other Classwork

Tie pronunciation in with practice of:

1. Count and noncount nouns and describing quantities using *how much* and *too much*.

2. Questions with *which*.

3. Asking for prices, as in a store or restaurant, using *How much*.

Word Stress Practice

Write large and small circles on the board showing these four stress patterns:

A ● •   B • ●   C ● • •   D • ● •

Read the following words. Students say whether they heard stress pattern A, B, C, or D.

1. sandwich (A)	6. special (A)
2. mixture (A)	7. chocolate (A)
3. naturally (C)	8. vegetable (C)
4. delicious (D)	9. commercial (D)
5. kitchen (A)	10. of course (B)

UNIT 34 /dʒ/ • joke

Didja (*did you*); Wouldja (*would you*); Didncha (*didn't you*); Doncha (*don't you*)

Student Difficulties

Many students have difficulty with the sound /dʒ/.

- ◾ Portuguese, French, Vietnamese, and sometimes Dutch speakers may pronounce it as /ʒ/.

- ◾ Thai speakers often replace it with /tʃ/.

- ◾ Korean speakers may confuse /dʒ/ and /z/.

- ◾ Speakers of Greek often substitute /ʃ/ or /dz/.

- ◾ Spanish speakers may confuse /dʒ/ and /y/ or may substitute /tʃ/ for /dʒ/, especially at the ends of words.

- ◾ German and Swedish speakers often substitute /y/ for /dʒ/, while Danish and

Norwegian speakers tend to pronounce it as /dy/. These problems may be reinforced by the spelling. The letter *j*, which in English usually represents /dʒ/, represents the sound /y/ in some other languages, including German, Dutch, Norwegian, Danish, and Swedish.

Making the Sound

Have students read the directions for making the sound /dʒ/ as they listen to the audio and look at the illustrations. Emphasize that the first part of this sound is a /d/.

If students have difficulty with the sound /tʃ/, instead of following the directions in the Student's Book, you may want to start by having them first practice /d/ and /ʒ/. Tell them to begin to make /d/. Then they should slowly move their tongues away from the roof of the mouth as they say /ʒ/.

If students substitute /dz/ for /dʒ/, tell them to move their tongues back just a little and make their lips round to say /dʒ/.

A **Word Pairs** See Overview, p. viii.

Word pairs for additional practice:

/tʃ/ – /dʒ/: cherry/Jerry, chess/Jess, choice/Joyce, chain/Jane, chill/Jill, chunk/junk, cello/Jell-O, etch/edge, match/Madge, March/Marge, rich/ridge, larch/large, lunch/lunge

See the notes for Unit 25, task A, for pairs that contrast /d/ and /dʒ/.

B **Test Yourself** See Overview, p. ix.

Step 1

> **ANSWERS**
>
> | | | |
> |---|---|---|
> | 1. joke | 3 cheap | 5. badge |
> | 2. jeer | 4. cherry | 6. H's |

Step 2

> **ANSWERS**
>
> 1. I was <u>choking</u>.
> 2. The crowd <u>jeered</u>.
> 3. They didn't say their <u>ages</u>.
> 4. Do you need another <u>batch</u>?
> 5. The car was <u>cheap</u>.
> 6. Are those <u>Jerry's</u>?

Step 3 In contrasting the sounds /tʃ/ and /dʒ/ at the end of words, make sure that students make the vowel longer before /dʒ/.

C **Vocabulary** See Overview, p. ix.

Step 1 Go over any unfamiliar vocabulary. Some of the items here are more difficult than the everyday words used elsewhere in the Student's Book, but many of these are words that students in an academic environment are likely to encounter.

If students have difficulty with the pronunciation, backward or forward buildup may be helpful, for example:

-gy, -ogy, -CHOLogy, psychology; psy-, psyCHOL-, psyCHOLo-, psychology

-als, -duals, -VIduals, -diVIduals, individuals; in-, indi-, indiVI-, indiVIdu-, individuals

Note that *knowledge* rhymes with *college*; it does not have the same vowel sound as *know*.

Step 2

> **ANSWERS**
>
> The sound /dʒ/ can be spelled with the letter *j* or with the letter ____*g*____ before *e* or with the letter ____*d*____ before *u*.

Extra practice Students may need help with stress, especially in some of the longer words. Play the audio. Ask students to underline or put a circle over the stressed syllable in all the words with more than one syllable (that is, all the words except for *job* and *change*).

D **Dialog** See Overview, pp. ix–x.

Step 1 Tell students they are going to read a conversation between Jess and her friend George. Have students work with a partner to fill in the blanks. Encourage them to say the words aloud as they fill them in.

Step 2

> **ANSWERS**
>
> | | |
> |---|---|
> | **George** | Did you call about the job? |
> | **Jess** | Which job? |
> | **George** | The job managing the travel <u>agency</u>. |
> | **Jess** | Oh, that job. Yes, I did. |
> | **George** | What did you find out? |
> | **Jess** | They want someone who graduated from <u>college</u>. |
> | **George** | Well, you just <u>graduated</u> in June. |
> | **Jess** | They're looking for someone who majored in business management. |
> | **George** | Didn't you major in management before you changed your major to psychology? |
> | **Jess** | Actually, I didn't change majors. I had a double major – I majored in management *and* <u>psychology</u>. |
> | **George** | If you get the <u>job</u>, would you arrange travel for individuals? Or would you just do group tour packages? |

Continued on page 84

Jess	Oh, I'd make all kinds of travel arrangements. They want someone who's energetic and <u>enjoys</u> challenges.
George	Anyone who majors in two subjects enjoys a challenge!
Jess	And they want someone with a <u>knowledge</u> of foreign languages.
George	You speak <u>Japanese</u>, don't you?
Jess	Yes. And a little German.
George	So, did you arrange for an interview?
Jess	Yes, for <u>July</u> 6th.
George	July 6th? Are you <u>joking</u>? That was yesterday!
Jess	I'm not joking. I had the interview, and I got the job!
George	Hey, congratulations! Why didn't you tell me?

E Didja (*did you*); Wouldja (*would you*); Didncha (*didn't you*); and Doncha (*don't you*)

Background notes Native speakers link words together when they talk. In informal, relaxed speech, consonant sounds are sometimes blended together to make a different sound when words are linked. When one word ends in the sound /d/ or /t/ and the next word begins with the sound /y/, the /d/ or /t/ is often blended with /y/ to make the sound /dʒ/, as in *did you* ("didja"), or /tʃ/, as in *don't you* ("doncha"). This happens especially when the second word is the unstressed word *you* or *your*.

Blended forms like these are very common in conversation. It is not important for students to use these forms in their own speech (and they may sound awkward in speech that is not very fluent) but they need to recognize them to understand native speakers. Practice with the pronunciation will help students become more familiar with the forms.

Steps 1 and 2 Students listen to and repeat blended forms with the sounds /dʒ/ and /tʃ/. Explain that blended forms like these are very common in conversation and that being able to understand forms like these will help their listening comprehension.

Encourage students to link words together and make the weak forms short. Note that *you* has the short, unstressed vowel /ə/ in almost all the sentences here. In *Would you arrange travel?*, it may have the vowel /uw/ because the next word begins with a vowel. Show respellings on the board (*didja*, *doncha*, etc.) to illustrate the blended pronunciations. Demonstrate the difference between the unblended and blended forms by saying the words in the phrases first by themselves and then linked together.

Extra practice In fast speech, *did you* can be reduced even further, to /dʒə/ – for example, *What did you do?* can sound like "Whaja do?" If your students are more advanced, you may want to give them some fast speech forms to "translate." You can use this classic exchange as an example.

A   Jeet yet? (= Did you eat yet?)
B   No, joo? (= No, did you?)

Say phrases such as the ones below; students write the conventionally spelled form of the words.

1. Howja do on the test? (How did you do on the test?)

2. Whereja go? (Where did you go?)

3. Wouldja like some? (Would you like some?)

4. Didncha like it? (Didn't you like it?)

5. Doncha know? (Don't you know?)

6. Gotcha! (I've got you!)

F Scrambled Conversations

Step 1 Working in pairs, students find the best response on the right to each question on the left. Go over the example. You may want student A to cover B's sentences, and student B to cover A's sentences while they practice.

While they practice, move around the room monitoring pronunciation of the sound /dʒ/ and blending. Encourage students to link words together where possible.

Step 2 After students listen and check their answers, ask them to underline the words that could be blended together to make the sound /dʒ/ or /tʃ/. Then play the audio again so they can check their answers.

G Role-Play

In small groups of two or three people, students role-play a job interview. If possible, have students rearrange desks and chairs to make the setting more realistic. Students should decide on what the job is before they begin their interviews. It would be helpful for them to write down a few questions they will ask before they begin. Students can do this within their groups, or you can divide students into two main groups (interviewers and job applicants) with each group brainstorming the kinds of questions they will ask. Remind students that this is a role play; the applicant does not have to answer the questions truthfully.

After students practice in groups, ask for volunteers to perform their job interviews for the class.

H Spelling

The letter *g* before *e*, *i*, or *y* usually has the sound /dʒ/, but there are some common exceptions in which it is pronounced /g/, including *get, forget, give, begin,* and *together*. See the Unit 34 Web Site Worksheet (at www.cambridge.org/pp/student) to practice the two pronunciations of the letter *g*.

I Common Expressions See Overview, p. xii.

Further Practice

Linking /tʃ/ and /dʒ/ sounds: Unlike many other consonants, the sounds /tʃ/ and /dʒ/ are not linked and pronounced as one long sound when they come together between words. Each sound is pronounced separately. Have students listen to and repeat phrases such as the following:

orange juice	which chair	which job
a large jar	rich children	teach German
change jobs	how much cheese	a large chicken

Linking Pronunciation with Other Classwork

Tie pronunciation in with practice of:

1. Simple past tense questions with *did you*.

2. *Would you*.

3. Structures using *just*.

Word Stress Practice

See *Extra practice* under task C, on page 83.

UNIT 35 Review /s/, /z/, /ʃ/, /ʒ/, /tʃ/, and /dʒ/

This unit provides additional practice and review of the consonants /s/, /z/, /ʃ/, /ʒ/, /tʃ/, and /dʒ/. These are the sibilant (hissing) and affricate (a combination of a stop and a sibilant) consonants in English. Note that these are the consonants after which *-s* endings are pronounced as a separate syllable /əz/.

A Test Yourself

Step 1 Play the audio. Students circle the words they hear. They can check the meaning of unfamiliar words, but they do not have to understand every word to do the task.

Extra practice Have individual students say the words, choosing a word from each numbered item. Other students write down the word they heard. This can be done with the whole class or in small groups.

B Vocabulary

Step 1 Students sort the words, grouping words with the same consonant sound together. Some of the words, like the example *cheese*, have more than one of the consonant sounds shown at the top of the table and belong in more than one column.

Step 2

C Thoughts

Step 1 Introduce the situation. Susan is trying to decide what to do today. The words in the bubbles show what she is thinking.

Students cover the thought bubbles in their books and listen to the audio. You may want to give them questions to direct their listening. For example, tell them to listen to Susan's thoughts and then answer these questions:

1. What does Susan usually do at the gym? (*Answer*: She usually goes swimming.)

2. What does she decide to have for dinner? (*Answer*: shrimp)

Step 2 Students read the thought bubbles and then write their own questions showing the choices they think about on their days off. You may want to specify the number of questions that they write – for example, at least three.

Ask students to read some of their questions aloud. Monitor pronunciation of the target sounds

and the intonation in choice questions (practiced in Unit 9, task C, and Unit 29, task E). If necessary, use hand gestures to show the direction of the intonation.

You may want to ask other students to keep track of words in the questions that have the sound /s, z, ʃ, ʒ, tʃ, or dʒ/ when they listen.

Extra practice Have students add more words from the thought bubbles in step 1 to the table in task B. Here is a list, but don't expect students to find all of these.

/s/: so, stay, swimming, let's, see, sandwich, some, house, guess, salmon, smell, just, salad, Je<u>ss</u>'s, said, skirt, Saturday, de<u>c</u>isions

/z/: is, as, use, chores, easier, dishes, news, Jess'<u>s</u>, was, jeans, decision<u>s</u>

/ʃ/: fish, shrimp, cash, sure, dishes, she

/ʒ/: usual, usually, casual, deci<u>s</u>ions

/tʃ/: lunch, chicken, sandwich, chores, which, check

/dʒ/: just, Jess's, jeans

D Puzzle

Students circle or say the word in each group in which the -s ending has a different pronunciation from the other words. Go over the example. If necessary, remind students that the -s ending has three pronunciations. Students can work alone or with a partner.

Check the answers at the end. If students need the practice, have them listen to and repeat the words when checking answers. Ask them to identify the pronunciation of the ending in the odd one out and in the other words in the line. Note that most of the items focus on whether the -s ending adds an extra syllable or not, since that is the most important feature for students to master.

Further Practice

Tell students the following anecdote. Read it only once.

A new shopping center has three shoe stores next to each other. The name of each shop owner is Joe. When the three shoe stores open, the first shop owner puts a sign on his store: "Joe's – the Largest Shoe Store." The second shop owner writes above his store: "Joe's – the Cheapest Shoes." The third shop owner writes above his store in large letters: "Joe's Shoes – Main Entrance."

Write the following symbols on the board: /s/, /z/, /ʃ/, /tʃ/, and /dʒ/. Ask students to say all the words they remember. As they list the words, ask them which column to add each word to.

/s/:   center, stores, next, first, puts, sign, store, second, writes, cheapest, entrance

/z/:   has, stores, is, his, Joe's, shoes, letters

/ʃ/:   shopping, shoe, shop, shoes

/tʃ/: each, cheapest

/dʒ/: Joe, Joe's, largest, large

Read the anecdote again. Have students add words they missed the first time. Ask for a volunteer to retell the anecdote, or ask students to work in pairs or small groups and try to write out the complete story. Then ask for volunteers to

tell it. Finally, provide students with the original version.

Word Stress Practice

Write large and small circles on the board showing these two stress patterns:

A ● • •   B • ● •

Give students the list of words below, either on the board or a paper handout. Ask them to decide which stress pattern each word has and to write A or B in the blank.

1. _____ casual (A)   5. _____ delicious (B)
2. _____ decisions (B) 6. _____ easier (A)
3. _____ exercise (A)   7. _____ vegetable (A)
4. _____ usual (A)   8. _____ Saturday (A)

Then read the words aloud and have students check their answers.

/y/ • yes   Useta (*used to*)

Student Difficulties

Learners may show some of the following interference from their first language:

■ The sound /y/ is pronounced as /dʒ/, or a sound close to /dʒ/, by many Spanish speakers.

■ Some Portuguese speakers may tend to omit the sound /y/.

■ Chinese and Japanese speakers may find the consonant /y/ difficult before the sound /iy/ or /ɪ/, as in *year*.

Making the Sound

Have students read the directions for making the sound /y/ as they listen to the audio and look at the illustrations. Show students that the tongue position for this sound starts in a position similar to the vowel /iy/. Emphasize that unlike the sound /dʒ/, the front of the tongue should not touch the roof of the mouth for /y/. If students tend to substitute the sound /dʒ/ for /y/, have them compare the rounded lip position shown for /dʒ/ in Unit 34 with the spread lip position shown for /y/.

Begin by practicing some words that start with /iy/ (e.g., *eat, easy*). Then write a word, such as *yes* or *you* on the board, erasing the letter *y* and replacing it with *EE*: *EEes, EEou*. Have students try saying the words that way, using the sound /iy/ to replace the /y/ and gradually making the /iy/ sound shorter.

Note that /y/ is a glide sound. In producing a glide, the mouth is not in a fixed position. The tongue glides smoothly as it moves from /y/ into the vowel that follows. If students confuse words like *ear* and *year*, have them push their tongues farther forward to make the sound /y/.

Variation in the sound Speakers of British English use the sound /y/ in words like *new* /nyuw/ and *student* /ˈstyuw•dnt/; U.S. and Canadian speakers generally do not.

A Word Pairs See Overview, p. viii.

Word pairs for additional practice:

/dʒ/ – /y/: Jell-O/yellow, juice/use (noun), jet/yet, jewel/you'll, Jack/yak, jell/yell, jarred/yard

B Test Yourself See Overview, p. ix.

Step 1

Step 2

C Vocabulary See Overview, p. ix.

Step 1 Note that all of the words in step 1 have the sound /y/, even though they don't all have the letter *y*.

Go over any unfamiliar vocabulary – for example, *peculiar* (= strange, odd), *familiar* (= known, easy to recognize because you've seen the person or thing before), or *millionaire* (= a person who has a million dollars; a very rich person).

Step 2 The sound /y/ often occurs as part of the spelling *u*. See task G, on page 89.

D Dialog See Overview, pp. ix–x.

Step 1 Play the audio. Students read the dialog and listen. Some of the words in the book are different from the words on the recording. Students can call out "Stop" or signal when they hear a word that is different. Pause the recording to give students time to write, or have students dictate the correction for you to write on the board. You may need to play the dialog several times for students to catch all the incorrect words.

Step 2 Play the audio again and go over the answers to step 1.

If students tend to substitute the sound /y/ for /dʒ/, check their pronunciation of *Jack, jeep,* and

jazz. Make sure, for example, that they do not use the same sound for *Jack* and *Yoko.*

Note the blending of /d/ and /y/ to make the sound /dʒ/ in *did you*, practiced in Unit 34, task E.

E Useta (*used to*)

Background notes *Used to* is pronounced as if it were a single word: /ˈyuw•stə/. When it comes before a vowel sound or at the end of a sentence (as in "Do you play the piano?" "No, but I used to"), it often ends with a clearer vowel sound: /ˈyuw•stuw/. The spelling *use to*, used in questions and negatives, is pronounced the same way. (Many people, including native speakers, use the spelling *used to* even in questions and negatives.)

Students listen and repeat after the recording. If necessary, check their understanding of *used to* to describe past states or habits by asking questions, such as: "Did you use to live in (student's hometown)?" "Where did *X* use to live?" "Does *X* live there now?" Students should understand that "He used to play the piano" means that he played the piano in the past but probably does not play now.

F Conversation Practice

Explain the task. Students try to find people who fit the descriptions in the sentences in step 2. To do that, they will need to move around the room and ask questions. Go over any unfamiliar vocabulary before they begin.

Write one or two of the descriptions from step 2 on the board, for example, "used to play the piano." Ask students what question they would ask, but tell them to just ask, and not answer, the question now. Notice that the question has two clauses, each pronounced as a separate intonation group:

When you were younger, /

did you use to play the piano? /

When students find someone who answers "yes" to a question, they should write the person's name in the blank and ask a different person a different question. Each person's name should be used only once; if there aren't enough students, change the directions to "Try to fill in as many different names as you can."

Set a time limit of about 10 minutes. If some students finish early, encourage them to ask people on their lists follow-up questions (e.g., "How long was your hair?" for number 6). After students finish, ask questions about what they found out, for example, "Did you find someone who used to have an unusual job? What was it?"

G Spelling

The sound /y/ as part of the spelling u is confusing for many students, who often find it hard to know when to use a /y/ sound and when not to. The spelling u has the sound /y/ (pronounced either /yuw/ or /yə/):

1. at the beginning of a word: *use, university, usually* (but not in the prefix *un-*: *unhappy*)

2. after the consonant sounds /p, b, k, g, f, v, h, m/ (consonants made without using the front of the tongue): *computer, popular, ambulance, cute, excuse, executive, argue, regular, future, confuse, human, huge, music* (but not when /k/ is spelled with the letter q or when *gu* is followed by a vowel, as in *guess*)

3. in the middle of a word, also after the consonants /n/ and /l/, if the u vowel does not

have strong stress: *January, annual, continue, menu, value, volume*. The /y/ sound also occurs, but more rarely, with a few other consonant sounds: /d/ (*pendulum*), /θ/ (*Matthew*), /r/ (*erudite*).

Rules 1 and 2 do not apply – that is, the sound /y/ does not occur – if the letter u is followed by two consonants (*upper, umbrella, butter, husband,* etc.) or by a single final consonant (as in *us or but*).

British speakers and a small number of Canadian and American speakers, use rules slightly different from these. These speakers use the sound /y/ in more places, for example after the consonants /t/, /d/, and /n/, as in *student, due,* or *news*.

Present the rules according to the level of your students; you will probably not want to give them all the rules above. Check their understanding of the rules by asking them to try pronouncing some additional words, ones with and without the /y/ sound, for example: *upset, unite, unkind, uniform, cute, husband, ruler, puppy, human, fuel, funny, value*.

H Common Expressions See Overview, p. xii.

Note that the sound /y/ is used to link words ending in the sounds /iy/, /ey/, /ay/, and /ɔy/ (sounds that end in /y/) to a vowel sound at the beginning of the next word, for example:

He isn't here.   Say it again.   I agree.

Further Practice

The sounds /y/ and /dʒ/ contrast in *do you* / *did you* when *did you* is pronounced "didja" (see Unit 34, task E). (In very rapid speech, the phrases may be reduced to *do you* /dyə/ vs. *did you* /dʒə/.) To practice this, see the exercise on the Unit 36 Web Site Worksheet (at www.cambridge.org/pp/student).

Linking Pronunciation with Other Classwork

Tie pronunciation in with practice of:

1. Talking about the past using *used to*.

2. Talking about being or becoming accustomed to things, using *be used to* or *get used to*.

3. Sentences with *usually*, for example in talking about present routines or past activities.

4. Questions beginning *Do you* / *Are you* /

Can you / Have you and affirmative answers beginning with *yes*. For example, play 20 Questions, with one student going to the front of the room and pretending to be a famous person. The other students ask *Yes / No* questions (e.g., "Are you American?" "Do you live in Hollywood?") to try to figure out who the famous person is. The number of questions is limited to 20.

Word Stress Practice

Write large and small circles on the board showing these three stress patterns:

A ● • •   B • ● •   C • • ●

Read the following words. Students say whether they heard stress pattern A, B, or C.

1. computer (B)   6. opinion (B)
2. musician (B)   7. peculiar (B)
3. familiar (B)   8. piano (B)
4. yesterday (A)   9. interview (A)
5. millionaire (A or C) 10. popular (A)

UNIT 37 /f/ • fan Intonation in Long Sentences

Student Difficulties

Although many students do not have problems with the sound /f/, it is difficult for speakers of Korean, Tagalog, Indian languages, and some other Asian languages (but not Chinese). Speakers who have difficulty usually confuse /f/ with the sound /p/. Japanese speakers, however, often confuse it with /h/, especially before vowels made in the back of the mouth like /uw/ or /ɔ/.

Making the Sound

Have students read the directions for making the sound /f/ as they listen to the audio and look at the illustrations.

If students confuse /f/ and /p/, have them compare the illustrations, especially the front views of the lips, for /f/ and /p/ (see Unit 22). When saying /f/, the front teeth are visible, touching the lower lip. Demonstrate that the sound /f/ can be a long sound (/fffff/), with air continuing to escape from the mouth. In making the sound /p/, the air is stopped completely and the two lips are pressed together. For /f/, the upper lip does not touch anything. Encourage students to practice in front of a mirror.

A Word Pairs See Overview, p. viii.

Word pairs for additional practice:

/p/ – /f/: put/foot, pill/fill, past/fast, pin/fin, pine/
fine, pat/fat, pool/fool, pour/four, pork/
fork, paint/faint, pear (*or* pair)/fair, pile/
file, prize/fries, supper/suffer, cheap/chief,
leap/leaf, lap/laugh

/h/ – /f/: hill/fill, heel/feel, hat/fat, heat/feet, hall/
fall, hold/fold, hey/Fay, honey/funny, her/
fur, hire/fire, hair/fair, hear/fear, he/fee,
hue/few, height/fight, hit/fit, home/foam,
horse/force, halt/fault, who'll/fool, who'd/
food

B Test Yourself See Overview, p. ix.

Step 1

ANSWERS		
1. pan	3. pull	5. copy
2. feel	4. cuff	6. fast

Step 2

ANSWERS
1. The sign said "Full".
2. Is that an electric pan?
3. Peel this orange.
4. They walked fast.
5. The copy machine is broken.
6. Are the cuffs clean?

C Vocabulary See Overview, p. ix.

Step 1 Go over any unfamiliar vocabulary. For example, ask students to find a word that means "happy" (*cheerful*) or a word for someone who takes pictures professionally (*photographer*). Note the different stress in **pho**tographs and pho**tog**rapher.

Step 2

The letters *f* (*funny*), *ph* (*phone*), and *gh* (*laugh*) spell the sound /f/ here.

D Dialog See Overview, pp. ix–x.

Step 1 Have students work with a partner to fill in the blanks. Encourage them to say the words aloud as they fill them in.

Step 2

Fred	I'd like a photo of <u>myself</u> and my family.
Photographer	Fill out this <u>form</u>, please. What size <u>photographs</u> would you prefer – 4 x 6 or 5 x 7?
Fred	If there isn't a big difference in price, I'd <u>prefer</u> the 5 x 7.
Photographer	We're offering a special this week. <u>If</u> you pay for four photos, you get the fifth one free.
Fred	(*filling out the form*) Sounds fine.
Frankie	Sophie stepped on my foot!
Sophie	Frankie stepped on my foot <u>first</u>.
Faith	Stop fighting!
Photographer	Can the four of you sit on this sofa, please?
Sophie	I can't fit. Frankie's taking up the whole sofa!
Frankie	Am not! Your head is in <u>front</u> of my face.
Fred	That's <u>enough</u>! If you two don't stop fighting, we'll never get finished.
Photographer	Are you comfortable now? (*Frankie and Sophie frown.*)
Photographer	Mr. and Mrs. Freeman, try to laugh.
Faith	That's difficult. If you say something <u>funny</u>, I'll laugh.
Photographer	Frankie and Sophie, look <u>cheerful</u> and friendly! (*Fred and Faith laugh.*)
Photographer	Perfect!
Fred	Will the photographs be ready by <u>February</u> 1st?
Photographer	Definitely. If you don't hear from us by Friday, <u>phone</u> my office.

Extra practice Ask students to think of names for family members that have the sound /f/ (wife, father, grandfather, nephew).

E Intonation in Long Sentences

Background notes Breaking up a long sentence into phrase groups (see Unit 10, task F) is helpful for both the speaker and the listener, making the sentence easier to say and showing the listener which words belong together. Each phrase group has a stressed word, with a lengthened vowel, and a change in intonation. There may also be a pause at the end of a phrase group, especially in slower speech. The intonation at the end of a phrase group either rises a little or falls a little; there is not as much of a change in pitch as there is at the end of a sentence.

When a clause with *if* begins a sentence, it can end with either slightly rising or slightly falling intonation. In either case, the vowel in the last stressed word of the *if* clause is lengthened and there is often a pause where the comma is shown in writing.

Students listen and repeat sentences that begin with *if* clauses. Use gestures or arrows on the board to show the direction of the intonation. Check to make sure students lengthen the stressed syllables, shown in bold in the Student's Book.

F Scrambled Sentences

Step 1 Working in pairs, students find the clause in the second column that best finishes the sentence beginning in the first column. Go over the example. Students should take turns reading the sentences.

ANSWERS

If you need help, ask your father.
If you're finished, feel free to leave.
If I'm free on Friday, I'll go to my friend's party.
If I have enough money, I'll go to France.
If I drink coffee after dinner, I can't fall asleep.
If I feel nervous, I often laugh.
If you forget the phone number, call 555-1212.
If you go shopping for food, don't forget to buy fish.
If you get some fresh air, you'll feel better.
If you don't finish your homework, you can't watch TV.

Step 3 Working individually or with a partner, students write endings to three of the sentence beginnings on the left. Have some students read their sentences aloud. You may want to see how many different ways different students completed a particular sentence. Monitor the pronunciation of the sound /f/ and the phrasing and intonation when students read their sentences.

G Spelling

The pronunciation of the vowel in words that end with the spelling *gh* pronounced as /f/ is likely to cause confusion.

/æ/   laugh
/ʌ/   enough, rough, tough
/ɔ/   cough

In the words above, the letters *gh* spell the sound /f/, but in many other words, *gh* is silent (it does not make the sound /f/). The spelling *ough* may be pronounced as /ɔ/ (*thought, bought,* etc.), /ow/ (*though*), /uw/ (*through*), or /aw/ (*bough*). The spelling *augh* is usually pronounced /ɔ/ (*caught, taught,* etc.).

H Common Expressions See Overview, p. xii.

Further Practice

Students read the following groups of words from the board and say which word doesn't belong in each group and why.

1.	wife	knife	father	grandfather	(knife)
2.	fifty	four	first	fifteen	(first)
3.	fly	fish	fruit	beef	(fly)
4.	football	foot	finger	face	(football)
5.	left	fought	fell	forget	(forget: present tense)
6.	funny	fat	friend	careful	(friend: noun)

Linking Pronunciation with Other Classwork

Tie pronunciation in with practice of:

1. Conditional sentences using *if.*

2. The words *before, after* (*that*), *first,* and *finally* used in describing a sequence of events or explaining the steps involved in doing something.

Word Stress Practice

Write large and small circles on the board showing these three stress patterns:

A ● •   B • ●   C ● • •

Read the following words. Students say whether they heard stress pattern A, B, or C.

1. prefer (B)	6. forget (B)
2. myself (B)	7. difficult (C)
3. cheerful (A)	8. finished (A)
4. difference (C)	9. enough (B)
5. comfortable (C)	10. photograph (C)

UNIT 38 /v/ • very Weak and Strong Pronunciations of *have*

Student Difficulties

The sound /v/ is difficult for speakers of Arabic, Chinese, Japanese, Hindi, Punjabi and other Indian languages, Korean, Spanish, Thai, Lao, and Khmer.

■ Many students, such as speakers of Arabic, tend to substitute /f/ for /v/. Chinese speakers may also substitute /w/.

■ Japanese, Korean, and Spanish speakers often replace /v/ with /b/, pronouncing *very* as *berry*. Spanish speakers may pronounce both the letters *b* and *v* as a /b/ sound at the beginning of a word, but as a sound closer to /v/ – but made with the two lips, rather than the lips and teeth – between vowels.

- Dutch, German, and Turkish speakers may also have difficulty with the sound, especially at the end of words, where /v/ is likely to be replaced by /f/, so that *leave* sounds like *leaf*.

- Many students, including speakers of German, Indian languages, Russian, Thai, Farsi, Turkish, and Scandinavian languages, confuse /v/ and /w/, most often replacing /w/ with /v/, but sometimes replacing /v/ with /w/ or producing a sound somewhere between the two.

Making the Sound

Have students read the directions for making the sound /v/ as they listen to the audio and look at the illustrations.

If students confuse /v/ and /f/, emphasize the use of the voice in /v/ but not in /f/. Students can place their fingers on their throats to feel the voicing. They should feel their lower lips vibrate when they say /v/ but not when they say /f/. Also note that a lot of air is produced when saying /f/, but not when saying /v/.

For students who confuse /b/ and /v/, contrast the lip positions, using the illustrations in the Student's Book (see Unit 23) or a physical demonstration. Tell students to press their lips together for /b/, but to "bite" the lower lip with their teeth to say /v/. Also show that /v/ can be a long sound (/vvvv/) but /b/ cannot.

For students who confuse /v/ and /w/, contrasting the lip positions is helpful (see Unit 39). Encourage students who confuse /v/ with /b/ or /w/ to practice in front of a mirror.

A and B **Word Pairs 1 and 2** See Overview, p. viii.

Word pairs for additional practice:

/b/ – /v/: berry/very, bet/vet, bat/vat, bent/vent, bolts/volts, bow/vow, marble/marvel, cupboard/covered, curb/curve

/f/ – /v/: ferry/very, fee/V, feel/veal, fail/veil, fast/vast, fault/vault, fat/vat, surface/service, refuse/reviews, rifle/rival, safe/save, half/halve, life/live (adj.), belief/believe, proof/prove

C **Test Yourself** See Overview, p. ix.

Step 1

ANSWERS		
1. boat	3. vine	5. belief
2. cabs	4. leaf	6. van

Step 2

ANSWERS
1. One person – one vote.
2. I want to get the best.
3. This room has a few.
4. Do you want to leave?
5. We use our fan in the summer.
6. We saw two calves on the road.

Step 3 In contrasting the sounds /f/ and /v/ at the end of words, make sure that students make the vowel longer before /v/.

D **Vocabulary** See Overview, p. ix.

Step 1 Students listen and repeat words from the dialog in task E.

Step 2 Students look at the picture and describe it, using as many words with the sound /v/ as they can. Write any new words with /v/ on the board; students can add these to the list in step 1. Additional words and phrases might include: *village, driving a van, waving, vine, five leaves, seven roofs, evening.*

With less advanced students, you may want to give them a paragraph (e.g., on a handout) to help with describing the picture. Students read the paragraph below aloud, choosing the correct words to describe the picture.

This is a picture of a woman (arriving at / leaving) a village in the (forest / valley). She's driving a (bus / van) and (waving / laughing). It's a beautiful (evening / afternoon), but it's November, and the leaves have fallen from the (fir tree / vine). There are (five / seven) leaves on the ground.

After one or two volunteers read the paragraph aloud, ask one or more students to describe the picture without looking at the paragraph.

E **Dialog** See Overview, pp. ix–x.

Step 1 Students often fail to notice final consonants and reduced words. If their native language does not allow many different consonants at the ends of words, they may tend to drop final consonants in English. The task here focuses attention on differences in verb tense signaled by final consonants and reduced forms.

Have students work with a partner to circle the correct words in parentheses. Encourage them to say the words aloud as they circle them.

Step 2

ANSWERS	
Vivian	How long <u>have you lived</u> here?
Victor	Five and a half years. <u>We moved</u> here on November first.
Vivian	You have a fantastic view.
Victor	Thanks. Look, Vivian, you can see the river down in the valley.
Vivian	It's a beautiful view. <u>I've traveled</u> all over, and this is one of my very favorite places.
Victor	Yes, <u>I love</u> living here.
Vivian	And <u>I love</u> visiting!

F Weak and Strong Pronunciation of *have*

Background notes Native speakers generally use contractions or weak forms where possible. After a pronoun, the auxiliary *have* is normally contracted to *-'ve,* pronounced as the sound /v/ (e.g., *I've* / ɑyv/). In speech, though not usually in writing, the contracted form is also used after *Wh-* words (e.g., "How've you been?"). Elsewhere, the auxiliary *have* is usually unstressed and has the weak pronunciation /əv/ when it comes after another word. Note that unstressed words beginning with *h*, like auxiliary *have*, often lose the /h/ sound after another word (see Unit 40, task E). At the beginning of a question, either a strong (/hæv/) or weak (/həv/) pronunciation can be used. At the end of a clause or sentence, or when it is a main verb rather than an auxiliary, *have* has a strong pronunciation with a clearer vowel sound: *Yes, I have* (/hæv/). The negative contraction *haven't* always has a strong pronunciation. Note that *has* follows the same patterns: *She's traveled a lot. / How long has* /əz/ *he lived there? / He has* /hæz/ *a great view.*

Students listen and repeat three pronunciations of *have.* You may want to write the weak form as a contraction to illustrate the pronunciation: *How long've you lived here?*

Extra practice Give students extra practice listening for the contraction *'ve.* Read sentences like the following aloud, choosing a word from the word pair. Students can also practice this with a partner.

1. (We / We've) lived in Vancouver for five years.
2. (We / We've) traveled to seven countries.
3. (I / I've) never liked driving.
4. (I / I've) worked as a cab driver.
5. (I / I've) always loved reading.
6. (They / They've) saved over $500.

G Conversation Practice

Step 1 Students use the prompts to make questions with *have.* In some of the questions, *have* is used as an auxiliary with another verb, but in other questions, *have* is the main verb. Make sure students understand that not all the questions will be formed the same way. You may want to do the first two items together with the whole class.

With less advanced students, check that they can form all the questions correctly and know where to use the weak pronunciation of *have* before they practice in pairs. Move around the room as students practice, checking the pronunciation of *have* and other words with the sound /v/. Remind students, if necessary, to link the weak pronunciation of *have* in items 1 and 6 to the word before it.

ANSWERS
1. How long <u>have you</u> lived here?
2. <u>Do you have</u> a house or an apartment?
3. <u>Do you have</u> a good view from your house?
4. <u>Have you</u> lived in a lot of places?
5. <u>Have you</u> traveled a lot?
6. How many countries <u>have you</u> visited?

Steps 2 and 3 Students work in pairs to write short conversations similar to the dialog in task E and then practice the conversations with their partner. Ask for volunteers to perform their dialogs for the class at the end.

H Spelling

The sound /v/ is written with the letter *v*, except in the word *of.* Note that the letter *v* is never doubled, even after a vowel like /ɪ/, /ɛ/, or /æ/, as in *river, giving, never,* or *having* (compare *dinner, sitting, better, happen*).

Call attention to the fact that when the sound /v/ comes at the end of a word, the letter *e* is added in the spelling, even in words with the vowels /ɪ/, /æ/, and /ʌ/, as in *give, have,* and *love.*

Note that the word *have* is pronounced with the sound /f/ in *have to.*

1 Common Expressions See Overview, p. xii.

Further Practice

1. Related words ending in /f/ and /v/: Nouns ending in the sound /f/ often change the /f/ to /v/ in the plural (*leaf – leaves, knife – knives, shelf – shelves,* etc.) or have related verbs ending in the sound /v/ (*belief – believe, proof – proves, life – lives,* etc.). See the Unit 38 Web Site Worksheet (at www.cambridge.org/pp/student) for practice.

2. If students confuse the sounds /b/ and /v/, dictate scrambled spellings of words with the letters *b* or *v*, for example:

   RYVE (very)   VEMO (move)

   ABBY (baby)   ISTIV (visit)

   BULE (blue)

   Students unscramble the words. To check the answers, they dictate the words or the spellings of the words to a student who writes the answers on the board.

Linking Pronunciation with Other Classwork

Tie pronunciation in with practice of:

1. Present perfect:

   a. "How long have you lived / been here?" "Have you lived here for a long time?" "How long have you been studying English?"

   b. Talking about past experience: "Have you ever . . . ?" "Yes, I have / No, I haven't." "I've never . . ." (see Unit 45 under *Linking Pronunciation with Other Classwork*)

2. *very*: for example, in contrasting *very* and *too*

3. Modal perfect: *should have / shouldn't have / could have / couldn't have.* Note that after a modal, *have* can be reduced to just /ə/; for example, *should have* is often pronounced like "shoulda" in relaxed speech.

Word Stress and Syllable Practice

Give students the list of words below. Ask them to first write the number of syllables in the space and then underline the stressed syllable, if the word has more than one syllable.

1. <u>val</u>ley	2	6. moved	1
2. <u>vis</u>it	2	7. view	1
3. loves	1	8. No<u>vem</u>ber	3
4. <u>eve</u>ning	2	9. <u>fa</u>vorite	2
5. be<u>lieve</u>	2	10. <u>trav</u>eled	2

UNIT 39 /w/ • wet   *Wh-* Questions with Rising Intonation

Student Difficulties

Speakers of many languages, including German, Dutch, Hebrew, Hungarian, Turkish, Farsi, Japanese, Spanish, Portuguese, Greek, and Indian, Slavic, and Scandinavian languages, tend to have difficulty with this sound.

- Many learners, including speakers of German, Slavic and Scandinavian languages, Turkish, and sometimes Italian, replace /w/ with /v/, pronouncing *west* as *vest*, but they may also sometimes replace /v/ with /w/, pronouncing *vest* as *west.*

- Dutch, Lao, and Farsi speakers also confuse /w/ and /v/ or make an intermediate sound for both.

- Spanish and Greek speakers may replace /w/ with /gw/, /g/, or a similar sound, saying *good* for *wood* or *would.*

- Some students may confuse /w/ with /r/ or use a sound resembling /b/.

- Speakers of Spanish, Japanese, and some other Asian languages have particular difficulty in pronouncing /w/ when it is followed by /uw/ or /ʊ/, as in *woman.*

Even speakers who do not have trouble with the sound /w/ in isolation may have difficulty saying it in clusters such as /tw/, /kw/, /sw/, or /skw/, as in *twenty, quiet, sweater,* or *squirrel*.

Making the Sound

Have students read the directions for making the sound /w/ as they listen to the audio and look at the illustrations. The sound /w/ is a glide sound. It is close to the English sound /uw/. Have students first practice /uw/. Tell them to make their lips round and hard for /w/. The sound /w/ is a short sound. The lips quickly move into position for the next sound.

For many students, seeing the correct lip position through both physical demonstration and diagrams is helpful. If students tend to confuse /w/ and /v/, have them compare the lip diagram in this unit with the lip diagram shown for /v/ in Unit 38. Students who replace /w/ with /v/ should be careful not to let their bottom lip touch their upper teeth at all for /w/.

It may also be helpful to have students start by saying /uw/ smoothly before vowels (for example, "you – /uw/ – all – wall," "you – /uw/ – ill – will") or to practice /w/ after a word ending in /uw/, for example *new words, two weeks*.

Variation in the sound Some North American speakers pronounce the *wh* in *what, where, when,* and so on, as the sound /hw/, distinguishing between words like *which* (with /hw/) and *witch* (with /w/). Most speakers, however, pronounce the *wh* spelling as /w/. It is probably best for students to follow their teacher's pronunciation model. This book does not practice the sound /hw/. Even among speakers who distinguish between the sounds /w/ and /hw/, using /w/ in place of /hw/ is very unlikely to cause misunderstandings.

A Word Pairs See Overview, p. viii.

Word pairs for additional practice:

/v/ – /w/: verse/worse, veal/wheel, vent/went, vile/while, vault/Walt, veered/weird, visor/wiser

/b/ – /w/: ball/wall, B (*or* be)/we, best/west, bell/ well, bill/will, bird/word, bent/went, buy/ Y (*or* why), bet/wet, big/wig, bake/wake, bear/wear, born/worn

/g/ – /w/: good/wood (*or* would), gun/won (*or* one), guest/west, gate/wait, gave/wave, get/ wet, guide/wide

B Test Yourself See Overview, p. ix.

Step 1

ANSWERS

1. S (V, V)
2. D (wine, vine)
3. S (wet, wet)
4. S (veil, veil)
5. D (vest, west)
6. D (worse, verse)

Step 2

ANSWERS

1. Does this say "we"?
2. Look for it in the vest.
3. What kind of vine is this?
4. The whales were gray.
5. The other book was worse.
6. I think she's a vet.

C Vocabulary See Overview, p. ix.

Step 1 Go over the example. Make sure students understand that they should focus on the sound, not the spelling, when counting.

Step 2 Play the audio again. After students repeat and check their answers, ask them to list the different spellings of the sound /w/ here (*w* as in *wool, o* as in *one, u* as in *quiet*).

Note that *w* does not have the sound /w/ in *saw*; it is just part of the *aw* spelling for the vowel /ɔ/. Also note that *wh* has the sound /h/ rather than /w/ in *whole, who,* and words formed from *who* (e.g., *whose*).

ANSWERS

2	a heavy wool sweater
1	very windy
2	went for a walk
1	near the highway
0	the whole day
2	watched the squirrels
1	around one
1	saw him on Wednesday
1	twelve
2	it was very quiet
2	walking in the woods
3	we walked quickly

D Dialog See Overview, pp. ix–x.

Step 1 Have students work with a partner to fill in the blanks. Encourage them to say the words aloud as they fill them in.

Step 2 If students tend to confuse the sounds /v/ and /w/, you may want to check their pronunciation of words with /v/: *very, heavy, love, everywhere, twelve.*

ANSWERS

Valerie	What's happening with William? Did you see him this week?
Wendy	Yes, I saw him on Wednesday. We went for a walk.
Valerie	What did you do?
Wendy	I said we went for a walk.
Valerie	Where did you walk?
Wendy	In the woods.
Valerie	Where?
Wendy	In the woods. You know, the woods near the highway.
Valerie	Wasn't it cold and wet on Wednesday?
Wendy	Well, it was cold and very windy, but not wet. I wore a heavy wool sweater, and we walked quickly to keep warm.
Valerie	I love walking in the woods. It's so peaceful and quiet.
Wendy	Yeah, it was very quiet once we got away from the highway. There were birds and squirrels everywhere.
Valerie	Wow, it sounds wonderful. Did you spend the whole day in the woods?
Wendy	No. William had to work in the afternoon. I went home around one.
Valerie	What did you do for lunch?
Wendy	We brought sandwiches with us. We stopped for lunch around twelve, and we sat and watched the squirrels for a while, but it was too windy to sit long.
Valerie	Well, it sounds like a very nice walk, anyway.
Wendy	It was.

E *Wh-* Questions with Rising Intonation

Background notes *Wh-* questions usually have falling intonation when they ask for new information. The main stress and intonation change typically go on the last important word in the sentence; the intonation jumps up on the stressed syllable of that word and then continues to fall until the end of the question. *Wh-* questions are often said with rising intonation to ask someone to repeat or to express surprise. When a *Wh-* question has rising intonation, the *Wh-* word has the main stress, with the rise in intonation starting on that word and continuing until the end of the question. Being able to ask someone to repeat information that you didn't hear clearly or understand is, of course, very useful for a language learner.

Steps 1 and 2 Have students listen to the two short conversations illustrating the use of the two intonation patterns. Play the audio again and have students repeat the questions. Check that they use the correct stress as well as intonation in each question. Note that if the rising intonation in the second *Wh-* question rises too sharply or too high, it may suggest disbelief or surprise rather than a simple request for repetition. If students have difficulty with the stress or intonation, write the sentence on the board using capital letters for stressed syllables and making the words curve up or down according to the intonation.

F Conversation Practice

Step 1 Working in pairs, students draw the appropriate arrow for each of B's questions – falling if B is asking for new information, rising if B is asking A to repeat. Go over the first two lines that A and B say in the conversation as an example.

Step 2 After students listen to the recording and check their answers, have them practice saying the conversation with a partner. Alternatively, have them practice in groups of three, with one person monitoring the intonation and students switching roles. After students practice, ask for a few volunteers to say the conversation. Encourage students to look up when they say their lines.

A I'm going to a wedding this weekend.

B What? (⤴)

A I'm going to a wedding.

B Who's getting married? (⤵)

A Willa.

B Who? (⤴)

A Willa – a woman I work with.

B When did you say the wedding was? (⤴)

A This weekend.

B When? (⤵)

A Sunday at twelve.

B What are you going to wear? (⤵)

A A black-and-white wool suit.

Extra practice For practice in listening for the two intonation patterns in *Wh-* questions, see the Unit 39 Web Site Worksheet (at www.cambridge.org/pp/student).

G Spelling

1. Students may find the spellings of /w/ with a vowel letter (*u* or *o*) confusing. Note that the *u* in *qu* regularly represents the sound /w/, but that the *u* in *gu* and *su* has the sound /w/ only in a few words.

2. The letter *w* is silent in some common words. Practice the words with silent *w* in the Student's Book with the class. At a later time, give students a list of words such as the one below. Ask them to draw a line through the silent *w*'s.

   1. sweater
   2. two
   3. write
   4. twelve
   5. whole
   6. answer
   7. which
   8. woman
   9. wrong
   10. whose

H Common Expressions See Overview, p. xii.

Further Practice

1. Give students questions such as those below, and ask them to fill in the blank with one of these *Wh-* words: *what, when, where,* or *why*. (There may be more than one correct choice.) Then have students practice asking and answering the questions in groups of three or four people. If they don't hear someone's answer, they should use a *Wh-* question with rising intonation to ask the person to repeat.

_____ do you like to go for walks?

_____ kind of weather do you like?

_____ do you like to do in the winter?

_____ is your favorite thing to wear?

_____ do you work?

_____ do you want to learn English?

_____ in the world would you most like to live?

2. Practice linking with /w/. The sound /w/ is used to link words ending in the sounds /ow/, /uw/, and /ɑw/, (sounds that end in /w/) to a vowel sound at the beginning of the next word. For example:

   Go away!   Who is it?   How are you?

Linking Pronunciation with Other Classwork

Tie pronunciation in with practice of:

1. Questions with *what, where, when, which, why*.

2. Talking about the weather: For example, "What's the weather like in . . . ?" "It's (very) warm / wet / windy."

3. Questions with *will* or *would*, for example in offering things: "Would you like some . . . ?" "What would you like to drink?"

4. Identifying individual things or people using *which one*; for example:

   a. identifying items when shopping: "Which one do you want?" "This one / the one with the . . ."

   b. identifying people in a photograph: "Which one is your mother?" "The one with the red sweater."

Word Stress Practice

Read the following pairs of words. Students indicate whether the stress pattern for the two words is the same or different.

1. highway, away (D)
2. sandwiches, wonderful (S)
3. Wednesday, window (S)
4. sweater, windy (S)
5. around, quiet (D)
6. anyway, everywhere (S)

/h/ • how   Dropped /h/; Intonation in Exclamations

Student Difficulties

The sound /h/, which occurs very frequently in such common words as *he, her, his, have, how,* and *who,* is very difficult for some students to pronounce.

■ Speakers of French, Portuguese, Italian, Hebrew, and some African languages, as well as some speakers of Turkish, tend to omit the sound /h/ or overcompensate by adding it unnecessarily in front of words beginning with a vowel. Learners tend to put /h/ in the wrong place more frequently as they get more self-conscious about not saying this sound when they should. Encourage those who omit /h/ to connect words smoothly in phrases, without stopping their breath.

■ Speakers of Greek, Spanish, Slavic languages, Arabic, and Chinese tend to pronounce /h/ as a harsh sound, like the non-English sound /x/ in *Bach.*

■ Japanese speakers tend to confuse the sound /h/ with /f/ when it occurs before back vowels like /uw/, but they may confuse it with /ʃ/ before /iy/ or /ɪ/. Chinese speakers also often confuse the sounds /s/, /ʃ/, and /h/ when they occur before the sounds /iy/ or /ɪ/. This confusion is particularly noticeable with the words *he* and *she.*

Making the Sound

Have students read the directions for making the sound /h/ as they listen to the audio and look at the illustrations. Note that the exact position of the tongue and lips for /h/ depends on the sound that follows.

For students who tend to omit /h/, emphasize the fact that a lot of air is needed to produce this sound.

For students who tend to pronounce /h/ as a harsh sound, like the non-English sound /x/ in *Bach*, emphasize the fact that the tongue is not used in producing /h/. Practicing /h/ first before vowels made with the tongue low in the mouth will help students keep the back of the tongue down. Tell them to keep the tongue down as they say *hot, happy,* and *how.* Show that a lot of air is

needed to make /h/. Hold a strip of paper in front of your mouth and make the sounds /x/ and /h/ to show the difference in effect.

For students who tend to confuse /h/ with /ʃ/ before /iy/ or /ɪ/, call attention to the difference in mouth positions. For /h/ before /iy/ or /ɪ/, the tongue is arched, and the tip of the tongue touches the lower teeth. For /ʃ/ (see Unit 31, *Making the Sound*), the front of the tongue is grooved, and the tip does not touch the lower teeth. The lips for /h/ are slightly spread; for /ʃ/ they are slightly rounded.

A Word Pairs See Overview, p. viii.

Word pairs for additional practice:

(no /h/) – /h/: I/high, art/heart, ate/hate, ill/hill, all/hall, and/hand, ear/hear, ow!/how, it/hit, at/hat, Ed/head, I'd/hide, eel/heel, arm/harm

/ʃ/ – /h/: she/he, she's/he's, sheet/heat, ship/hip, sheep/heap, sheer/hear, she'll/he'll (*or* heel), she'd/he'd

B Test Yourself See Overview, p. ix.

Step 1

ANSWERS		
1. I	3. heat	5. hate
2. old	4. hair	6. art

Step 2

ANSWERS
1. It was <u>high</u>.
2. What nice clean <u>air</u>!
3. Did you <u>heat</u> the soup?
4. What did they say about his <u>art</u>?
5. I <u>hate</u> eggs for breakfast.
6. There's something wrong with my <u>hearing</u>.

C Vocabulary See Overview, p. ix.

Step 1 The silent letter *h* is difficult for many students, who may be confused about when to pronounce /h/ and when not to. Explain that sometimes the letter *h* does not have the sound

/h/. Working in pairs, students make an *X* through the *h*'s that are usually silent. Go over the example.

Step 2 Some native speakers pronounce the *h* in *vehicle*. In the other words below, however, the *h* is always silent. Point out that *hours* is pronounced like *ours*.

D **Dialog** See Overview, pp. ix–x.

Step 1 Have students work with a partner to fill in the blanks. Encourage them to say the words aloud as they fill them in

Step 2 If students tend to insert an extra /h/ sound in words beginning with a vowel, check the pronunciation of words and phrases like *hi, Ellen; how awful; a horrible accident; having an operation; an ambulance.*

Helen	I <u>hope</u> Henry will be all right.
Ellen	I hope so, too.

Extra practice Use the dialog to practice questions with *how, who, who's,* and *whose.* For example, have students choose the correct word to begin questions like these:

_____ had an accident?

_____ did it happen?

_____ husband had an accident?

_____ in the hospital?

E **Dropped /h/**

The sound /h/ is often dropped in unstressed words like *he, her, have,* and *his* in connected speech. It is not dropped at the beginning of a sentence or after a pause.

Step 1 Students repeat phrases and sentences in which an /h/ sound is dropped. Make sure that they link the words together when they drop the /h/: "wuzzy" for *was he,* "hit'im" for *hit him.* The sound /h/ is dropped only if the words are linked together.

Step 2 Students repeat sentences in which /h/ is not dropped. In the second sentence, the /h/ could be dropped if the speaker does not pause after the word *No.*

Extra practice Play the recording of the dialog in task D again. Ask students to listen and make an *X* through the *h*'s that are not pronounced in the words *he, his,* and *him.* Or do this together with the class, pointing out places where the /h/ is dropped (e.g., *on his way home from work, Was he hurt?, hit him from behind*).

F **Intonation in Exclamation**

Background notes Exclamations often have a wider intonation range than ordinary statements. In an exclamation, the voice usually rises to a higher pitch on the last stressed syllable than it does in an ordinary statement, followed by a sharply falling tone. Exclamations expressing surprise and dismay, like the ones practiced here, are also often said rather slowly, with the stressed vowels prolonged.

The intonation of many learners may tend to sound flat to native English speakers. Reasons for this may include lack of confidence, feeling inhibited, differences in intonation patterns in their own languages, or simply lack of attention to intonation because of focus on other elements of speech.

Model the intonation. If students do not use a wide enough range of intonation, encourage them to exaggerate the intonation and to make the stressed vowels extra long. You can use hand gestures or draw arrows on the board to compare the restricted range they are using and the wider range they should be using. Or write examples on the board like this to show the intonation:

$$\text{HOR}_{ri}{}_{bl}{}_{e} \qquad \text{AW}_{fu}{}_{l}$$

Extra practice With more advanced students, you may want to contrast intonation in which the voice jumps up high and falls, to show strong feeling, and flat intonation, often used to show sarcasm. Compare, for example:

A I got the job!   **A** I can't find the tickets.

B Great!   **B** Great.

If the voice is flat and does not go up high on strong adjectives like *great* or *wonderful*, it can sound like you don't mean what you're saying. It can even sound like you mean the opposite.

G Conversation Practice

Step 1 Students listen to the example and then practice the conversation in pairs, substituting a name from the first column in the first line, a sentence from the second column in the third line, and an exclamation from task F in the last line. Students should take turns being A and B.

Step 2

> **ANSWERS**
>
> The sound /h/ could be dropped in:
> She fell off a horse and hit <u>h</u>er head.
> He hurt both <u>h</u>is <u>h</u>ands and can't hold anything.
> She and <u>h</u>er husband bought a huge house in Hawaii.
> A helicopter hit <u>h</u>is house.
> He spent <u>h</u>is whole vacation in the hospital.

H Spelling

The sound /h/ is usually spelled with the letter *h*. The letter *h* also occurs in the combinations *sh*,

ch, th, ph, and *wh,* where it does not usually have the sound /h/, with a few exceptions (*whole, who,* words derived from *who,* and words like *hothouse* in which these letters belong to different word parts).

For later review, give students a list such as the one below. Ask them which words have the sound /h/.

1. hour	6. how
2. hear	7. who
3. whole	8. hole
4. unhappy	9. phone
5. why	10. honest

I **Common Expressions** See Overview, p. xii.

Further Practice

Many learners have trouble distinguishing unstressed pronouns in rapid conversation, especially when the /h/ is dropped in pronouns like *he, him, his,* and *her.* To give students practice in listening for reduced pronouns, write sentences such as "Give _____ the book" and "I saw _____ brother" on the board. Tell students to listen and fill in the blank with the word they hear. Read each sentence a few times, varying the pronoun. Make sure to read the sentences rapidly, using reduced forms, for example:

1. Give her the book.	4. I saw your brother.
2. Give him the book.	5. I saw her brother.
3. Give her the book.	6. I saw his brother.

Linking Pronunciation with Other Classwork

Tie pronunciation in with practice of:

1. Questions beginning with *how, who, how much, how many, how often.*

2. Questions beginning with *whose* and answers with the possessive pronouns *his / hers.*

3. The greetings *Hi, Hello,* and *How are you?*

4. Exclamations beginning with *how.*

Word Stress Practice

Write large and small circles on the board showing these four stress patterns:

A ● •   B • ●   C ● • •   D • ● •

Read the following words. Students say whether they heard stress pattern A, B, C, or D.

1. hospital (C)
2. vehicle (C)
3. behind (B)
4. happened (A)
5. unhappy (D)

6. husband (A)
7. herself (B)
8. horrible (C)
9. exhausted (D)
10. accident (C)

UNIT 41 /θ/ • think   Using Stress and Intonation to Show Surprise

Student Difficulties

Nearly all learners, except speakers of Greek and Castilian Spanish, have great difficulty with the sound /θ/, usually replacing it with /s/, /t/, or /f/. Students find the sound particularly difficult to pronounce in final consonant clusters, as in *fifth, sixth,* or *months.* Note that some ordinal numbers contain very difficult final clusters. Even native English speakers often simplify these in some way, for example, pronouncing *fifth* as /fɪθ/. It is probably best not to insist that students carefully pronounce every sound in these clusters.

Making the Sound

Have students read the directions for making the sound /θ/ as they listen to the audio and look at the illustrations.

Showing students the tongue position is important in teaching the sound /θ/. Give students a physical demonstration of how to make the sound, showing them how the tip of your tongue is placed between your teeth, lightly touching the top teeth. Students may resist doing this, considering it to be crude or embarrassing to stick their tongue out. Point out that the tongue protrudes just slightly. If possible, have students use small hand mirrors to check their tongue position. You can use the symbol for the sound as a visual reminder of the mouth position, with the line across the middle of the symbol /θ/ representing the tongue protruding between the teeth.

Spend some time practicing the sound /θ/ in isolation. Demonstrating how the sound can be prolonged (by saying it for about five seconds without stopping) helps students distinguish it from /t/. Knowing that the sound they are aiming at is a quiet sound may also help students.

A and B Word Pairs 1 and 2

See Overview, p. viii.

Word pairs for additional practice:

/s/ – /θ/: sank/thank, sing/thing, seem/theme, sin/thin, saw/thaw, sigh/thigh, sought/ thought, mass/math, bass/bath, face/ faith, moss/moth, worse/worth

/t/ – /θ/: tick/thick, tin/thin, taught/thought, team/ theme, true/through, pat/path, mat/math, boat/both, boot/booth, tent/tenth, debt/ death, mitt/myth, fort/fourth, wit/with, brought/broth

/f/ – /θ/: fought/thought, first/thirst, free/three, fin/thin, Fred/thread, frill/thrill, froze/ throws, deaf/death, roof/Ruth, miff/myth

C Test Yourself See Overview, p. ix.

Step 1

ANSWERS		
1. think	3. tree	5. sick
2. mouse	4. bath	6. thank

Step 2

ANSWERS

1. I hope they're not too <u>thick</u>.
2. Send <u>tanks</u>.
3. She <u>thought</u> for a long time.
4. I always <u>sink</u> in the pool.
5. It's not <u>true</u>, is it?
6. The <u>bath</u> was very small.

D **Vocabulary** See Overview, p. ix.

Check stress in the words *anything* and *something*. Both words are stressed on the first syllable.

Extra practice Ask questions that can be answered by words in tasks A, B, C, and D, for example: "What's the opposite of *thin*?" (thick); "What's the opposite of *nothing*?" (something).

E **Dialog** See Overview, pp. ix–x.

Step 1 In the dialog, Beth and Ethan are talking about Kathy Roth and her husband. Call attention to the title and the meaning of the word *gossip* (talk about other people's private lives, often not meant in a friendly way).

Review the features that make the most important word in a sentence stand out: The stressed syllable of this word is loud and slow and the intonation changes (jumps up or down) on this word (see Unit 5, task E).

Students listen to the dialog and underline the most important word in the numbered sentences. You may need to pause the recording to give them time to do this. The numbered sentences are all said by Ethan, who shows surprise at what Beth tells him.

Step 2 Play the recording of the dialog again. Point out or elicit that Ethan puts strong stress on the information that contrasts with (or is different from) what Beth said.

ANSWERS

1. I thought she was <u>forty</u>-three.
2. I thought it was last <u>month</u>.
3. I thought he was her <u>fourth</u> husband.
4. I thought it was worth about <u>one</u> hundred thousand dollars.
5. I thought he was an <u>athlete</u>.

F **Using Stress and Intonation to Show Surprise**

Background notes To express interest in what someone has said, people often use a short question with rising intonation, for example, "I spoke to Kathy." "Did you?" To express surprise, the intonation rises sharply, finishing at a high pitch: **Is** she?

In neutral English sentence stress, the last important word in the sentence usually has the main stress. But if the speaker wants to emphasize something or make a contrast, the main stress and intonation change goes on the information being contrasted or emphasized (see Unit 11, task F).

Step 1 Students listen to short questions used to express interest and surprise. Note that the word *be* is stressed in the question. You may want to point out that the form of the verb *be* in B's question agrees with the form in A's sentence.

Step 2 Students listen to and repeat two exchanges between A and B. Point out that B makes the word that contrasts with what A said extra loud and slow and says it at a high pitch.

Extra practice Prepare a paper handout with the scrambled conversations below.

Working with a partner, students match each sentence in column A with the best response in column B. When they find the best response, they should underline the most important word in the sentence in column B. (The most important word is already underlined in the sentences in column A.)

Students practice the short conversations with their partner.

A	**B**
His birthday was last <u>month</u>.	Is it? I thought it was 533-4136.
Ethan is thirty-<u>three</u>.	Was it? I thought it was <u>next</u> month.
Beth was at the <u>theater</u>.	Are you? I thought you drank something.
My house is <u>north</u> of here.	Is it? I thought it was worth three thousand dollars.
My birthday is May <u>30</u>th.	Is he? I thought he was thirty-six.
Their phone number is 533-412<u>6</u>.	Is it? I thought it was south of here.
My car is only worth three hundred <u>dollars</u>.	Was she? I thought she was at Ethan's house.
The math test is on <u>Tuesday</u>.	Is it? I thought it was June 30th.
I'm so <u>thirsty</u>.	Is it? I thought it was on Thursday.

G Conversation Practice

When a person says something that is not correct and you want to correct it, you put extra stress on the correct information. The extra stress is like highlighting or underlining in writing. Each of the sentences here has information that is not correct. Explain the task: Student A says the incorrect sentence. Student B should show surprise with a short question ("Is it?" "Was it?" etc.) and correct the mistake. Students should switch roles while they practice. Have students listen to the example on the recording before they begin. You may also want to model the example with a student, or have students start by practicing the example with their partner.

If necessary for your students, go over the form of B's short questions before they practice in pairs. Note that the subject and verb in the short question need to agree with the subject and verb in the sentence: *Is it?* (sentences 1, 2, 4, 6, 7), *Are there?* (sentence 3), *Was she?* (sentence 5), *Was it?* (sentence 8).

While students practice, move around the room monitoring the pronunciation of the sound /θ/ and making sure student B makes the correct word stand out. If necessary, remind students to make the information that is different stand out. Encourage student A to read each sentence silently first and then say it aloud without reading word by word from the book.

H Spelling

See the notes for Unit 42, task H.

I Common Expressions See Overview, p. xii.

Further Practice

Students listen to the following sentences read by the teacher and respond to each with this sentence: "Oh, no. Their house is worth thirty thousand dollars." Students should stress the appropriate word in the response to each of the teacher's sentences.

Teacher's sentences:

a. The Roths' house is worth thirty thousand euros.

b. The Roths' house is worth thirty million dollars.

c. The Roths' house is worth sixty thousand dollars.

d. The Roths' house isn't worth thirty thousand dollars.

e. The Roths' car is worth thirty thousand dollars.

Linking Pronunciation with Other Classwork

Tie pronunciation in with practice of:

1. Ordinal numbers, for example, in practicing dates, fractions, or the results of a race. To practice dates using birthdays, have students give their birthdays (month and ordinal number) while a student at the board writes the dates down. After all students have given their birthdays, students try to remember whose birthday was on which date.

2. Directions: For example, use familiar place names to practice "Is it north or south of here?" "What direction is it (in)?" (north, south, southeast, etc.)

3. Structures with *anything, something, nothing, everything*.

4. Saying "Thank you."

5. Expressing opinions, beginning with *I think*.

Word Stress Practice

Ask students to find at least five words in the unit that have the strong stress on the first syllable. (Answers might include: *thousand, thirsty, Thursday, author, anything, something, birthday, athlete, thank you*.)

Remind students, or elicit, that most words in English have stress on the first syllable.

/ð/ • the other   Weak Pronunciations for *the* and *than*

Student Difficulties

Nearly all students except Greek and Spanish speakers have great difficulty with the sound /ð/. They usually replace it with /z/, /d/, or sometimes /v/, for example, pronouncing *then* as *Zen* or *den* or *clothing* as "cloving." Japanese speakers may also substitute /dʒ/ before the vowel /iy/ or /ɪ/, saying *this* as "jis." Consonant clusters with /ð/, as in *bathed* or *bathes*, are particularly troublesome; fortunately, these are not very common in English.

Spanish speakers should not have difficulty making the sound /ð/, but since the letter *d* in Spanish is pronounced as the sound /d/ at the beginning of a word and as /ð/ between vowels, they may be confused about the difference between the sounds /d/ and /ð/ in English.

Making the Sound

Have students read the directions for making the sound /ð/ as they listen to the audio and look at the illustrations. Point out that the sound /ð/ occurs in some very common words like *the, this, that,* and *other.*

As with the sound /θ/ in Unit 41 (see *Making the Sound*) showing students the tongue position is very helpful. When practicing the sound in isolation, show how the voice is used to produce /ð/. Demonstrating that /ð/ can be a long sound (/ðððð/) also helps students to distinguish it from /d/.

A and B Word Pairs 1 and 2

See Overview, p. viii.

Word pairs for additional practice:

/d/ – /ð/: D's/these, dough/though, Dave/they've, Dan/than, letter/leather, riding/writhing, udder/other, wordy/worthy, side/scythe, load/loathe, sued/soothe

/z/ – /ð/: Z's/these, Zen/then, rising/writhing, size/scythe, close/clothe, seize/seethe, sues/soothe

/v/ – /ð/: veil/they'll, van/than, vat/that, sliver/slither, clove/clothe, lithe/live, loaves/loathes

C Test Yourself See Overview, p. ix.

Step 1

ANSWERS

1. day
2. leather
3. tease
4. closing
5. these
6. breathe

Step 2

ANSWERS

1. The sign said "Clothing".
2. We waited until they came.
3. The child was just teething.
4. Try to pronounce Z's more clearly.
5. They're breeding like rabbits.
6. Did you see the letter?

D Vocabulary See Overview, p. ix.

Step 1 Explain that the spelling *th* can spell either /ð/ or /θ/. Working in pairs, students try to find the word in each column that has the sound /θ/; the other words have the sound /ð/. You may want to do the first column together with the class.

Step 2 Go over the answers. Discuss the spelling rules (see the notes for task H, below) according to the level of your class.

ANSWERS

The words *think, three, anything,* and *Thursday* have the sound /θ/.

E Dialog See Overview, pp. ix–x.

Step 1 Have students work with a partner to fill in the blanks. Some of the words in task D will need to be used more than once. Encourage them to say the words aloud as they fill them in.

Step 2

ANSWERS	
Heather	I'd like to buy that jacket in the window.
Salesclerk	Well, <u>there</u> are three jackets <u>together</u> in the window. Do you want the one with the feather collar?
Heather	No. The other one. The leather one.
Salesclerk	The one with the zipper?
Heather	No, not <u>that</u> one either. That one over <u>there</u>. The one that's on sale.
Salesclerk	Oh, that one. Now, here's <u>another</u> leather jacket that I think you'd like.
Heather	But this one is more expensive than the one in the window.
Salesclerk	It's a better jacket than the other one. The <u>leather</u> is smoother.
Heather	I'd <u>rather</u> get the one in the window, though. I think that one is better for cold <u>weather</u>.
Salesclerk	Well, fine, if <u>that's</u> the one you want. But we don't take <u>anything</u> out of the window until three o'clock on Thursday.

Extra practice Students role-play short conversations used in shopping. For example, bring in or collect from students a number of items, such as several pairs of gloves, notebooks, cell phones, hats, scarves, and so on. Have students practice conversations such as the following:

Customer	Can I see that scarf?
Salesclerk	Which one? This one?
Customer	No. The red one.
Customer	How much are these gloves?
Salesclerk	Which ones? These?
Customer	No. The brown leather ones.
Salesclerk	$13.95.
Customer	Can I try them on?

F **Weak Pronunciations for *the* and *than***

Background notes Students practice sentence stress and the weak pronunciations of *the* and *than*. Note that some native speakers use the pronunciation /ðə/ for *the* before vowels as well as before consonants.

The stress marked in the sentences in the Student's Book is not the only possible choice; for example, a speaker might stress the pronouns *you* and *I* in the question and response and not stress the word *think*. Words like *do, the, is, with,* and *than* would not normally be stressed, however.

Students repeat the phrases and sentences. If necessary, remind them that unstressed words generally take less time to say and have vowels that are less clear than stressed words. Tap or clap to demonstrate the stress.

The Student's Book shows backward buildup to practice part of the sentences. If students have difficulty with the rhythm or stress, you can use this technique to practice the parts they find difficult, for example:

think – do you think – do you think is better – do you think is better than the others

which jacket – Which jacket do you think is better than the others?

G **Conversation Practice**

Students practice in pairs or small groups, as in the model. Have them practice the words in the list first. Check stress as they practice.

H **Spelling**

Since the letters *th* can spell either /ð/ or /θ/, students are likely to need help predicting when *th* is pronounced /ð/ and when it is pronounced /θ/. Discuss the following rules, according to the level of the class.

1. At the beginning of words, the spelling *th* is almost always pronounced /ð/ in structure (function) words: *the, this, these, that, then, there, therefore, they, them, though,* and so on. At the beginning of content words, *th* is pronounced /θ/: *think, thing, thirsty, three, Thursday, thank, thumb, thin,* and so on.

2. At the end of a word, *th* is almost always pronounced /θ/: *south, north, mouth, path, month, worth, tooth, fourth.* Exceptions are *with,* which is pronounced either /wɪθ/ or /wɪð/, and *smooth.* If *th* is followed by *e,* it has the sound /ð/. Compare these pairs of related nouns and verbs, with /θ/ in the noun and /ð/ in the verb: *breath / breathe, teeth / teethe, bath / bathe, cloth / clothe.* Note that when plural *-s* is added to words ending in *th* (like *path* or *mouth*), the *th* often changes its pronunciation from /θ/ to /ð/.

3. In the middle of a word, *th* can have either the sound /ð/ or /θ/. It is usually pronounced /ð/ before *-er*: *mother, father, rather, leather, southern, weather, together.* It is usually pronounced /θ/ before other sounds: *nothing, author, athlete, method, sympathy* (exceptions include *worthy*).

See the Unit 42 Web Site Worksheet (at www.cambridge.org/pp/student) for practice of some of these spelling rules.

I Common Expressions See Overview, p. xii.

Linking Pronunciation with Other Classwork

Tie pronunciation in with practice of:

1. this / that / these / those.

2. another / the other.

3. I'd rather . . . (than . . .).

4. Making comparisons; for example, "This car is bigger than the other one."

5. Talking about family photographs; for example, "This is / that's my mother / father / brother / grandmother / grandfather."

6. Identifying people in group pictures or photographs; for example, "Which one is your brother?" "The one with the hat / the one on the left / the one with the glasses," etc.

Word Stress Practice

Students listen to the following pairs and say whether the stress pattern for the two words is the same or different.

1. together / example (S)
2. another / anything (D)
3. practical / expensive (D)
4. comfortable / attractive (D)
5. dressier / casual (S)

UNIT 43 Review /y/, /f/, /v/, /w/, /h/, /θ/, and /ð/

This unit provides additional practice and review of the consonants /y/, /f/, /v/, /w/, /h/, /θ/, and /ð/. All of these sounds are made without completely stopping the breath. The sounds /y/ and /w/ are glides. The other consonants are *fricatives*, sounds made by forcing the air through a narrow space to make a noisy sound.

A Test Yourself

Play the audio. Students circle the words they hear. They can check the meaning of unfamiliar words, but they do not have to understand every word to do the task

ANSWERS		
1. vest	5. you	9. leaf
2. berry	6. ear	10. tense
3. fine	7. tree	11. breed
4. who'll	8. Zen	12. teethe

Extra practice Have individual students say the words, choosing a word from each numbered item. Other students write down the word they heard. This can be done with the whole class or in small groups.

B Conversations

Step 1 Explain the task: For each item, students hear what speaker B says and underline the word that stands out the most in the sentence. Then they read the two choices for what A said and decide which sentence B was responding to. Knowing the word that stands out in B's response should help them guess what A probably said.

Go over the example with the class.

Step 2

ANSWERS
1. **A** Did you use to live in New York?
B No, but I used to <u>work</u> there.
2. **A** Does he have any brothers or sisters?
B He has four <u>brothers</u>.
3. **A** How long have they lived here?
B More than five <u>years</u>.
4. **A** Her interview is at 1:30.
B I think it's at <u>12:30</u>.

Continued on page 108

5. **A** I think he has three brothers.
   B He has <u>four</u> brothers.

6. **A** When is her interview?
   B I think it's at 12:<u>30</u>.

7. **A** Do you work in New York?
   B No, but I <u>used</u> to work there.

8. **A** They've lived here for five years.
   B <u>More</u> than five years.

Step 3 Students practice the short conversations in step 1 with a partner. For each item, student A chooses one of A's sentences. Student B says B's response, making the correct word stand out. Student A should not always choose the sentence checked in step 1. Partners should switch roles.

C Puzzle

Students circle or say the word in each group that does not have the same consonant sound that is underlined in the first word. Go over the example. If necessary, remind students to focus on sounds, not spellings. Students can work alone or with a partner.

Check the answers at the end. If students need the practice, have them listen to and repeat the words when checking answers

ANSWERS

1. there	5. only
2. often	6. nothing
3. thought	7. quickly
4. why	

UNIT 44 /m/ • me   Using Intonation to Change Meaning

Student Difficulties

Students generally do not have difficulty pronouncing the sound /m/, but some students have problems involving /m/ and other nasal sounds.

- Spanish, Portuguese, and Japanese speakers may confuse /m/ with /n/ or /ŋ/ at the end of words. Spanish speakers tend to replace /m/ with /n/ or /ŋ/ in final position and before consonants not made with the lips – for example, pronouncing *I'm* in *I'm going* as /ɑyŋ/ or *some* in *sometimes* with the sound /n/.

- Some students do not pronounce nasal consonants clearly at the end of a word. Portuguese speakers may strongly nasalize the vowel before /m/ or other nasal consonants, often making the /m/ itself too weak. Chinese speakers may also nasalize the vowel before /m/ and either drop the /m/ itself or replace it with /n/ or /ŋ/.

- Some students, such as speakers of Lao, may strongly nasalize vowels after /m/ or /n/.

- Speakers of Greek, Italian, and Spanish, may tend to voice /s/ when it is followed by /m/, as in *small*, pronouncing the /s/ more like a /z/.

Making the Sound

Have students read the directions for making the sound /m/ as they listen to the audio and look at the illustrations. Point out that the lips are firmly closed.

If students have difficulty with final /m/, emphasize the lip position. Explain that final nasal sounds like /m/ are pronounced clearly in English.

A Vocabulary   See Overview, p. ix.

Check that students pronounce final /m/ sounds clearly. Note that the two /m/ sounds in the middle of *homemade* are pronounced together as one long /m/.

B Dialog   See Overview, pp. ix–x.

Step 1 Explain any unfamiliar vocabulary. For example, *homemade* means "made at home" and *Maine* is a state in the northeastern United States (you can show or sketch a map). A *muffin*, illustrated in the Student's Book, is a small, slightly sweet kind of bread that is often eaten in the morning.

Have students work with a partner to fill in the blanks, saying the words aloud as they fill them in.

Step 2

ANSWERS	
Sam	Mom?
Mom	Mm?
Sam	Can my friend Tom come <u>home</u> with me for lunch tomorrow?
Mom	Mm, I guess so. Have I <u>met</u> Tom before?
Sam	Mm-hm. You met him in the <u>summer</u>. He's small and really <u>smart</u> in math.
Mom	Mm, I <u>remember</u> Tom. His family <u>comes</u> from Maine, right?
Sam	Mm-hm, that's him. Oh, um, Mom? Can you <u>make</u> some <u>homemade</u> muffins tomorrow?
Mom	Mm . . . maybe. If I have <u>time</u>.
Sam	But <u>Mom</u>, I told Tom about your muffins. That's why he's coming for lunch <u>tomorrow</u>!

C Using Intonation to Change Meaning

Background notes By varying the length and intonation, *mm* and other nasal sounds can be used to express a variety of meanings. Note that other meanings are possible for some of the intonations shown.

Some of the intonations here have been practiced earlier in the book, with similar meanings, using words rather than sounds – for example, rising intonation to ask someone to repeat (see Unit 39, task E). Making *mm*, *um*, or a word extra long, without making the pitch go up or down, is a common way for speakers to show that they're thinking and plan to continue speaking. This is a useful technique for learners to use when they're trying to think of how to say something in English.

D Conversation

Step 1 Students listen to the conversation, identifying the meaning that *mm* has in B's answers.

Before going on to step 2, give students the chance to say *mm* with the various meanings shown in task C. Write the various *mm*'s and their meanings on the board. Ask individual students to choose one of the *mm*'s and say it; other students guess which meaning *mm* had.

You may want to add other uses of *mm* or other nasal sounds, such as *Hm*! ("I'm surprised"), *Mm-hm* ("Yes"), *Unh-unh* ("No"), *Um* . . . (hesitation).

Step 2 Students practice the conversation in pairs. Have a few volunteers perform it for the class.

Extra practice Students look at or listen to the dialog in task B again and say what meaning each *mm* sound has.

E Spelling

1. The sound /m/ is written with the letter *m*. Note the doubling of *m* in words like *summer* and *swimming* to preserve the lax pronunciation of the vowel (see the notes for Unit 22, task F).

2. Students often pronounce consonant letters that should be silent. Note the silent *b* in the spelling *mb* (as in *comb*) and the silent *n* in the spelling *mn* (as in *column*). In both cases, the two consonants together make one sound – /m/.

F Common Expressions See Overview, p. xii.

Further Practice

Practice from the board:

Would you like some . . . ?
   muffins / more / milk / mustard / money / matches
   coffee / tea / water / sugar / cream / jam / cake /
   gum / help / food / vegetables / French fries /
   flowers

Note that when two /m/ sounds link words, they are pronounced as one long /m/. Before /f/ or /v/ (as in *comfortable*), the sound /m/ is often made with the lips and teeth in position for the /f/ or /v/ sound instead of in the usual position for /m/. Before other sounds, however, the pronunciation of /m/ does not change; students should pronounce /m/ clearly.

Linking Pronunciation with Other Classwork

Tie pronunciation in with practice of:

1. Invitations or commands using the verb *come*: for example, *Come in / Come here / Come with me / Come to my house / Come home.*

2. Questions with *How much / How many.*

3. Object pronouns *him* and *them.*

4. Modal auxiliaries *may, might, must.*

Word Stress Practice

Write large and small circles on the board showing these three stress patterns:

A ● • B ● • • C • ● •

Read the following words. Students say whether they heard stress pattern A, B, or C.

1. summer (A)
2. remember (C)
3. important (C)
4. sometimes (A)
5. tomorrow (C)
6. family (A)
7. familiar (C)
8. comfortable (B)

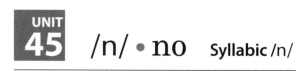

UNIT 45 /n/ • no Syllabic /n/

Student Difficulties

Most students do not have trouble with the sound /n/ at the beginning of words, although some students pronounce it with the tongue touching the top teeth (dental /n/) rather than with the tongue behind and not touching the teeth, giving it a slightly foreign sound.

Students are more likely to have difficulty with /n/ at the ends of words. Some students, including speakers of Spanish, Portuguese, Japanese, and Turkish, do not pronounce final /n/ clearly enough. They may pronounce the vowel before the /n/ as a nasal vowel, with the /n/ itself disappearing, or they may replace the sound /n/ with /m/ or /ŋ/, depending on the sounds around it. Some Chinese and Thai speakers may replace /n/ with /l/ at the end of words; speakers of some Chinese dialects (though not Mandarin) may have difficulty with /n/ in all positions.

If students tend to drop final /n/, explain that final nasal sounds like /n/ are pronounced clearly in English. Practice with pairs of words such as *play/plane, my/mine, see/seen, show/shown, lie/line, law/lawn* can be helpful.

Many students have difficulty with syllabic /n/ (see task E) in words like *garden* or *written*, usually inserting a vowel before the /n/.

Making the Sound

Have students read the directions for making the sound /n/ as they listen to the audio and look at the illustration. The tip of the tongue is on the tooth ridge (or alveolar ridge) just behind the upper front teeth. The sides of the tongue touch the side teeth.

A **Word Pairs** See Overview, p. viii.

Word pairs for additional practice:

/m/ – /n/: M/N, mice/nice, might/night, meet/neat, moon/noon, met/net, mile/Nile, some (*or* sum)/sun, dumb/done, seem/seen, them/then, jam/Jan, foam/phone, team/teen, dime/dine, lime/line, same/sane, warm/warn, dimmer/dinner, mummy/money

B **Test Yourself** See Overview, p. ix.

Step 1 Try saying one of the words in each pair silently and have students identify the word you said. Students can also practice this with a partner.

ANSWERS

1. mail	3. mine	5. gun
2. knee	4. comb	6. N

Step 2

ANSWERS

1. Can you pick up the <u>mail</u>?
2. I'd like two <u>cones</u>, please.
3. I'll give you <u>nine</u>.
4. Be careful – don't step on the <u>gum</u>!
5. Isn't the homework <u>done</u>?
6. Do you spell that with one <u>M</u> or two?

C **Vocabulary** See Overview, p. ix.

Words like *don't* and *can't* are often pronounced with a nasalized vowel instead of a clear /n/ sound. Otherwise, however, the consonant sound /n/ is usually clearly pronounced. Make sure that students do not cut off the ends of words in step 2 or simply nasalize the vowel without saying the consonant /n/ at the end.

D Dialog See Overview, pp. ix–x.

Step 1 The task here focuses attention on contractions and when they are and aren't used. Students sometimes resist using contractions, believing that full forms are more correct. In ordinary conversation, however, native speakers almost always use contractions where possible, with uncontracted forms used chiefly for emphasis.

Introduce the topic of the dialog: renting an apartment. You may want to begin by asking students questions such as the following: "Do you live in a house or apartment?" "Do you rent or own it?" "How did you find your apartment (or house)?" "In your native country, do most people live in apartments or houses?" Check their understanding of *rental agency* and *rental agent*.

Play the audio. Students listen to the dialog and circle the words they hear.

Alternatively, have students read the dialog before they listen, either working alone or in pairs, and circle the words they expect to hear. Then have students listen and check their answers.

Step 2 Point out or elicit that the speakers use contractions wherever possible in the conversation. Tell students that using contractions will help their speech sound more natural.

Explain that English speakers use contractions very often in conversation, but that there are rules about when contractions can and can't be used. Depending on the level of your class, you may want to help them formulate some rules, for example:

- *Be* is almost always contracted after a pronoun: *I'm a student. It's on a bus line.*

- The contraction *'s* for *is* is also used after other words: *There's a garden. Martin's a student.* Compare: *There are two bedrooms. Friends are forbidden.*

- *Have* is contracted after a pronoun when it is an auxiliary used with another verb: *We've got one apartment. Have* is not contracted when it is a main verb (see Unit 38, task F): *We have a nice apartment. It has big windows.*

- *Not* is almost always contracted: *I don't know. I couldn't pay. No, it isn't.*

- Contractions aren't used in *Wh-* questions ending with the word *it*: *Where is it?* (Compare: *Where's the apartment?*)

Note that the /t/ sound is often dropped in these common words and phrases: *twenty*; *want to* (sounds like "wanna"); *I don't know*.

ANSWERS

Martin Good morning. <u>I'm</u> interested in renting a one-bedroom apartment downtown.

Agent Certainly. <u>We have</u> a nice apartment on the corner of Main Street and Central Avenue. <u>It has</u> big windows, a new kitchen, and a very convenient location. And <u>it's</u> only $1,120 a month.

Martin I <u>couldn't</u> pay $1,120 a month. <u>I'm</u> a student.

Agent A student, hmm. . . . How much can you spend?

Martin Well, I <u>didn't</u> want to spend more than $700 a month.

Agent $700 a month? We <u>don't</u> often have apartments as inexpensive as that. Not in the center of town, anyway. <u>We've</u> got one apartment for $790 a month.

Martin <u>Where is</u> it? Is it in the same neighborhood?

Agent No, it <u>isn't</u>. <u>It's</u> on Seventh Avenue, near the train station.

Martin I <u>don't</u> know. I mean, I need to be near the university.

Agent <u>It's</u> on a bus line. <u>It has</u> a kitchen, but the kitchen <u>doesn't</u> have an oven.

Martin No oven? Well, a nice kitchen <u>isn't</u> that important to me.

Agent <u>There's</u> a garden in the front, but the tenants <u>can't</u> use it. The landlord lives downstairs. Friends are forbidden in the apartment after midnight. No noise and no television after 11:15. No –

Martin No, thank you! I want an apartment, not a prison!

E Syllabic /n/

Background notes In words with syllabic /n/, the /n/ forms a syllable by itself, without any vowel. In the words in task E, syllabic /n/ comes after the sound /t/, /d/, or /z/ – sounds made with the tip of the tongue just behind the top teeth, as for /n/. The difference between pronunciations with and without a syllabic /n/ is particularly noticeable after the sounds /t/ and /d/, as in *certainly* or *garden*. Students who expect to hear a vowel sound may have difficulty understanding words like these when said by a native English speaker.

To say syllabic /n/ after /t/ or /d/, the tongue goes to the roof of the mouth to make /t/ or /d/, but no air is released from the mouth. The tongue stays in the same place to make /n/, and the air for both sounds escapes through the nose as /n/ is pronounced. Note that if syllabic /n/ comes after the sound /t/, the /t/ is pronounced as a glottal stop. A glottal stop – the sound at the beginning of each syllable in *uh-oh* – is made by quickly closing and opening the space between the vocal cords.

Step 1 Students repeat words with syllabic /n/. Respell words on the board, showing the stress, if students have difficulty; for example:

● •   ● •   ● • •
gardn   prisn   certnly

Step 2 Students repeat phrases with *and*. The word *and* is typically pronounced as a syllabic /n/ when it comes after a word ending in the sound /t/, /d/, /s/, or /z/.

F Conversation Practice

Students practice in pairs, asking and answering *Yes / No* questions about the dialog. Depending on the level of your students, you may want to do this as a whole class activity or practice some short answers before students get into pairs. Note the syllabic /n/ in words like *didn't, isn't,* and *couldn't* in the negative short answers. Point out or elicit that contractions aren't used in affirmative short answers (*Yes, he is* – not * *Yes, he's*).

Move around the room while students practice, monitoring the short answers and use of syllabic /n/. Students who finish early can be asked to add their own questions to the list.

G Discussion

Students practice in small groups, talking about the features that are important to them in an apartment. You could ask students to rank the items by number in order of importance (note that the numbers 1, 7, and 9 have the sound /n/).

After students practice in groups, ask a few students to report on the things that people in their group thought were important and not important. You can extend the discussion to talk about students' homes and whether they have

the features in task G, adding questions such as: "What do you like about your apartment?" "What would you like to change about it?"

H Spelling

1. Note the doubling of *n* in words like *funny, dinner,* and *beginning* to keep the lax sound of the vowel (see Unit 22, task F). Compare the pronunciation of words like *diner / dinner*.

2. Syllabic /n/ is commonly spelled: *-n* (*didn't, couldn't, isn't, hasn't*), *-en* (*garden, listen, student, sudden, written*), *-on* (*person, lesson, cotton, button*), *-in* (*Latin*), *-an* (*important*), or *-ain* (*certainly, mountain, curtain*).

Extra practice Introduce the idea of *homophones* – words that sound alike but are spelled differently. Demonstrate with a pair like *see / sea* or *meet / meat*. Write the first word in each pair below on the board. Working alone or with a partner, students try to find a homophone for each word. You may want to allow them to use dictionaries.

Example: know; Homophone: no

knows – nose	sun – son
knot – not	won – one
knew – new	nun – none
knight – night	scene – seen

I Common Expressions See Overview, p. xii.

Further Practice

Game: Bingo Students first practice saying some or all of the numbers below. Check that they say the final /n/ clearly in words like *nine* and *eleven*. If necessary, review the difference in stress between numbers like *seventeen* and *seventy* (see Unit 2, task E).

1	7	9	10	11	13	14	15	16	17
19	20	21	27	29	70	71	77	79	90
91	97	99	101	120	121	700	790	900	970

To play, follow the directions in the Student's Book on page 11.

A

9	20	90
970	79	71
97	19	120

B

1	79	700
16	29	7
99	27	101

C

77	10	99
18	121	97
11	91	29

D

1	79	9
17	790	900
99	21	70

Linking Pronunciation with Other Classwork

Tie pronunciation in with practice of:

1. Negative short answers using: "No . . . isn't / doesn't / didn't / haven't / hasn't / shouldn't / couldn't," and so on. For example, students give short answers to questions about a picture, such as the one in Unit 38, task D.

2. Asking and talking about abilities, using *can* and *can't* (see Unit 8, task C).

3. Negative questions and tag questions (see, for example, Units 14 and 21).

4. Present perfect with past participles ending in *-en* (*taken, been, written,* etc.): For example, after first practicing the past participles, prepare a list of phrases such as the following on the board or a handout:
   Have you ever . . .

   > ridden a horse / eaten snails / written a song / driven a truck / gotten a prize / given a speech in English / spoken to a famous person / fallen asleep in class?

Students circulate around the room asking and answering questions ("Have you ever ridden a horse?" "Yes, I have. / No, I haven't."). Their goal is to find other students who have done each of the things listed.

Word Stress Practice

Write large and small circles on the board showing these three stress patterns:

A ● • •   B • ● •   C • • ●

Read the words below. Students say whether they heard stress pattern A, B, or C.

1. apartment (B)
2. avenue (A)
3. agency (A)
4. understand (C)
5. convenient (B)
6. location (B)
7. important (B)
8. interested (A)
9. certainly (A)
10. forbidden (B)

UNIT 46 /ŋ/ • sing   Weak Pronunciation and Contraction of *be*

Student Difficulties

The sound /ŋ/ occurs frequently, especially in the *-ing* form of verbs. Although mistakes rarely cause confusion in meaning, they are noticeable. Arabic, French, some German, Farsi, Greek, Hebrew, Italian, Turkish, West African, and Slavic speakers may have difficulty with this sound, usually pronouncing it /ŋg/, /ŋk/, or /n/. Some students may pronounce it as /n/ + /g/ because of the spelling.

For students who add /g/ or /k/ to /ŋ/, it may help them to practice words such as *longer* and *thinker*, gradually slowing down the pronunciation and increasing the gap between the first and second syllables. It also sometimes helps to get students to sing the sound (e.g., in the word *sing*), gradually getting softer at the end.

While some students tend to add a /g/ after every /ŋ/ sound, speakers of Dutch and German tend to omit /g/ after /ŋ/ where it should be

pronounced, as in *hunger, finger,* or *longer*. Portuguese speakers may strongly nasalize the vowel before a nasal consonant (/m/, /n/, or /ŋ/), leaving the final consonant itself very indistinct. Spanish speakers may replace other nasal sounds with /ŋ/, or vice versa, depending on what sounds surround it (also see the *Student Difficulties* sections in Units 44 and 45). They may also tend to drop the /k/ after /ŋ/ in words like *think*, creating confusion between words like *thing* and *think*.

Making the Sound

Have students read the directions for making the sound /ŋ/ as they listen to the audio and look at the illustration. Note that the sound /ŋ/ does not occur at the beginning of words in English.

Variation in the sound In informal speech, some people pronounce the *-ing* verb ending, as in *doing, eating,* or *laughing*, as /ɪn/ rather than /ɪŋ/.

Word pairs for additional practice:

/n/ – /ŋ/: sun/sung, run/rung, ton/tongue, sin/
sing, lawn/long, hand/hanged, banning/
banging, sinning/singing, sinner/singer

/ŋk/ – /ŋ/: winks/wings, sunk/sung, sank/sang,
rank/rang, stink/sting, tank/tang,
sinking/singing

C Test Yourself See Overview, p. ix.

Step 1

ANSWERS

1. D (thin, thing)		4. S (wins, wins)
2. D (think, thing)		5. D (sink, sing)
3. S (rang, rang)		6. D (fan, fang)

Step 2

ANSWERS

1. Don't let him sink!
2. They banged the books.
3. Watch out for those fangs.
4. I want to win.
5. The rink was a perfect circle.
6. They should ban it.

D Vocabulary See Overview, p. ix.

E Dialog See Overview, pp. ix–x.

Step 1 Play the audio. Students read the dialog and listen. Some of the words in the book are different from the words on the recording. Students can call out "Stop" or signal when they hear a word that is different. Pause the recording to give students time to write, or have students dictate the correction for you to write on the board. You may need to play the dialog several times for students to catch all the incorrect words.

Step 2 Note that in the words *finger* and *angrily*, the *-ng* spelling is pronounced /ŋg/. In words like *singing, bringing, hanging*, and *singer*, however, where the *-ing* or *-er* ending is added to a word that ends in the sound /ŋ/ (e.g., *sing* /sɪŋ/), the *ng* spelling in the middle of the word is pronounced /ŋ/ by most native speakers: *singer* /sɪŋər/, *singing* /sɪŋɪŋ/. Check that students do not add a /g/ sound in these words.

ANSWERS

Frank (*angrily*) Bang! Bang! Bang! What are the Kings doing? It's seven o'clock on Sunday morning, and we're trying to sleep!

Ingrid They're talking very loudly.

Frank Yes, but what's the banging noise, Ingrid?

Ingrid (*looking out the window*) Ron is standing on a ladder and banging some nails into the wall with a hammer. Now he's tying some strong string on the nails.

Frank What's Ann doing?

Ingrid She's bringing something pink for Ron to drink. Now she's putting it down. He's reaching for the drink and – Oh, no!

Frank What's happening?

Ingrid The ladder is falling!

Frank Is Ron still standing on it?

Ingrid No, he's . . . he's hanging from the string. Oh, my goodness. He's holding onto the string by his fingers and yelling.

Frank Isn't Ann helping him?

Ingrid No. She's running toward our house.

Frank You're joking!

Bell (*Ring! Ring! Ring!*)

Ingrid That's her ringing the bell!

Frank Well, I'm not answering it. I'm sleeping.

F Weak Pronunciation and Contraction of *be*

Background notes The word *be,* both as a main verb and an auxiliary, is almost always unstressed and pronounced as a contraction or weak form, unless the speaker wants to give it special emphasis. After a pronoun, *be* is contracted to *'m* (pronounced as the sound /m/), *'re* (pronounced as the sound /r/), or *'s* (pronounced /s/ after *it* and /z/ after *he* or *she*). The contraction *'s* is also used after *Wh-* words and nouns – for example, *What's happening? Ann's ringing the bell.* The word *are* usually has the weak pronunciation /ər/ when it comes after another word.

Step 1 Note that *What are they doing?* sounds like "Whater they doing?" Make sure that students do not stress the unstressed words or syllables in the sentences. Tap with a ruler or clap to show the rhythm. Since students are concentrating on the /ŋ/ sound in this unit, they may tend to overstress the last syllable of the verbs ending in *-ing*; the *-ing* syllable should not be stressed.

Step 2 Students practice asking and answering *Wh-* questions about the pictures, as in the example, either in pairs or as a whole class. Encourage them to do this without referring back to the dialog. Check that they use falling intonation on both the *Wh-* questions and the answers.

Note that the dialog and the questions provide practice of the nasal sounds /m/ and /n/ as well as /ŋ/. If students tend to confuse these sounds, ask additional questions about the dialog that elicit answers with these sounds (e.g., "What time of day is it?"). Or have students practice the dialog, working in small groups. They can then act it out, providing appropriate sound effects.

G Conversation Practice

Step 1 Working either in pairs or small groups, students take turns making true sentences about themselves. Tell them to try to remember the things that their partner says. Encourage students to ask each other follow-up questions. For example, if student A says "I'm reading an interesting book," student B could ask "What are you reading?"

Step 2 Students report on the things they have in common with their partners. If step 1 was done in small groups, students can tell the rest of the class about the things that are true for all of them, some of them, and none of them. For example: "All of us are studying more than one language." "One of us is wearing something pink." "None of us is planning a long trip."

H Spelling

The sound /ŋ/ is usually written with the letters *ng*. Before a /k/ or /g/ sound, it is spelled with the letter *n*.

The letters *ng* can represent either the single sound /ŋ/ (as in *ring*) or the sounds /ŋ/ + /g/ (as in *hungry, anger,* or *English*). Note that when the *-er* and *-est* endings are added to adjectives or adverbs (*younger, longest*), a /g/ sound is added in the pronunciation: *young* /yʌŋ/, *younger* /'yʌŋ•gər/. This does not happen when endings are added to verbs: *ringing* /'rɪŋ•ɪŋ/, *singer* /'sɪŋ•ər/.

I Common Expressions See Overview, p. xii.

Linking Pronunciation with Other Classwork

Tie pronunciation in with practice of:

1. Continuous tenses with *-ing* verb endings, for example:

   a. asking and answering questions about people in a picture or people students know: "What is your husband / wife / sister / father doing (now or at a hypothetical time)?"

   b. asking and answering questions about the future: "What will you be doing at nine o'clock tonight / this time tomorrow?" etc. "I'll (probably) be . . ."

2. Asking and talking about preferences in sports and other leisure activities:

   "Do you like swimming / playing tennis / watching football / dancing / playing ping pong?" and so on. "What are your favorite things to do on the weekend?" "Going to the movies / going to museums / going dancing / going shopping" and so on.

3. Complaining about problems in an apartment or a house; for example, "The kitchen sink is dripping / The ceiling is falling down / The paint is peeling / My washing machine isn't working." "There's something wrong with the phone / the intercom" and so on.

4. Greetings ("Good morning / Good evening / Good night" etc.) or times of day ("seven o'clock in the morning / one in the afternoon" etc.).

5. Structures with *anything, something, nothing, everything.*

Word Stress Practice

Review the usual stress pattern of:

1. Two-syllable words ending in *-ing*:

   ● • talking, singing, holding, doing, standing, shouting, running, sleeping, morning

2. Two-syllable words ending in *-er* / *-or*:

   ● • singer, neighbor, finger, hammer, ladder, longer

UNIT 47 /l/ • light, fall Weak Pronunciation and Contraction of *will*

Student Difficulties

Speakers of Vietnamese, Thai, and Lao have difficulty distinguishing /n/ and /l/ at the end of words. They usually substitute /n/ for /l/, for example pronouncing *tell* as *ten*. Speakers of some Chinese dialects also confuse /n/ and /l/.

Speakers of Japanese, Chinese, Korean, Thai, and other Asian languages, as well as speakers of some African languages, tend to confuse /r/ and /l/ (see Unit 48, *Student Difficulties*).

Students who have trouble with /l/ tend to have particular difficulty with /l/ in consonant clusters, as in *glass* or *cold*, or in final position, as in *feel* or *pull*. Even students who do not otherwise have problems with /l/ may have difficulty with it in those positions. Many students, including those who speak Arabic, Turkish, Farsi, Japanese, Chinese, Thai, Indian languages, and African languages, tend to insert a vowel between consonants in a cluster. Dutch speakers may insert a vowel in some final clusters, such as in *milk* or *film*. Some students may drop one of the consonants in clusters, especially in final clusters, for example dropping the /l/ in *cold*. Other students, including speakers of Portuguese, may replace /l/ in final position or before a consonant with a vowel resembling /ʊ/. Some students (e.g., speakers of Chinese) may drop a final /l/ or add a vowel after it. Syllabic /l/ (/l/ pronounced as a syllable by itself, without any vowel, as in *bottle*) often causes particular difficulty. Learners often add a vowel – sometimes a full, stressed vowel – before the /l/.

Many languages have only one /l/ sound, either a clear /l/ or a dark /l/. Speakers of these languages will tend to use the sound found in their language in all positions in English. Speakers of French, German, Farsi, and Scandinavian and Indian languages, for example, tend to use clear /l/ only. Other languages, such as Russian, Turkish, and Dutch, have both /l/ sounds, but not in the same places as in English. Students who speak these languages may substitute dark /l/ for clear /l/ or vice versa. Many students pronounce /l/ with the tongue in a slightly different position than for English /l/ (e.g., farther forward or back in the mouth), giving it

a foreign sound. The use of only clear /l/ or dark /l/, the substitution of one /l/ sound in place of the other, or the use of a non-English /l/ will not cause misunderstandings, but may contribute to a non-native accent.

Making the Sound

Have students read the directions for making the sound /l/ as they listen to the audio and look at the illustrations. Note that the sides of the tongue should not touch the side or back teeth.

The instructions on page 178 of the Student's Book describe "clear /l/," as it is usually pronounced at the beginning of a word or after a consonant. The instructions on page 179 describe "dark /l/," as it is usually pronounced at the end of a word or before a consonant. For dark /l/, have students raise the back of the tongue closer to the roof of the mouth as they say /l/, keeping the tip of the tongue just behind the front teeth. Note that some English speakers produce dark /l/ with the whole tongue a little farther back in the mouth than for clear /l/.

If students tend to drop final /l/ or replace it with a vowel, have them check the position of their tongues as they finish saying words like *I'll* or *pull*. The front of the tongue should be touching the roof of the mouth just behind the front teeth.

If students have difficulty producing dark /l/, tell them to say the sound /l/ and, as they say /l/, to try to say the sound /uw/. Some native English speakers add a slight /ə/ sound when /l/ comes after a front vowel like /iy/ or /ey/, as in *feel* or *tail*, as the tongue moves from the front of the mouth to dark /l/. It may be easier for students to achieve the correct /l/ sound if they add this /ə/.

Variation in the sound There are two kinds of /l/ sound in English. At the beginning of a word or after a consonant, as in *leave* or *class*, /l/ usually has a clear, light sound. At the end of a word or before a consonant, as in *pull* or *old*, /l/ has a darker, heavier, "swallowed" sound. Some people also use a darker /l/ before vowels made in the back of the mouth, as in *look* or *low*.

British speakers tend to make a sharper distinction between clear /l/ and dark /l/ than American speakers, using clear /l/ at the beginning of all words and dark /l/ at the end of words or before consonants.

A and B Word Pairs 1 and 2 See Overview, p. viii.

Word pairs for additional practice:

/n/ – /l/:   not/lot, knock/lock, need/lead, knee/Lee, nap/lap, nice/lice, knit/lit, niece/lease, snacks/slacks, snob/slob, Jenny/jelly, tenor/teller, winning/willing, win/will, in/ill, rain/rail, Ben/bell, mean/meal, been/bill, fine/file, fin/fill, main/mail, phone/foal, even/evil

(no /l/) – /l/:   row/roll, bow/bowl, mow/mole, sew/soul (or sole), toe/toll, road/rolled, code/cold, toad/told, wide/wild, head/held, odor/older, boat/bolt, coat/colt

C Test Yourself See Overview, p. ix.

Step 1

ANSWERS		
1. low	3. connect	5. bone
2. light	4. tell	6. snow

Step 2

ANSWERS
1. Is it <u>night</u> already?
2. Write it under the <u>line</u>.
3. I dropped a <u>pin</u>.
4. That's the dog's <u>bowl</u>.
5. There were <u>no</u> tables in the room.
6. He <u>collected</u> the pieces.

D Vocabulary See Overview, p. ix.

Step 1 Students repeat words with a clear /l/ sound. Check that they do not add an extra vowel sound before or after the /l/ in consonant clusters in the words in the last column. If students have difficulty with the clusters, try practicing the following from the board:

lllock clllock   clock   llllass clllllass   class

Step 2 Students repeat words with a dark /l/ sound. If they add a full vowel sound in the second syllable of words like *people, trouble,* and *simple,* try respelling the words on the board: "**peo**pl," "**trou**bl," "**sim**pl."

E Dialog See Overview, pp. ix–x.

Step 1 Introduce the topic of the dialog: difficulty sleeping. You can begin by asking students questions about their sleep habits, for example: "Do you ever have trouble sleeping?" "What do you do if you can't sleep?" "How many hours of sleep do you usually get?" "Do you usually sleep late on the weekend?" "Do you use an alarm clock to wake up?" "Are you a light sleeper or a heavy sleeper?"

Before students listen to the dialog, have them read questions 1 and 2 and the possible answers. Explain that they will listen for the answers to these questions as they listen to the dialog. You can ask students to predict which items in question 2 Dr. Lopez will suggest to help Lilly sleep better.

Students should not look at the dialog in their books when they listen. Since this dialog is longer than many others in the book, you may need to play it more than once, pausing the recording occasionally to allow students to answer the questions.

Step 2 Play the audio again and go over the answers to the questions in step 1. Ask students if they have other ideas to help someone who has trouble falling asleep.

ANSWERS
1. She has trouble falling asleep.
2. Follow a regular schedule.
Turn all the lights off.
Drink a glass of milk.
Go to bed later.
Sleep in a cool room.
Don't lie in bed looking at the clock.
Don't watch television in bed.

F Weak Pronunciation and Contraction of *will*

Background notes The sound /l/ is pronounced as dark /l/ in *will* and contractions of *will*. *Will* is usually contracted to *'ll* after a pronoun. It is also sometimes contracted after *Wh-* words: *What'll you do?* After a noun, *will* is usually reduced to /əl/ or a syllabic /l/ in speech, but it is usually written as *will* rather than as a contraction. The reduced form is linked smoothly to the noun.

When *will* is contracted after a pronoun, the vowel in the pronoun often sounds weaker or more relaxed: *I'll* /ɑl/ (rhymes with *doll*), *you'll* /yʊl/ (rhymes with *full*), *he'll* /hɪl/ (sounds like *hill*), *she'll* /ʃɪl/, *we'll* /wɪl/ (sounds like *will*), *they'll* /ðɛl/ (rhymes with *shell*).

Have students listen to and repeat the sentences with contractions of *will*. The word *that'll* has a syllabic /l/. To say syllabic /l/ here, the tongue goes to the roof of the mouth for /t/ and then stays there for /l/, with the air for /t/ escaping over the sides of the tongue as /l/ is pronounced. Note that /t/ is usually voiced before syllabic /l/ and pronounced more like a quick /d/ (see Unit 24, task A).

For practice of the weak and contracted forms of *will*, see the Unit 47 Web Site Worksheet (at www. cambridge.org/pp/student). After students do the exercise on the Web site for this unit, print out the audio script and have students practice the dialog in pairs.

G Quiz

Step 1 Explain that students will take a quiz that shows whether they are night owls, who naturally tend to stay up late, or early birds, who are most alert early in the day. Go over any unfamiliar vocabulary before they begin, as well as the pronunciation of the words that go in the blanks: *always* / *usually* / *occasionally* / *hardly ever* / *never*.

Have students read the sentences to themselves before they get into pairs. Working with a partner, students take turns completing the sentences in the quiz. While they practice, move around the room monitoring the pronunciation of words with /l/.

Step 2 Have students report on the results of the quiz for themselves and their partners. Ask them if they agree with the results. If you haven't already discussed sleep and problems sleeping (see the notes for task E, step 1), you may want to do that now.

H Spelling

1. Doubling of *l*: Note that the letter *l* is often doubled at the end of a word after the vowels /ɛ, ɪ, ʌ, ɑ, ɔ, ʊ/: *bell, fill, dull, doll, fall, pull*.

   In American English, when *-ed* or *-ing* is added to a verb ending in *l*, the *l* is doubled only if the vowel before it is stressed. In British English, the *l* is doubled even if the vowel is not stressed. Compare American *traveled* / *traveling* and British *travelled* / *travelling*.

2. Syllabic /l/ is spelled: *-le* (*little, candle, puzzle, apple, table, uncle, example*), *-al* (*final*), *-el* (*travel*), *-il* (*pencil*), or *-ol* (*symbol*).

3. Silent *l*: Many students pronounce *l* where it should be silent; others may drop *l* in consonant clusters where it should be pronounced. For later review, give students a list of words such as the one below. Have them either listen as you read the words aloud or just look at the words in written form. Explain that the letter *l* is silent in some words. Tell students to make an *X* through the silent *l*'s in these words.

1.	could	6.	cold
2.	talk	7.	half
3.	milk	8.	chalk
4.	calm	9.	help
5.	felt	10.	folk

Then say the words; students repeat the words and check their answers. Note that some native speakers pronounce the *l* in *calm* and *palm*.

I Common Expressions   See Overview, p. xii.

For additional practice, have students learn these common sayings: *Last but not least. Live and let live. All's well that ends well.*

Linking Pronunciation with Other Classwork

Tie pronunciation in with practice of:

1. Talking about likes and dislikes: For example, students could make sentences from cues on the board, beginning "I like / love / don't like":

   salad / lettuce / lamb / lemon / apples / melon / plums / chili / cauliflower / celery / clams / olives / garlic / chocolate / vanilla / cold milk

   the color blue / black / yellow / purple

   yellow flowers / difficult puzzles / old films / large hotels / plastic plates / old buildings

   flying / sleeping late / complaining / traveling / cleaning / playing tennis / climbing mountains.

2. Requests with *please*.

3. Telling the time using *o'clock*.

4. Questions with *long*: for example, "How long have you lived here?" "Have you lived here for a long time?"

5. Asking and talking about the future, using *will*.

6. Adjectives in descriptions, for example: *small, old, clean, yellow, black, blue, plastic, slow, full, cold, little, difficult, simple, clever, careful, sensible, wonderful, beautiful, dull, unusual*

7. *myself / yourself / herself / himself.*

Word Stress Practice

Write large and small circles on the board showing these two stress patterns:

A ● •   B • ●

Read the words below. Students say whether they heard stress pattern A or B.

1. collect (B)   5. asleep (B)
2. o'clock (B)   6. hello (B)
3. relax (B)   7. schedule (A)
4. college (A)   8. always (A)

UNIT 48 /r/ • right   Stress in Long Words

Student Difficulties

Almost all learners have difficulty with English /r/.

- Speakers of many Asian languages, including Japanese, Chinese, Thai, Korean, and Lao, confuse /l/ and /r/. Speakers of Japanese, for example, usually substitute the Japanese /r/, a flapped /r/ sound, for both /l/ and /r/ in English. Thai speakers tend to substitute /l/ for /r/. Speakers of Korean may say either /l/ or /r/, depending on the position of the sound in the word. Speakers of some African (especially West African) languages may also confuse /l/ and /r/.

- French, German, Danish, Hebrew, some Portuguese, and many Dutch speakers often make a sound produced too far back in the mouth (uvular /r/). At the beginning of words, Portuguese speakers may use a voiceless sound that sounds like a strong /h/.

- Many students, including speakers of Arabic, Greek, Italian, Portuguese, Spanish, Turkish, Farsi, Norwegian, and Swedish, as well as African, Indian, and Slavic languages, trill /r/ or pronounce it as a short flap sound resembling the /d/ sound in *ladder*.

A trilled or flapped /r/ does not prevent students from being understood. This sound actually occurs in some varieties of English, such as Scottish English. It is, however, often a noticeable part of a foreign accent, and if students want to acquire a native-sounding accent, the English /r/ sound must be mastered.

Uvular /r/ also does not cause misunderstandings in meaning. But the sound /r/ occurs so frequently that it can be distracting to listen to English pronounced this way.

Confusing /l/ and /r/ can easily lead to misunderstandings and may even be subject to ridicule. Students tend to have particular difficulty when /r/ is in a consonant cluster or in a word that also has an /l/ sound.

A less common problem among nonnative speakers is confusion of /r/ with /w/.

Making the Sound

This unit practices the sound /r/ before a vowel; the following unit practices /r/ when it is not followed by a vowel.

Students will probably need to spend some time practicing the correct mouth position for /r/. Demonstrate the tongue position or direct attention to the illustration in the book, emphasizing that the front of the tongue should not touch the roof of the mouth. This is especially useful for students who use a trilled or flapped /r/ or who confuse /l/ and /r/. The tongue is curled slightly back, and the sides of the tongue lightly touch the upper back teeth, forming a hollow space in the middle of the tongue. The lips are pushed forward a little into a circle. This describes the mouth position most speakers use for initial /r/. In the middle of a word, as in *parent*, the tongue may point up without being curled back and the lips may not be rounded.

For students who confuse /l/ and /r/, note that with /l/ the air passes over the sides of the tongue;

with /r/ the air moves over the center of the tongue. This can be felt if the tongue is held in position for the sound and the breath is sharply inhaled. In consonant clusters with /r/ (as in *grass* or *friend*), the mouth often starts to form an /r/ while making the first sound. Tell students to try saying both sounds at the same time.

Tell students who substitute /w/ for /r/ to make the sound with their tongues, not just their lips; the lips also should not form so tight a circle.

For students who use a uvular /r/, demonstrating the correct tongue position and practicing the /l/ – /r/ word pairs should help students learn to use the front of the tongue rather than the back.

A Word Pairs See Overview, p. viii.

Word pairs for additional practice:

/l/ – /r/: lock/rock, low/row, load/road, lead/read, led/red, lied/ride, late/rate, lace/race, law/raw, lice/rice, lime/rhyme, lane/rain, lip/rip, list/wrist, liver/river, loyal/royal, collect/correct, jelly/Jerry, belly/berry, alive/arrive, elect/erect, palace/Paris, fly/fry, climb/crime, flute/fruit, clown/crown, flame/frame, flight/fright, flea/free, play/pray, bleed/breed, bland/brand, glow/grow, glue/grew, glamour/grammar

/w/ – /r/: wing/ring, wide/ride, which/rich, waist/raced, wink/rink, ways/raise, way/ray, wait/rate, one (*or* won)/run, west/rest, went/rent, wise/rise

B Test Yourself See Overview, p. ix.

Step 1

ANSWERS		
1. S (light, light)	4. D (pirate, pilot)	
2. D (glass, grass)	5. S (cloud, cloud)	
3. S (wrong, wrong)	6. S (correct, correct)	

Step 2

ANSWERS

1. That sentence is <u>long</u>.
2. Don't walk on the <u>grass</u>.
3. He was a famous <u>pilot</u>.
4. I'm going to <u>collect</u> the homework.
5. I couldn't see because of the <u>crowd</u>.
6. Did you take the <u>right</u> suitcase?

C Vocabulary See Overview, p. ix.

Go over any unfamiliar vocabulary. Note that stress in many of the longer words is practiced later in the unit. If students have difficulty with the pronunciation of some of the longer words here, backward or forward buildup may be helpful, for example:

-pher, -grapher, -TOgrapher, phoTOgrapher; pho-, phoTOG-, phoTOGra-, phoTOGrapher

-cian /-ʃən/, -TRIcian, -lecTRIcian, elecTRIcian; elec-, elecTRI-, elecTRIcian

Students may have particular difficulty with the sound /r/ in the words in step 2, which contain both /l/ and /r/ sounds.

D Dialog See Overview, pp. ix–x.

Step 1 Explain the task: Students listen to the dialog, looking at the vocabulary words in task C as they listen. They should put a check mark next to the words Rose and Laura use to describe their children and a circle around the jobs their children have. Check that students know which kinds of words (adjectives) would be used to describe people.

Step 2 Point out the frequent use of the word *really* in conversation, for emphasis (e.g., "what he really wants to do"), as a question to show surprise or interest ("He's an air traffic controller." "Really?"), and in the negative *not really*. Explain that English speakers tend to use conversational fillers like "Really?" quite often to show that they are listening and interested. Said with sharply rising intonation, "Really?" also expresses surprise. To practice this briefly, tell students either true or imaginary things (especially surprising things), about yourself or students in the class.

ANSWERS

Words used to describe their children: married, bright, creative, practical

Jobs their children have: reporter, librarian, translator, air traffic controller

E Stress in Long Words

Many long words in English are formed by adding prefixes or suffixes to a base word. Here, students practice stress patterns in words when some common suffixes are added.

Read or summarize the information in the box with the class. Remind students, if necessary, of the importance of using the correct stress in English words. Putting the stress on the wrong syllable can make a word very hard to understand. On the other hand, putting the stress on the correct syllable can help listeners understand a word, even if some of the consonant or vowel sounds aren't pronounced correctly.

Note that some of the longer words here also have a second, lighter stress (the syllable with the main stress is underlined): re**spon**si**bi**lity, con**grat**u**la**tions.

Step 1 Students practice adding the suffixes -*er,* -*or,* -*ing,* -*ful,* and -*ly.* These endings generally do not cause the stress pattern to change. Note that the vowel sound at the end of *beauty* changes both in spelling and sound, with the /iy/ sound reduced to /ə/, when the ending -*ful* is added. The placement of the stress stays the same, however. And though the stress doesn't change when *photographer* is formed from *photography,* it does shift between *pho**to**graph* and *pho**tog**rapher.*

Step 2 Students practice adding the suffixes -*ian,* -*ic,* -*ical,* -*ion,* and -*ity.* In words with these endings, stress generally falls on the syllable just before the ending. Point out that when the stress changes, the pronunciation of some of the vowels may also change. For example, the vowel in the stressed first syllable of *pol**it**ics* has the sound /ɑ/, but the vowel is reduced to /ə/ when the stress shifts in *po**lit**ical.*

Note that -*cian* and -*tion* are both pronounced /ʃən/.

Step 3 Students can work individually or in pairs to underline the stressed syllables.

Extra practice Add other words with these endings that your students are familiar with, for example: *musician, musical, technician, technical, economic, possibility, electricity, security,* etc.

F Discussion

Step 1 Students practice in groups of two or three; this could also be done in larger groups. Each student completes the sentence "I'd like a job that . . ." listing three of the items shown in their books. Tell students to try to remember what the other people in their group say, because they will need this information for step 2.

Move around the room while students practice, monitoring pronunciation of the sound /r/ and stress in words. You may also want to check their intonation when they list items (see Unit 22, task C).

After students practice for a few minutes, ask a student from each group to report on the choices made by the people in their group. At the end, ask students to say which choices were the most and least popular.

Step 2 Tell students to think of a job that each person in their group would like to have, based on their answers to step 1. They do not have to restrict their choices to the jobs mentioned in the unit. If they name other jobs with the endings practiced in this unit, write the word on the board and ask students to identify the stressed syllable.

At the end, ask if students agreed with their partners' choice of jobs for them.

G Spelling

The sound /r/ is usually written with the letter *r* or, in the middle of a word, with *rr.* At the beginning of a word it is sometimes spelled *wr* or *rh,* with the *w* or *h* silent.

H Common Expressions See Overview, p. xii.

Further Practice

Practice antonyms that have the sounds /r/ and /l/. Give students one of the words in pairs such as the following. Students think of a word that has the opposite meaning.

right / wrong	single / married
false / true	ugly / attractive
boring / interesting	(*or* pretty *or* beautiful)
relaxing / stressful	polite / rude
	dull / bright

Linking Pronunciation with Other Classwork

Tie pronunciation in with practice in:

1. Talking about jobs/occupations.

2. Talking about colors: For example, students ask each other about their favorite colors or find objects in the room that are specified colors. Color names with the sounds /l/ and /r/ include: red, green, gray, brown, orange, cream, purple, yellow, blue, black, lilac, lavender, light blue, pale yellow.

3. Replies to "How are you?": "All right. / Pretty good."

Student Difficulties

Almost all students have difficulty with /r/ and the way it affects the pronunciation of a preceding vowel. Learners commonly substitute an /r/ sound from their own language, replace /r/ with /l/, or drop /r/ after a vowel. If students use a trilled or flapped /r/, it is likely to interfere with their ability to pronounce vowels before /r/ correctly.

Students may need practice in:

1. distinguishing final /l/ and final /r/.

2. distinguishing words with a vowel + /r/ in the same syllable from words with no /r/ after the vowel.

3. distinguishing various vowels before /r/ from others (e.g., the vowels in *here* and *there*); spelling difficulties often add to students' confusion.

For more about difficulties with /r/, see Unit 48, *Student Difficulties*.

Making the Sound

When the sound /r/ follows a vowel in the same syllable in a word, it often affects the way the vowel is pronounced.

It may be easiest to begin practice of /r/ after the vowel /ɑ/. Have students start by saying the sound /ɑ/. Tell them to move their tongues up slowly as they say /ɑ/ and curl the tip of the tongue back – but without touching the roof of the mouth. They can then practice this using different vowels. In each case, students should make sure that they do not touch the roof of the mouth with their tongues.

If students have previously practiced the sound /ər/, it should be easier for them to pronounce the vowels in this unit. Adding the unstressed sound /ər/ after each of the vowels practiced in this unit can help them to make the correct sound.

Note Many native English speakers make the sound /r/ a little differently after a vowel than before a vowel. Instead of curling the tongue back, they may bunch up the tongue in the middle toward the roof of the mouth or pull it back a little.

Variation in the sounds

1. British speakers and some American speakers pronounce /r/ only when it comes before a vowel sound. They do not pronounce /r/ before a consonant or a pause (as in *airport* or *here*). For these speakers, /r/ would be silent in most of the words in this unit. Most speakers of North American English, however, do not drop /r/ in these words.

2. There is a great deal of dialect variation in the way vowels are pronounced before /r/. Some speakers, for example, pronounce the word *hear* with a vowel much like /ɪ/, some use a vowel closer to /iy/, and others use a sound somewhere between /iy/ and /ɪ/. Similar variation occurs between /ɛ/ and /ey/ in the word *there* and between /ʊ/ and /uw/ in *poor*. Many English speakers do not say *poor* with either /ʊ/ and /uw/, instead using the same vowel as in *pour* (/ɔr/). Some people use three different vowels in the words *Mary, merry,* and *marry*, but many North American speakers pronounce all three words with the same vowel (/ɛ/, or a vowel close to that). In general, most North American speakers do not use as many different vowel sounds before /r/ as they do before other consonants. As with other sounds, it is probably best for students to follow the pronunciation model of their teacher.

3. Many people add a slight /ə/ sound between a vowel and a following /r/, especially in words with diphthongs, such as *fire* or *hour*.

A **Word Pairs** See Overview, p. viii.

The exact words that form minimal word pairs here will be different for different native speakers, depending on what vowel sounds they use before /r/. For many speakers, for example, the words *hill / hear* and *tell / tear* (verb) would have more similar vowels than the pairs *heel / hear* and *pail / pear* shown in the Student's Book.

/l/ – /r/:   feel/fear, real/rear, we'll/we're, fill/fear, hill/here, will/we're, tail/tear, fail/fair, tell/tear (verb), bell/bear, well/wear, fell/fair, wall/war, tall/tore,

Paul/pour, pole/pour, stole/store, mole/more, pool/poor, tool/tour, pull/poor, tile/tire, while/wire, owl/hour

vowel – vowel + /r/: cheese/cheers, E/ear, bead/beard, tea/tear (noun), bee/beer, his/hears, bid/beard, days/dares, pays/pears, stayed/stared, dead/dared, shed/shared, cot/cart, hot/heart, dock/dark, caught/court, sauce/source, saw/sore, coat/court, so/sore, two's/tours, lose/lures, shut/shirt (and see Unit 21, task C)

Some contrasting vowels before /r/:

ear/air, hear/hair, tear (noun)/tear (verb), cheers/chairs, dear/dare, beer/bear, fear/fair

wear/were, hair/her, fair/fur, stair/stir, pear (or pair)/purr

care/car, fair/far, stair/star, scare/scar, bear/bar

(For pairs contrasting other vowels, see Units 11, task A, and Unit 21, tasks A and B.)

B Test Yourself See Overview, p. ix.

Step 1

ANSWERS		
1. four	3. file	5. towel
2. hear	4. pear	6. poor

Step 2

ANSWERS

1. Put this paper in the <u>fire</u>.
2. I put the <u>pail</u> in the kitchen.
3. <u>Fall</u> is the best time to go there.
4. Did you find the <u>tower</u>?
5. You shouldn't <u>fear</u> it.
6. We need more money for the <u>pool</u>.

C Vocabulary See Overview, p. ix.

Step 1 Working in pairs, students sort the words by sound, grouping words with the same vowel sound + /r/ together.

Step 2

ANSWERS

1:/ɪr/	3:/ɑr/	5:/ɔr/
hear	far	four
here	start	morning
near	large	before
clear	aren't	toward
2:/ɛr/	**4:/ər/**	
chair	thirty	
there	first	
upstairs	worse	
where	clerk	

D Dialog See Overview, pp. ix–x.

Step 1 Call attention to the illustration to introduce the dialog. Ask questions about the information shown, for example: "What is the number of the flight?" "What time will it leave?"

Have students work with a partner to fill in the blanks. Encourage them to say the words aloud as they fill them in.

Step 2

ANSWERS

Announcement	Good <u>morning</u>. Passengers on Park Airways flight 434, scheduled to depart for New York at 12:30, there will be a short delay. That flight will now depart at 4:45. Passengers should remain here at the airport. We're sorry. . .
Aaron	Did you hear that? It wasn't very <u>clear</u>.
Mary	There's going to be a short delay. We <u>aren't</u> leaving until a quarter to five.
Aaron	SHORT delay?! That's more than <u>four</u> hours!
Mary	Well, I'm thirsty. Do you know if there's a coffee bar here?
Aaron	I'm not sure. Oh, there's an airline clerk. Ask her.
Mary	(*to the airline clerk*) Pardon me, is <u>there</u> a coffee bar here?

Continued on page 124

Airline clerk	A coffee bar? No, sorry. This isn't a very <u>large</u> airport. But there's a cafeteria <u>upstairs</u>, near the security check.
Mary	Thanks. *(to Aaron)* I'm going upstairs. Coming, dear?
Aaron	No. I'm tired. I'm going to find a comfortable <u>chair</u> and stay here. *(to the airline clerk)* Where's the nearest restroom?
Airline clerk	Right over there, <u>near</u> gate 14.
Aaron	Is there a problem with the airplane?
Airline clerk	Oh, no, sir. There's a storm moving toward here, and the weather forecast says it will get <u>worse</u> before it gets better. But it should clear up in a couple of hours.
Aaron	Are you sure?
Airline clerk	Oh, yes, sir. Flight 434 will be the <u>first</u> plane to leave after the storm. Our departure time is 4:45. We'll start boarding at quarter after four.

E Intonation in Polite Questions

Background notes Speakers often use a high voice range to show politeness. The intonation practiced here is polite and rather formal; it is typically used when asking a stranger a question. The intonation starts at a high pitch, dips down to a low pitch on the stressed syllable of the most important word, and then rises again at the end.

Explain that people often use a special intonation when they want to sound very polite. Read or summarize the information in the box with the class.

You may want to have students repeat the examples several times. To learn the tune of the sentences, it can be helpful for students to say the examples at the same time as they are said on the recording, or at the same time that you say them. Use hand gestures to show the direction of the falling and rising intonations.

F Conversation Practice

Students take turns asking for and giving directions. First practice the items in the list, explaining any new vocabulary. If necessary, review the stress pattern for noun compounds: strong stress on the first element, lighter stress on the second (**air**port, **tour**ist office, and so on). You may want to add other places to the list, such as *a* **super**market. Note that *Pardon me* and *Excuse me*, used to get someone's attention, are often said at a fairly high pitch or with a slight rise in pitch at the end, to show politeness or friendliness.

Move around the room while students practice, checking their pronunciation of /r/ after vowels and their intonation in polite questions. You can use the numbers for the sounds in the table in task C to help correct errors.

G Spelling

The variety and overlapping of spellings for vowels before /r/ is very confusing for students, especially since some spellings represent sounds before /r/ that they do not represent in other places. Only the most common spellings for each sound are shown.

Extra practice To review the spellings of vowels before /r/ at a later time, give students a list of words, either on paper or on the board, to sort by sound. Students sort the words, grouping words with the same vowel sound together. Alternatively, write each word on a card, preparing more than one set of cards for larger classes, and have students work in groups to sort them.

Sample words to be given in scrambled order:

hear, here, near, clearly, year
wear, there, stairs, care, their
were, early, word, bird, heard, learn
heart, hard, start, large
warm, four, more, short, store

H Common Expressions See Overview, p. xii.

Linking Pronunciation with Other Classwork

Tie pronunciation in with practice of:

1. Asking for and giving directions: "Where?" "Over there / right here / around the corner / near . . ." Practice the contrast of /l/ and /r/ in *left / right / straight ahead.*

2. Possessive pronouns: *hers, yours, ours, theirs.*

3. "Would you like some more . . . ?" in offering things and "Here you are" when giving something to someone.

4. Vocabulary used in looking for an apartment. For example, have students role-play calling about an apartment for rent. Note the /l/ and /r/ sounds in: *near, large, small, air-conditioning, security deposit, rooms, living room, bedroom* (etc.), *rent, electricity, separate kitchen, available, Is there . . . ?*

5. Describing people and what they are wearing: dress / shirt / skirt / scarf / sweater / blouse / sleeves / belt / glasses

   striped / plaid / print / solid / flowered / wool / short / long / straight / pleated

   Tell students to look at their classmates and remember as much about them as possible.

Ask one student to come to the front of the room and face away from the class. Choose another student; ask the student at the front to describe what that student is wearing.

Word Stress Practice

Write large and small circles on the board showing these four stress patterns:

A ● •   B • ●   C ● • •   D • ● •

Read the words below. Students say whether they heard stress pattern A, B, C, or D.

1. before (B)
2. departure (D)
3. passengers (C)
4. upstairs (B)
5. tourist (A)
6. remain (B)
7. library (C)
8. morning (A)
9. neighborhood (C)
10. delay (B)
11. important (D)
12. comfortable (C)

UNIT 50 Review /m/, /n/, /ŋ/, /l/, and /r/

This unit provides additional practice and review of the consonants /m/, /n/, /ŋ/, /l/, and /r/. These are the nasal and liquid consonants in English.

A Test Yourself

Play the audio. Students circle the words they hear. They can check the meaning of unfamiliar words, but they do not have to understand every word to do the task.

ANSWERS

1. sung	5. night	9. hears
2. ran	6. collect	10. salt
3. clam	7. rate	11. two's
4. rung	8. wide	12. wired

Extra practice Have individual students say the words, choosing a word from each numbered item. Other students write down the word they heard.

B Intonation

Explain the task. Students listen to each question and circle the question that shows the intonation used on the recording. Then students choose the most likely context for the intonation. Give students time to read the choices before they begin.

ANSWERS

1. b	5. b
2. a	6. b
3. c	7. a
4. c	8. c

Extra practice Have students work with a partner. Each pair chooses three of the questions in task B. For each question, they write a short conversation that includes the question said with one of the intonations shown in their books. They should try to use a different intonation for each question.

C Puzzle

Students circle or say the word in each group that does not have the same stress pattern as the others. They can work alone or with a partner.
   Check the answers at the end.

ANSWERS

1. oven	3. probably	5. relaxing
2. myself	4. practical	6. comfortable

Diagnostic Test

The purpose of this test is to identify students' difficulties with pronunciation, in order to determine which sounds need the most attention. The test can also be used at the end of the course to check students' progress.

Each item in the *Shopping List* tests one or two sounds, as indicated on the *Results* sheet. In item 1 in the *Shopping List*, for example, the *Results* sheet indicates that the teacher should listen for the sounds /iy/ (as in *tea*) and /tʃ/ (as in *chips*) and evaluate the student's pronunciation of those sounds. The sound /iy/ occurs in the words *Chinese*, *tea*, *cheese*, *cheapest*, and *please*. The sound /tʃ/ occurs in the words *Chinese*, *French*, *cheese*, and *cheapest*. Some items also show an additional feature to listen for, such as stress or intonation.

Administering the Test

Prepare a copy of the test for students. The test can be used in two forms, depending on the level of the class (or of individual students in a multi-level class). The *Shopping List* with the material in parentheses can be photocopied and given to more advanced students. The *Shopping List* without the material in parentheses can be given to less advanced students.

Allow students to read and practice saying the *Shopping List* until they are familiar with it. Have each student read the *Shopping List* aloud. If at all possible, record their performance, so that you can replay an item as many times as necessary to note the results. If necessary, students at a more elementary level could be asked to repeat the items in the *Shopping List* rather than read them.

Since errors in pronunciation are often due to confusion caused by spelling, it is a good idea to check errors by saying the mispronounced words correctly and asking the student to repeat them.

Suggested symbols for evaluating pronunciation

    ✓ = no difficulty with this sound
    ✗✓ = minor difficulty
    ✗ = moderate difficulty
    ✗✗ = extreme difficulty

Pronunciation Test

Shopping List

1. some Chinese tea; some French cheese (Get the cheapest cheese, please.)
2. milk; some little dishes; fish or chicken for dinner (If you get fish, make sure it's fresh.)
3. ten green peppers; eggs for breakfast (Get the biggest eggs again.)
4. eight potatoes; eight tomatoes; two steaks (Let's try to make the steak tonight.)
5. a jar of jam; a head of cabbage; a can of orange juice
6. cold soda; dog food; some good bread
7. some gum; mustard; maybe some mushrooms
8. a can of tuna; a pound of bananas; nine lemons; some bacon (I can make bacon and eggs in the morning.)
9. another sweater for my mother; a leather jacket for my father (not the one with the zipper)
10. a laptop; a box of pasta; a lot of popcorn for the party, please
11. some strong string; four long forks; more coffee for the morning
12. frozen yogurt; yellow onions (just a few)
13. a newspaper; two soup spoons; some fruit juice (maybe grapefruit juice)
14. a cookbook; a box of sugar cookies; cream to put in coffee
15. a watch; a white wool sweater (I want a warm one.)
16. ice cream; rice for making fried rice (Try to buy brown rice, not white rice.)
17. baby oil; some toys for the boys (maybe a blue ball for Bob)
18. about four pounds of ground beef; half a pound of coffee; some flowers for the house
19. some frozen peas; a dozen roses, please
20. a vegetable to have this evening; vitamins for everyone; a couple of DVDs (What's your favorite movie?)
21. a purple shirt; a purse; a skirt (to wear to work)
22. lettuce for a salad; plastic glasses; a bottle of olive oil (a small bottle, please)
23. spaghetti; strawberries; six steaks; some snacks (Let's stop at the drugstore first.)
24. honey; hot dogs; a whole ham (I hope they have it.)
25. three things: toothpaste, bath soap, and something for Kathy (I think her birthday is on Thursday.)
26. pears; more beer; cereal; flour; four chairs for the party
27. a television; a tape measure

Pronunciation Test

Shopping List

1. some Chinese tea; some French cheese
2. milk; some little dishes; fish or chicken for dinner
3. ten green peppers; eggs for breakfast
4. eight potatoes; eight tomatoes; two steaks
5. a jar of jam; a head of cabbage; a can of orange juice
6. cold soda; dog food; some good bread
7. some gum; mustard; maybe some mushrooms
8. a can of tuna; a pound of bananas; nine lemons; some bacon
9. another sweater for my mother; a leather jacket for my father
10. a laptop; a box of pasta; a lot of popcorn for the party, please
11. some strong string; four long forks; more coffee for the morning
12. frozen yogurt; yellow onions
13. a newspaper; two soup spoons; some fruit juice
14. a cookbook; a box of sugar cookies; cream to put in coffee
15. a watch; a white wool sweater
16. ice cream; rice for making fried rice
17. baby oil; some toys for the boys
18. about four pounds of ground beef; half a pound of coffee; some flowers for the house
19. some frozen peas; a dozen roses, please
20. a vegetable to have this evening; vitamins for everyone; a couple of DVDs
21. a purple shirt; a purse; a skirt
22. lettuce for a salad; plastic glasses; a bottle of olive oil
23. spaghetti; strawberries; six steaks; some snacks
24. honey; hot dogs; a whole ham
25. three things: toothpaste, bath soap, and something for Kathy
26. pears; more beer; cereal; flour; four chairs for the party
27. a television; a tape measure

Results

1. /iy/ (tea) _____
   /tʃ/ (chips)_____

2. /ɪ/ (sit)_____
   /ʃ/ (shoe) _____
   Intonation in long sentences_____

3. /ɛ/ (yes)_____
   /g/ (good) _____

4. /ey/ (day) _____
   /t/ (two)_____

5. /æ/ (hat) _____
   /dʒ/ (joke)_____
   Linking a final consonant to a vowel _____

6. /d/ (did)_____

7. /ʌ/ (cup) _____
   /m/ (me) _____

8. /ə/ (a banana) _____
   /n/ (no) _____
   /ə/ in unstressed words _____

9. /ər/ in unstressed syllables and words _____
   /ð/ (the other) _____
   Weak pronunciation of *the*_____

10. /ɑ/ (hot) _____
    /p/ (pop) _____

11. /ɔ/ (ball) _____
    /ŋ/ (sing)_____

12. /ow/ (go) _____
    /y/ (yes)_____

13. /uw/ (too) _____

    Stress in compound nouns _____

14. /ʊ/ (book) _____

    /k/ (key) _____

15. /w/ (wet) _____

16. /ay/ (fine) _____

    /r/ (right) _____

    Using stress to show a contrast _____

17. /ɔy/ (boy) _____

    /b/ (baby) _____

18. /aw/ (house) _____

    /f/ (fan) _____

19. /z/ (zoo) _____

20. /v/ (very) _____

    Silent syllables _____

21. /ər/ (word) _____

22. /l/ (light, fall) _____

23. /s/ (sun) _____

    Consonant clusters with /s/ _____

24. /h/ (how) _____

25. /θ/ (think) _____

    Phrase groups _____

26. /r/ after vowels _____

27. /ʒ/ (television) _____